CENSORSHIP

Opposing Viewpoints®

Other Books of Related Interest in the Opposing Viewpoints Series:

American Government
American Values
Civil Liberties
The Mass Media
Sexual Values

Additional Books in the Opposing Viewpoints Series:

Abortion
AIDS
American Foreign Policy
America's Elections
America's Future
America's Prisons
Animal Rights
Biomedical Ethics
Central America
Chemical Dependency
China
Constructing a Life Philosophy
Crime and Criminals
Criminal Justice
Death and Dying
The Death Penalty
Drug Abuse
Eastern Europe
Economics in America
The Elderly
The Environmental Crisis
Euthanasia
Genetic Engineering
The Health Crisis
The Homeless
Immigration
Israel
Japan
Latin America and U.S. Foreign Policy
Male/Female Roles
The Middle East
Nuclear War
The Political Spectrum
Poverty
Problems of Africa
Religion in America
Science & Religion
Social Justice
The Soviet Union
The Superpowers: A New Detente
Teenage Sexuality
Terrorism
The Third World
The Vietnam War
Violence in America
War and Human Nature
War on Drugs

CENSORSHIP

Opposing Viewpoints ®

David Bender & Bruno Leone, *Series Editors*

Lisa Orr, *Book Editor*

OPPOSING VIEWPOINTS SERIES ®

Greenhaven Press, Inc.   PO Box 289009   San Diego, CA 92198-9009

Library of Congress Cataloging-in-Publication Data

Censorship : opposing viewpoints / Lisa Orr, book editor.
    p. cm. — (Opposing viewpoints series)
    Includes bibliographical references and index.
    Summary: Presents opposing viewpoints about various aspects of censorship and freedom of speech. Includes critical thinking skill activities and a list of organizations to contact.
    ISBN 0-89908-454-0 (pap.). — ISBN 0-89908-479-6 (lib.)
    1. Censorship—Juvenile literature. [1. Censorship.] I. Orr, Lisa, 1966-   . II. Series: Opposing viewpoints series (Unnumbered)
Z657.C42   1990
363.3'1—dc20   90-42854

"Congress shall make no law . . .
abridging the freedom of speech,
or of the press."

First Amendment to the U.S. Constitution

The basic foundation of our democracy is the first amendment
guarantee of freedom of expression. The Opposing Viewpoints
Series is dedicated to the concept of this basic freedom and the
idea that it is more important to practice it than to enshrine it.

Contents

Page

Why Consider Opposing Viewpoints?   9

Introduction   12

Chapter 1: Should There Be Limits to Free Speech?

Chapter Preface   16

1. Speech Should Be Limited   17
   Rod Davis

2. Speech Should Not Be Limited   22
   American Civil Liberties Union

3. Censoring Obscene Music Is Justified   28
   John Leo

4. Censoring Obscene Music Is Not Justified   32
   Clarence Page

5. The Government Should Restrict Funding of   36
   Objectionable Art
   Jesse Helms

6. Restricting Art Funding Is Censorship   42
   Robert Brustein

A Critical Thinking Activity: 49
   Distinguishing Between Fact and Opinion

Periodical Bibliography   51

Chapter 2: Should the News Media Be Regulated?

Chapter Preface   53

1. Freedom of the Press Must Be Unlimited   54
   Mario M. Cuomo

2. Freedom of the Press Must Be Limited   62
   John C. Merrill

3. Broadcasting Should Be Regulated   70
   The Spotlight

4. Broadcasting Should Not Be Regulated   75
   John Fund

5. Libel Laws Should Be Strengthened   79
   Michael Ledeen

6. Libel Laws Should Not Be Strengthened   85
   Lois G. Forer

A Critical Thinking Activity: 92
  Recognizing Stereotypes
Periodical Bibliography   94

Chapter 3: Does National Security Justify Censorship?

Chapter Preface   96

1. National Security Justifies Censorship   97
  Elmo R. Zumwalt & James G. Zumwalt

2. National Security Does Not Justify Censorship   101
  Joseph C. Spear

3. Security Leaks to the Press Should Be Punished   106
  Michael Ledeen

4. Security Leaks to the Press Should Not Be Punished   110
  CBS, Inc., The Washington Post, et al.

A Critical Thinking Activity: 115
  Evaluating Censorship and National Security
  Concerns

Periodical Bibliography   118

Chapter 4: Is School and Library Censorship Justified?

Chapter Preface   120

1. Library Censorship Is Justified   121
  Will Manley

2. Library Censorship Is Not Justified   126
  Peter Scales

3. Libraries Should Reflect Majority Values   133
  Phyllis Schlafly

4. Libraries Should Reflect Diverse Views   136
  American Library Association

5. Colleges Should Censor Racist Speech   140
  Darryl Brown

6. Colleges Should Not Censor Racist Speech   147
  Nat Hentoff

7. America's Textbooks Are Censored in Favor of the Left   154
  William F. Jasper

8. America's Textbooks Are Censored in Favor of the Right   160
  John H. Buchanan

A Critical Thinking Activity: 166
  Understanding Words in Context

Periodical Bibliography   169

Chapter 5: Should Pornography Be Censored?

Chapter Preface   171

1. The First Amendment Should Protect Pornography   172
   Geoffrey R. Stone

2. The First Amendment Should Not Protect   178
   Pornography
   Alan E. Sears

3. The Feminist Case for Censoring Pornography   186
   Andrea Dworkin

4. The Feminist Case Against Censoring Pornography   194
   Barbara Dority

5. The Harm Pornography Causes Justifies Censorship   202
   Deana Pollard

6. Harm Does Not Justify Censoring Pornography   211
   Alan Wolfe

A Critical Thinking Activity: 221
   Distinguishing Bias from Reason

Periodical Bibliography   223

Organizations to Contact   225

Bibliography of Books   230

Index   233

Why Consider Opposing Viewpoints?

> *"It is better to debate a question without settling it than to settle a question without debating it."*
>
> Joseph Joubert (1754-1824)

The Importance of Examining Opposing Viewpoints

The purpose of the Opposing Viewpoints Series, and this book in particular, is to present balanced, and often difficult to find, opposing points of view on complex and sensitive issues.

Probably the best way to become informed is to analyze the positions of those who are regarded as experts and well studied on issues. It is important to consider every variety of opinion in an attempt to determine the truth. Opinions from the mainstream of society should be examined. But also important are opinions that are considered radical, reactionary, or minority as well as those stigmatized by some other uncomplimentary label. An important lesson of history is the eventual acceptance of many unpopular and even despised opinions. The ideas of Socrates, Jesus, and Galileo are good examples of this.

Readers will approach this book with their own opinions on the issues debated within it. However, to have a good grasp of one's own viewpoint, it is necessary to understand the arguments of those with whom one disagrees. It can be said that those who do not completely understand their adversary's point of view do not fully understand their own.

A persuasive case for considering opposing viewpoints has been presented by John Stuart Mill in his work *On Liberty*. When examining controversial issues it may be helpful to reflect on this suggestion:

The only way in which a human being can make some approach to knowing the whole of a subject, is by hearing what can be said about it by persons of every variety of opinion, and studying all modes in which it can be looked at by every character of mind. No wise man ever acquired his wisdom in any mode but this.

Analyzing Sources of Information

The Opposing Viewpoints Series includes diverse materials taken from magazines, journals, books, and newspapers, as well as statements and position papers from a wide range of individuals, organizations, and governments. This broad spectrum of sources helps to develop patterns of thinking which are open to the consideration of a variety of opinions.

Pitfalls to Avoid

A pitfall to avoid in considering opposing points of view is that of regarding one's own opinion as being common sense and the most rational stance, and the point of view of others as being only opinion and naturally wrong. It may be that another's opinion is correct and one's own is in error.

Another pitfall to avoid is that of closing one's mind to the opinions of those with whom one disagrees. The best way to approach a dialogue is to make one's primary purpose that of understanding the mind and arguments of the other person and not that of enlightening him or her with one's own solutions. More can be learned by listening than speaking.

It is my hope that after reading this book the reader will have a deeper understanding of the issues debated and will appreciate the complexity of even seemingly simple issues on which good and honest people disagree. This awareness is particularly important in a democratic society such as ours where people enter into public debate to determine the common good. Those with whom one disagrees should not necessarily be regarded as enemies, but perhaps simply as people who suggest different paths to a common goal.

Developing Basic Reading and Thinking Skills

In this book, carefully edited opposing viewpoints are purposely placed back to back to create a running debate; each viewpoint is preceded by a short quotation that best expresses the author's main argument. This format instantly plunges the reader into the midst of a controversial issue and greatly aids that reader in mastering the basic skill of recognizing an author's point of view.

A number of basic skills for critical thinking are practiced in the activities that appear throughout the books in the series. Some of the skills are:

Evaluating Sources of Information. The ability to choose from among alternative sources the most reliable and accurate source in relation to a given subject.

Separating Fact from Opinion. The ability to make the basic distinction between factual statements (those that can be demonstrated or verified empirically) and statements of opinion (those that are beliefs or attitudes that cannot be proved).

Identifying Stereotypes. The ability to identify oversimplified, exaggerated descriptions (favorable or unfavorable) about people and insulting statements about racial, religious, or national groups, based upon misinformation or lack of information.

Recognizing Ethnocentrism. The ability to recognize attitudes or opinions that express the view that one's own race, culture, or group is inherently superior, or those attitudes that judge another culture or group in terms of one's own.

It is important to consider opposing viewpoints and equally important to be able to critically analyze those viewpoints. The activities in this book are designed to help the reader master these thinking skills. Statements are taken from the book's viewpoints and the reader is asked to analyze them. This technique aids the reader in developing skills that not only can be applied to the viewpoints in this book, but also to situations where opinionated spokespersons comment on controversial issues. Although the activities are helpful to the solitary reader, they are most useful when the reader can benefit from the interaction of group discussion.

Using this book and others in the series should help readers develop basic reading and thinking skills. These skills should improve the reader's ability to understand what is read. Readers should be better able to separate fact from opinion, substance from rhetoric, and become better consumers of information in our media-centered culture.

This volume of the Opposing Viewpoints Series does not advocate a particular point of view. Quite the contrary! The very nature of the book leaves it to the reader to formulate the opinions he or she finds most suitable. My purpose as publisher is to see that this is made possible by offering a wide range of viewpoints that are fairly presented.

David L. Bender
Publisher

Introduction

"Abuses of the freedom of speech ought to be repressed; but to whom are we to commit the power of doing it?"

Benjamin Franklin

One of the founding precepts of the United States is freedom. Many of the people who originally settled here fled from repressive societies that did not allow them the freedom to practice or even to express their religious, political, and social beliefs. Consequently, the people who turned this raw country into a nation were determined to preserve all possible freedom for the inhabitants here. As testimony to their determination, the very First Amendment to the U.S. Constitution, added in 1791, pledged that "Congress should make no law. . .abridging the freedom of speech, or of the press."

In spite of this seemingly clear prohibition against abridgement of free speech and press, censorship has been a controversial issue throughout American history. For example, the First Amendment did not prevent the nation's second president, John Adams, from signing into law the Alien and Sedition Acts in 1798. Passed during a time of turmoil and uncertainty, the laws, in part, made it a crime to speak, write, or publish materials "with intent to defame. . .or bring into contempt or disrepute" members of the government. Such criticism was deemed "sedition" and thus was not protected by the Constitution. Under these acts, some newspapers were shut down and their editors jailed.

The laws were allowed to expire in 1801 by Adams's successor Thomas Jefferson, the author of the Declaration of Independence. In contrast to Adams and others who worried that the power of the press might, in some situations, endanger the nation, Jefferson considered it a strength. Jefferson was strongly against censorship of any kind, believing that people should have free access to all information. He argued that people could then sort through information and make wise decisions. He did not fear that they would be seduced by false and possibly malicious claims in newspapers. Instead, he argued, common people would be able to recognize falsehood from the truth. After he left the presidency, he wrote in a letter, "When the press is free and every man able to read all is safe."

The philosophical differences between two of our nation's founders, Adams and Jefferson, are echoed today in debates over exactly what forms of speech "shall not be abridged" according to the Constitution. In areas as disparate as pornography, espionage, education, and art, Americans are still divided over whether the government has the right to restrict individual expression to protect its citizens or to protect national security.

One example of a recent controversy concerns treatment of the American flag. In 1989 the Supreme Court, in a five-to-four ruling, overturned the conviction of a political protester brought to trial because he had burned the flag. The Court's majority ruled that burning the flag in protest is a right guaranteed by the First Amendment to the Constitution. President George Bush was among many who disagreed with the Court's ruling. Bush and others were so concerned that they proposed a new amendment to the Constitution specifically prohibiting such actions. The controversy generated by the Court's ruling focused America's attention on highly charged arguments about patriotic feelings vs. freedom of expression.

Justice William Brennan, author of the Supreme Court's majority view, argued that burning the flag is a form of speech and that its offensiveness to other Americans is not enough to censor it. He wrote, "The government may not prohibit the expression of an idea simply because society finds the idea itself offensive or disagreeable. . . .Punishing desecration of the flag dilutes the very freedom that makes this emblem so revered." Justice Anthony Kennedy added that recent peaceful revolutions in Eastern Europe, in which flags were burned, prove that this is an "internationally recognized form of protest." These justices and others, as did Thomas Jefferson, believe that Americans should be free to voice any opinion, no matter how repugnant, as long as it does not directly cause harm to any individual. To act otherwise would be to tolerate censorship, an even greater affront to America's ideals.

People who believe flag burning should be illegal say that it is the epitome of disloyalty and perhaps even treasonous. In an opinion disagreeing with the Court's flag-burning ruling, Justice John Paul Stevens stated, "The flag uniquely symbolizes the ideas of liberty, equality, and tolerance. . .ideas that Americans have passionately defended and debated throughout our country." Chief Justice William Rehnquist agreed, stating, "Flag burning is the equivalent of an inarticulate grunt or roar that. . .is most likely to be indulged in not to express any particular idea, but to antagonize others." He argued that such expression is not protected by the Constitution. To these justices and others, permitting destruction of the flag is tantamount to sanctioning destruction of the nation itself. They believe that even in a nation whose chief value is freedom, certain things should not be tolerated.

This controversy is only one of many that have marked America's recent history. *Censorship: Opposing Viewpoints* examines contemporary controversies on freedom of speech and other censorship issues. This new book replaces Greenhaven's 1985 book of the same title with new viewpoints and several new issues. The questions debated are: Should There Be Limits to Free Speech? Should the News Media Be Regulated? Does National Security Justify Censorship? Is School and Library Censorship Justified? Should Pornography Be Censored? The controversies examined here show that censorship remains an emotional and important issue for the U.S. as the nation continues to try to live up to its historical visions of freedom.

Should There Be Limits to Free Speech?

CENSORSHIP

Chapter Preface

Freedom of speech is one of the basic privileges guaranteed to all Americans by the Bill of Rights in the U.S. Constitution. Traditionally, no form of speech should be censored unless it poses a direct harm to others. Shouting "fire" in a crowded theater (assuming no fire exists) is the most familiar example of harmful, and outlawed, speech.

But several questions are raised by this seemingly straightforward view of freedom of speech. One question often asked is whether some speech is so harmful that its censorship is justified. Writer Rod Davis, for example, believes that people espousing white supremacy and racial hatred do not deserve freedom of speech protections. But others, including civil libertarian Nat Hentoff, argue that even deeply offensive speech must be protected, and that preventing a white supremacist from speaking is one step toward censoring other unpopular kinds of speech as well.

The viewpoints in this chapter debate three topics on the critical issue of freedom of speech.

"A society that hates racism would not permit it to flourish."

Speech Should Be Limited

Rod Davis

Rod Davis is a free-lance writer and author. He formerly taught English at the University of Texas at Austin, and edited *The Texas Observer*, a biweekly magazine. In the following viewpoint, Davis argues that a country's values are reflected in its policies. If a country does not believe in racism, it should not protect racist speech, he states. Davis contends that the need to protect people from racist speech outweighs the abstract right of freedom of expression.

As you read, consider the following questions:

1. What evidence does the author give of the Klan's danger to society?
2. What does the author mean by his statement that "'free speech' is a rhetorical catchphrase . . . maintained by governments to fetishize concepts routinely abrogated in practice"?
3. What does Davis think should be done about groups such as the Klan?

Rod Davis, "Free Speech for the Klan Is a Fraud, Not a Right," *The Progressive*, July 1983. Reprinted by permission from *The Progressive*, 409 East Main Street, Madison, WI 53703. Copyright © 1983, The Progressive, Inc.

What should be done to prevent the resurgence of the Ku Klux Klan in the United States? Everything possible, by broad-based, organized, enthusiastic popular opposition. Whether or not the Government certifies such action through various facades of "legality" is irrelevant, just as official approval of mass action has been irrelevant from Mahatma Gandhi's India to Martin Luther King's America.

The issue before the Left is clear, but our line of vision must not wander. We must not be concerned with protecting the Klan from the abstract encroachments of governmental censorship, but with protecting the people—including all nonwhites and non-Protestants in this instance—from the real, documentable, historical violence of the Klan and its allies.

For more than 120 years, the Klan has murdered and organized, first in the South and later in the volatile racist North and East. Now it is organizing in the West as well: Marin County, California, has an active Klan which harasses the few black residents, and in Oregon the Klan has found a hate-wedge by recruiting against hippies and Orientals. . . .

Though estimates of current membership vary—the number is probably around 20,000, based on projections from a 1981 *New York Times* report—it is fair to guess that the Klan renaissance is significant.

Klan Infestation

The revival encompasses violent attacks, paramilitary camps, bookstores, frequent public and media appearances, and renewed perception of Klan strength at the community level. In my state, Texas, the Klan has run a media blitz with city council-approved rallies in three major cities, and in rural east Texas there is a virtual epidemic of Klan support. In Alabama, Georgia, the Carolinas, Michigan, Maryland, the Klan is a reality—an active malignant presence with an impact that reaches far beyond the firelight circle of white-robed racists and black-uniformed storm troopers. In some cases—for example, in Greensboro, North Carolina—the Klan has infested the law enforcement and judicial systems that are supposed to control it.

Is there any reason for society, and especially for the Left, not to oppose the Klan and the racism of which it is merely the ugly symbol with a ferocity equal to that mustered against the Vietnam war, segregation, the draft, child abuse, and sexism? Incredibly, there is a preferred reason. It is suggested that instead of *opposing* the Klan and racism, we ought to *defend* the Klan and the larger issue of "free speech."

This is absurd, it is insulting, and, insofar as it places the rituals of an arbitrary government above the real need for protec-

'Watsa matter, don't you like freedom of speech?'

Ollie Harrington/*People's Daily World*. Reprinted with permission.

tion of the non-WASP citizenry, it is racist. "Free speech." What rhetorical catchphrase is in greater need of deconstruction? "Free speech," unlike racial terror, is an abstraction, and abstractions are maintained by governments to fetishize concepts routinely abrogated in practice.

If free speech means anything, it can only refer to the expression of a hazy range of interpretations within the ideological parameters of an enforcing power. The "free speech" of the dominant class will never be the free speech of the oppressed and exploited, and saying so in the face of historical experience is dissembling. . . .

Government caprice regarding free speech is notorious. Were Japanese-Americans accorded free speech in their internment camps? Did the Smith Act, the Dred Scott decision, the CIA [Central Intelligence Agency] regulations provide unfettered dialogue for their respective targets? Are we supposed to wait for the Government to grant or withdraw permission to discuss social change? Did the Southern civil rights movement wait on the mighty shield of the First Amendment or just sit in those buses and at those lunch counters, and die in bullet-riddled cars?

What *is* this phantom? Just as some white-dominated city councils were giving the Klan "free speech" permits to rally, another governmental body, the State Department, denied an entry visa to Salvador Allende's widow because her scheduled speech to church groups in California was deemed "prejudicial to U.S. interests." That is, the Government tagged her as a communist.

The Privilege to Hate

There is no question that the First Amendment guarantees our right to free speech without fear, but does that right include the right to advocate hate and threats to harass and kill those whom we do not like? Why should the KKK have the privilege to incite its members to kill Jews, "Niggers," homosexuals?

After John Hinckley's attempt to assassinate Ronald Reagan, a huge protective shield was set up to guard the President. Blacks, Jews, and others feel they have the same right to protection from a group that openly advocates hate, violence, and death.

May Goldman, letter in *The Progressive*, August 1983.

Constitutional "free speech," in the daily, concrete world, consists of what the Government decides it to be. It is a fantasy to insist that in protecting our enemies we protect ourselves. We are already under attack. FBI [Federal Bureau of Investigation] guidelines implemented in March 1983 go so far as to equate political activism (including union membership) with organized crime as a proper focus for Federal scrutiny.

Play us no Nero violins of "free speech" while the Left is being systematically burned. Defending the Klan's "right" to appear publicly defends nothing more than the Klan, in the same way that pursuing peace with honor meant nothing more than pursuing war. As for "free speech" outside relations to the Government—who would claim there is free speech on the shop floor, in church, at school, or in the media?

Defeat of Racism

Stop the Klan, for it is not the grotesqueries of the Klan mentality which are being opposed but the acceptability of the Klan within its white host. If you feel that the defeat of racism is a greater priority to society than is continued worship of the legal fiction of "free speech," then you see the issue clearly. And you will not subscribe to the secondary liberal position that demonstrating against the Klan means "stooping to the Klan's level." One does not stoop to the level of an enemy by opposing it; the millions who fought and died in the war against Hitler so testify. . . .

A society creates itself—its tools, its language, its ideas. It is the responsibility of society to produce that which will reflect its values. A society that hates racism would not permit it to flourish and would, in particular, not allow a vanguard racist group to operate with official sanction and police protection. That our society does afford sanction is but a statement that we will employ anything, even the phantom fetish of the First Amendment, to let racism persist. The need actively to oppose the Klan, denying it any vestige of protection, is paramount. If you waver behind the mirage of "free speech," you must consider the possibility of complicity.

Right to Protection

If, on the other hand, you believe that "freedom" and "speech" are products of social interaction, not black-robed writ, and that a society which produces racist and fascist sects cannot possibly mean anything when it boasts "free speech," then you will have no more compunction about shutting out the Klan than a doctor would about injecting against smallpox.

Action against the Klan is a statement, long overdue, about the depth of our perception about race—a perception which must not be diluted by rational-sounding, legalistic discourse. This statement should not be left to fringe crazies; no tiny group should co-opt the obligation of society to resolve what is our greatest historical social disease. Even Woody Allen, nobody's casual thug, observed that the only way to deal with the Nazis and the Klan is with baseball bats. Especially the early, wooden ones.

> *"The duty of government is to permit speech and to restrain those who would disrupt it violently."*

Speech Should Not Be Limited

American Civil Liberties Union

Since its founding in 1920, the American Civil Liberties Union [ACLU] has championed the rights set forth in the Declaration of Independence and the Constitution, particularly the right to freedom of speech. In the following viewpoint, excerpted from an ACLU pamphlet, the authors explain why they defend freedom of speech even for racists and totalitarians. According to the ACLU, only a strict interpretation of the First Amendment will ensure that all voices, from the Ku Klux Klan to civil rights activists, are heard.

As you read, consider the following questions:

1. Why is it important that even speeches which may cause a violent reaction in the audience be protected, in the ACLU's view?
2. What is the Supreme Court's interpretation of the "fighting words" rule, according to the authors?
3. Why does the ACLU believe the government should not be allowed to restrict speech said to threaten national security?

American Civil Liberties Union, *Why the American Civil Liberties Union Defends Free Speech for Racists and Totalitarians,* 1978. Excerpted with permission.

In times and places where the views of civil rights activists, pacifists, religious and political dissenters, labor organizers and others have been unpopular, the ACLU [American Civil Liberties Union] has insisted on their right to speak.

Throughout the history of the ACLU, we have adhered to Voltaire's principle that "I may disapprove of what you say, but I will defend to the death your right to say it."

But does the First Amendment protect even those who urge the destruction of freedom? Does it extend to those who advocate the overthrow of our democratic form of government or who espouse violence?

In 1969, in an ACLU case involving a KKK [Ku Klux Klan] leader who had urged at a rally in Hamilton County, Ohio, that Black Americans be sent back to Africa, the United States Supreme Court unanimously established the principle that speech may not be restrained or punished unless it "is directed to inciting or producing imminent lawless action and is likely to incite or produce such action." (*Brandenburg v. Ohio*)

In this, and in earlier cases involving advocates of draft resistance in World War I and leaders of the Communist Party during and following World War II, the Supreme Court made it clear that before a speaker can be suppressed there must be a clear and present danger that the audience will *act illegally and do what the speaker urges*—not just *believe* in what is advocated.

A Clear and Present Danger?

When Nazis or others like them choose to demonstrate in places like Skokie, Illinois, where hundreds of survivors of the concentration camps live, are they not creating a clear and present danger of violent reactions?

Speaking or marching before a *hostile* audience is not the same as inciting a *sympathetic* crowd to engage in illegal acts. The audience is not being urged to become violent and do bodily harm to the demonstrators. Hostile crowds must not be allowed to exercise a veto power over the speech of others by themselves creating a clear and present danger of disorder. Otherwise any of us could be silenced if people who did not like our ideas decided to start a riot.

It is common practice for speakers and demonstrators to carry their messages to hostile audiences—perhaps in the hope of making conversions, perhaps to attract attention, or perhaps to test the potential for restraint or for ugliness in their adversaries.

In hundreds of cases, the ACLU has defended the right to speak even when the speakers were so unpopular that opponents reacted violently. The Wobblies carried their unionization message to Western mining towns. That message was so unpopular that some of them were lynched. Jehovah's Witnesses distributed their tracts in Roman Catholic neighborhoods. They were stoned. Norman Thomas spoke in Mayor Frank Hague's Jersey City. He was pelted with eggs and narrowly escaped serious violence. Paul Robeson sang at a concert in Peekskill, New York. There was a riot. Civil rights activists in the 1960s chose to demonstrate in Mississippi and Alabama. Some of them were murdered. Opponents of the Vietnam war picketed military bases. Many of them were beaten. Martin Luther King, Jr. marched in the most racist neighborhoods of Chicago. And there was racial violence.

The duty of government is to permit speech and to restrain those who would disrupt it violently. Opponents of a point of view must be free to have their say, but not to make any public place off-limits for speech they don't like.

But isn't a demonstration in an intensely hostile area the same as falsely shouting "fire" in a crowded theater?

Speaking or marching with offensive messages in public places is not at all the same as falsely shouting "fire" in a crowded theater. The members of the crowd are not in a tightly enclosed arena where a panic would almost certainly follow by a sudden and unexpected cry of danger before any contrary view could be heard. They have come to the scene freely, probably knowing what to expect, and they may freely turn away if they are upset by what they see or hear. Just as speakers have a right to express themselves, listeners have a right to ignore them or, if they choose, to hold peaceful counterdemonstrations.

Fighting Words

Hasn't the Supreme Court said that certain kinds of communication—like hurling epithets at another person—are so likely to lead to fighting that the speaker, and not the audience, is responsible? Isn't the display of a swastika or the burning of a cross the same as such "fighting words?"

The Supreme Court has made it clear that speech can be punished as "fighting words" only if it is directed at another person in an *individual, face-to-face encounter*. The Court has never applied this "fighting words" concept to nonverbal symbols displayed before a *general* audience (like the display of a swastika or a peace symbol or the burning of a cross or of an effigy of a political leader).

Why do the ACLU and the courts believe that prior restraints on free speech are so much worse than punishments after a speech has been made?

Prior restraints not only prevent *entirely* the expression of the would-be speaker, but they also deprive the public of its *right to know* what the speaker would have said.

When the Nixon Administration tried to impose a prior restraint on the Pentagon Papers, they told us that publication would injure the national security. When the Pentagon Papers were published, we discovered that they exposed misdeeds by the government, but did no damage to national security.

Group Libel

If the purpose of the First Amendment is to insure a free flow of ideas, of what value to that process are utterances which defame people because of their race or religion? Can't we prohibit group libel that merely stirs up hatred between peoples?

Legal philosopher Edmond Cahn dealt with this subject in a notable address delivered at the Hebrew University in Jerusalem in 1962. If there were a prohibition against group defamation, said Cahn:

> The officials could begin by prosecuting anyone who distributed the Christian Gospels, because they contain many defamatory statements not only about Jews but also about Christians; they show Christians failing Jesus in his hour of deepest tragedy. Then the officials could ban Greek literature for calling the rest of the

25

world 'barbarians.' Roman authors would be suppressed because when they were not defaming the Gallic and Teutonic tribes they were disparaging the Italians. For obvious reasons, all Christian writers of the Middle Ages and quite a few modern ones could meet a similar fate. Even if an exceptional Catholic should fail to mention the Jews, the officials would have to proceed against his works for what he said about the Protestants and, of course, the same would apply to Protestant views on the subject of Catholics. Then there is Shakespeare who openly affronted the French, the Welsh, the Danes. . . . Dozens of British writers from Sheridan and Dickens to Shaw and Joyce insulted the Irish. Finally, almost every worthwhile item of prose and poetry published by an American Negro would fall under the ban because it either whispered, spoke, or shouted unkind statements about the group called 'white.' Literally applied, a group-libel law would leave our bookshelves empty and us without desire to fill them.

History teaches us that group libel laws are used to *oppress* racial and religious minorities, not to protect them. For example, none of the anti-Semites who were responsible for arousing France against Captain Alfred Dreyfus was ever prosecuted for group libel. But Emile Zola was prosecuted for libelling the military establishment and the clergy of France in his magnificent *J'Accuse* and had to flee to England to escape punishment. . . .

A Dismaying Debate

In one sense, I find it remarkable—as well as dismaying—that censorship is still a subject for debate. The Constitution could not be more clear: "Congress shall make no law abridging the freedom of speech, or of the press," says the First Amendment. And that means, as Justices William O. Douglas and Hugo Black have consistently maintained, freedom of expression in any form. ("I read *no law abridging*," Justice Black added in the 1957 Roth case, "to mean NO LAW ABRIDGING.")

Nat Hentoff, *Censorship: For & Against*, 1971.

Why should someone who detests the Nazis and the KKK support defense of their right to speak?

In a society of laws, the principles established in dealing with racist views necessarily apply to all. The ACLU defended the right of Father Terminiello, a suspended Catholic priest, to give a racist speech in Chicago. In 1949, the U.S. Supreme Court agreed with our position in a decision that is a landmark in the history of free speech. Time and again, the ACLU was able to rely on the decision in *Terminiello v. Chicago* in defending free speech for civil rights demonstrators in the deep South. The Supreme Court cited its own decision in *Terminiello* in its leading decisions on behalf of civil rights demonstrators, *Cox v. Louisiana* and *Edwards v. South Carolina*. Similarly, the Supreme Court's decision in 1969 in *Brandenburg v. Ohio* upholding free speech for the KKK was the principal decision relied upon by a lower court the following year in overturning the conviction of Benjamin Spock for opposing the draft.

The principles of the First Amendment are indivisible. Extend them on behalf of one group and they protect all groups. Deny them to one group, and all groups suffer.

Increasing Public Interest

Doesn't providing racists and totalitarians with a legal defense give publicity to their cause and their ideas that they would otherwise not receive?

It is the attempts by communities to *prevent* such people from expressing themselves that gives them the press coverage they would ordinarily not receive. If providing a legal defense for their constitutional rights results in a continuation of the publicity, that is an unavoidable consequence of the events that were set in motion by the original denial of First Amendment guarantees. A fact that seems little understood by those who take a restrictive view toward speech they do not like is that attempts at suppression ordinarily increase public interest in the ideas they are trying to stamp out. . . .

We cannot remain faithful to the First Amendment by turning our backs when it is put to its severest test—the right to freedom of speech for those whose views we despise the most.

=====

*"Why should our daughters have to grow up
in a culture in which musical advice on the
domination and abuse of women is accepted
as entertainment?"*

=====

Censoring Obscene Music Is Justified

John Leo

John Leo is a columnist for the weekly magazine *U.S. News &
World Report*. In the following viewpoint, he argues that lyrics
which degrade women should be banned. He maintains that
rock music influences those who listen to it, which makes songs
that glorify abusing women particularly dangerous. Therefore,
he believes, First Amendment concerns about controlling offensive lyrics are outweighed by concerns for the well-being of
women.

As you read, consider the following questions:

1. How has the reticence to quote lyrics influenced the debate
   over banning them, according to Leo?
2. Why does the author believe lyrics which demean women
   are dangerous to blacks in particular?
3. What evidence does the author cite to show that liberals are
   inconsistent on the issue of censorship?

The issue at the heart of the controversy over the rap group 2 Live Crew is not censorship, artistic freedom, sex or even obscene language. The real problem, I think, is this: Because of the cultural influence of one not very distinguished rap group, 10- and 12-year-old boys now walk down the street chanting about the joys of damaging a girl's vagina during sex.

Abusing Women

What we are discussing here is the wild popularity (almost 2 million records sold) of a group that sings about forcing anal sex on a girl and then forcing her to lick excrement. The squeamishness of the press about sharing this rather crucial information with readers may be understandable; the subject is obviously loathsome. But it has distorted the case, making the censors look worse and the rappers look better than they really are. This is not about "expletive laced" or "raw" or "bawdy" language that shocks the bluenoses among us. It is about the degradation of women, packaged and beamed to kids as entertainment, and how a free society that cares about its future should respond.

You would never know any of this, or understand the outrage, if you read the bulk of what passes for social analysis in this country. "The history of music is the story of innovative, even outrageous styles that interacted, adapted and became mainstream," *The New York Times* said in a safely abstract, headache-inducing editorial. (Taking the tolerant long view, the *Times* is telling us an old story: New cultural expression shocks us first, then enters the mainstream. Hmm. Does this mean that woman-abuse will become conventional and the *Times* doesn't mind?) The *Los Angeles Times,* scrambling for the same high ground, tells us that much rap "often deals explicitly with violence and sexuality" (though, alas, none of this explicitness could be shared with readers). The president of Manhattan's New School for Social Research says we are witnessing a collision between those comfortable with change and those yearning for a simpler era.

Missing the Mark

Most other commentary was even worse. Colleen Dewhurst imagined that all American artists were under assault. Tom Wicker saw the nation yielding to "the persisting fear of difference." Richard Cohen, normally a sharp analyst of the culture, took the what's-the-harm approach, arguing that flag burning and 2 Live Crew (routinely lumped together by many writers) were merely "bubbles on the surface of the culture." Juan Williams, in a brilliant piece in *The Washington Post*, showed a better grasp of what the harm is. He argued that in a society in which the black family is falling apart, young black males are particularly vulnerable to the fear and hatred of women being fanned by 2 Live Crew.

Hateful Music

Another black commentator, Prof. Henry Louis Gates of Duke University, made the case that black culture has many referent points and styles (including in this case, hyperbole and humor) that whites can't understand and should be slow to attack. A valid point, except that the most telling criticism of 2 Live Crew has come from blacks, who presumably have less trouble reading black culture. Stanley Crouch, the prominent critic and essayist, calls 2 Live Crew "spiritual cretins" and "slime." Crouch says that "sadistic, misogynist, hateful music" adds to the problematic attitudes already burdening the black middle class.

Ramirez/Copley News Service. Reprinted with permission.

But the dominant opinion of the opinion industry, so far as I can see, is that no reaction is really called for: 2 Live Crew is, in Cohen's phrase, "yet another cultural day lily." Maybe so, but the group's misogyny does not take place in a vacuum. From Prince's pro-incest song to the pimp worship of some rap songs to Madonna's current ditty about how much girls like being tied up and spanked, some fashionably warped messages about women are pouring through the culture. Why are we so sure that tolerance of such attitudes has no consequences?

Attempting to argue that there is nothing new under the sun, some critics say that 2 Live Crew resembles Redd Foxx's scatological humor and is probably as harmless. But Foxx was talking to small audiences of adults. We are talking about a huge audience of young people in an era when the electronic media are hundreds of times more powerful than they were a generation ago. Much more is at stake. And since we are an entertainment society, venomous messages are more likely than ever to disguise themselves as harmless fun. Andrew Dice Clay's audiences seem to be mostly white, male, blue-collar and resentful. I admit they are not yet whistling the Horst Wessel song, but they bear watching.

This is an age in which many Americans are conflicted about censorship. Liberal opinion is firmly against all censorship, except when it comes to the restrictive speech codes recently embraced at certain liberal universities. (The only way 2 Live Crew could get in trouble with some commentators would be to enroll at Stanford and read their lyrics to a female student.)

A Red Herring

"Censorship is a red herring in this case," says Jewelle Taylor Gibbs, author of *Young, Black and Male in America: An Endangered Species.* "The real issue is values, the quality of life." Yes, indeed. Censorship is folly. So is standing around reciting the First Amendment as if that were the only issue.

The popular culture is worth paying attention to. It is the air we breathe, and 2 Live Crew is a pesky new pollutant. The opinion industry's advice is generally to buy a gas mask or stop breathing. ("If you don't like their album, don't buy it," one such genius wrote.) But by monitoring, complaining, boycotting, we might actually get the 2 Live Pollutants out of our air. Why should our daughters have to grow up in a culture in which musical advice on the domination and abuse of women is accepted as entertainment?

"I disapprove of what 2 Live Crew raps, but I will defend to the death the group's right to rap it."

Censoring Obscene Music Is Not Justified

Clarence Page

In the following viewpoint, Clarence Page argues against banning the sale of albums with lyrics which may be considered offensive. He also opposes arresting musical groups when they perform such lyrics. He contends that while some lyrics are sexist, there is no proof that they promote violence against women. Censoring rock lyrics, he writes, could lead to further censorship in other areas. Page is a columnist for *The Chicago Tribune.*

As you read, consider the following questions:

1. How has the controversy over 2 Live Crew's album actually benefited the group, according to Page?
2. Why does the author believe banning lyrics is an impractical way to fight sexism?
3. What future does Page foresee for censorship?

Clarence Page, "Today 2 Live Crew! Tomorrow This Column?" *Liberal Opinion,* June 25, 1990. Reprinted by permission: Tribune Media Services.

It is unfortunate that, as one astute civil libertarian once said, First Amendment cases often put you on the same side with people you would never invite to your home for dinner.

But those who want to curb the Bill of Rights are clever enough to single out the most objectionable and artless material they can find, hoping to pave the way to later assaults on the more commonplace and meritorious.

Today *Hustler*, tomorrow *Playboy*. Today Mapplethorpe, tomorrow *Time* magazine.

Today flag burning, tomorrow an essay that advocates flag burning.

The Controversy

That's how I find myself defending 2 Live Crew, a rap group that is growing quite wealthy enough without my help, thanks to the controversy surrounding its piece of work, an album called *As Nasty As They Wanna Be*.

A federal district judge in south Florida found the album to be obscene, a finding that helped sweep it from local record stores and led to the arrest of two band members after a performance in an adults–only club. Two days earlier, authorities also arrested a record store owner in Ft. Lauderdale who refused to stop selling the album.

The fuss has resulted in the album's becoming such a sellout success at record stores that I had a difficult time investigating the lyrics in question.

Fortunately, the Parents Music Resource Center, founded by Tipper Gore, wife of Sen. Al Gore Jr. and a tireless crusader against naughty rock lyrics, saved the day. The center offered to fax the lyrics to me, all nicely printed out like a Shakespearean sonnet.

I accepted the offer, although in hindsight I suppose a zealous prosecutor like Jack Thompson, the Florida attorney who spearheaded the drive to have 2 Live Crew declared obscene, could accuse us of conspiracy to transport indecent materials across state lines.

But it was worth the risk, just to examine the lyrics for myself and judge their merit, a right Jack Thompson seems intent on curtailing.

An Adult Audience

Here's my judgment: Thompson is right about the lyrics. They're filthy.

They're vulgar, awful, loathsome, odious, nasty, offensive, vile, putrid and disgusting. Oral and anal sex are described in graphic terms and women are treated as sexual playthings.

I wanted to wash my hands after reading these lyrics. But I

don't find them to be a jailable offense.

To paraphrase Voltaire, I disapprove of what 2 Live Crew raps, but I will defend to the death the group's right to rap it.

I am less offended by the filthy lyrics than by the arrest of the band members. They were not distributing their music, if you want to call it that, to children. Nor were they performing in a day care center.

They were performing in an adults–only club. If people like the young, multiracial crowd that attended the show in question want to spend their money on that, it should be their right, as long as they don't hurt anybody else.

Wiley Miller/*San Francisco Examiner*. Reprinted with permission.

Jack Thompson, who has represented abused women in the past, has convinced himself that filthy lyrics do hurt somebody else. He says he wants *As Nasty As They Wanna Be* banned because it might fall into the hands of children and he wants all performances of the lyrics banned because they glorify, in Thompson's view, the sexual brutalization of women.

Well, Thompson is right to call the album sexist. Its lyrics regard women as sexual playthings for the pleasures of men.

But if that makes it obscene, there would be a lot of books, videotapes, movies and, for that matter, television shows that would be banned, regardless of artistic merit, except perhaps for reruns of Lawrence Welk.

Like other censors in the past, Thompson argues without scientific evidence that a rise in dirty lyrics leads to a rise in rape and other violence against women. Actually, the rise in such reports is more likely caused by a growing awareness of the problem and a new willingness by victims to come forward and report their victimization.

Voicing the Problem

Unfortunately, Thompson has convinced himself that dirty lyrics are the cause of a social problem—sexism—when in reality they only are giving voice to the problem.

Once we begin to exempt from First Amendment protections words and ideas that offend some of us, the list of exceptions that affects all of us only grows longer. It does not shrink.

President Bush would outlaw flag burning.

Jesse Helms would outlaw homoerotic art.

Author and radical feminist Andrea Dworkin would censor any art, photos or films that, in her view, treat women as sex objects.

Some minority college students would censor all forms of expression that offend their sensibilities, including classroom discussions and student newspaper opinions.

Pretty soon, we wouldn't have much left to protect.

Who knows? Today 2 Live Crew. Tomorrow maybe this column.

*"Federal funding for sadomasochism, homo-
eroticism, and child pornography is an insult
to taxpayers."*

The Government Should Restrict Funding of Objectionable Art

Jesse Helms

In 1989 two government-funded works of art touched off a heated debate on whether the government should fund art which offended many people. Senator Jesse Helms of North Carolina introduced an amendment to restrict such funding, arguing that taxpayers should not have to support art portraying blasphemy or immoral behavior. The amendment failed, but Congress did decide to withhold $40,000 from the National Endowment for the Arts. The following viewpoint is taken from the speech Helms gave on the floor of the Senate in support of his amendment.

As you read, consider the following questions:

1. How does Helms respond to the charge that he supports censoring art?
2. How did the National Endowment deceive its review panel, according to the author?
3. What examples does Helms cite to demonstrate that the public agrees with him?

Jesse Helms, speech given to the U.S. Senate, July 26, 1989.

I believe we are all aware of the controversy surrounding the use of Federal funds, via the National Endowment for the Arts [NEA], to support so-called works of art by Andres Serrano and Robert Mapplethorpe. My amendment would prevent the NEA from funding such immoral trash in the future. Specifically, my amendment prohibits the use of the NEA's funds to support obscene or indecent materials, or materials which denigrate the objects or beliefs of a particular religion.

Senators' Efforts Appreciated

I applaud the efforts of my distinguished colleagues from West Virginia, Mr. Robert C. Byrd, and from Idaho, Mr. James A. McClure, to address this issue in both the Appropriations Subcommittee on the Interior, and the full Appropriations Committee. Cutting off funding to the Southeastern Center for Contemporary Art [SECCA] in Winston-Salem and the Institute for Contemporary Art in Philadelphia will certainly prevent them from misusing Federal funds for the next 5 years. However, as much as I agree with the measures, the committee's efforts do not go far enough because they will not prevent such blasphemous or immoral behavior by other institutions or artists with Government funds. That is why I have offered my amendment.

A Compromise

Frankly, I have fundamental questions about why the Federal Government is involved in supporting artists the taxpayers have refused to support in the marketplace. My concern in this regard is heightened when I hear the arts community and the media saying that any restriction at all on Federal funding would amount to censorship. What they seem to be saying is that we in Congress must choose between: First, absolutely no Federal presence in the arts; or second, granting artists the absolute freedom to use tax dollars as they wish, regardless of how vulgar, blasphemous, or despicable their works may be.

If we indeed must make this choice, then the Federal Government should get out of the arts. However, I do not believe we are limited to those two choices and my amendment attempts to make a compromise between them. It simply provides for some common sense restrictions on what is and is not an appropriate use of Federal funding for the arts. It does not prevent the production or creation of vulgar works, it merely prevents the use of Federal funds to support them.

I remind my colleagues that the distinguished Senator from New York and I called attention to Mr. Serrano's so-called work of art, which portrays Jesus Christ submerged in a bottle of the artist's urine, on May 18, 1989. We pointed out that the National Endowment for the Arts had not only supported a $15,000 award honoring Mr. Serrano for it, but they also helped promote and exhibit the work as well.

The Review System

Over 25 Senators—Democrats and Republicans—expressed their outrage that day by cosigning a letter to Hugh Southern, the Endowment's acting chairman, asking him to review their procedures and to determine what steps are needed to prevent such abuses from recurring in the future. Mr. Southern replied on June 6, 1989 that he too was personally offended by Mr. Serrano's so-called art, but that—as I have heard time after time on this issue—the Endowment is prevented by its authorizing language from promoting or suppressing particular points of view.

Chuck Asay, by permission of *The Colorado Springs Gazette Telgraph.*

Mr. Southern's letter goes on to endorse the Endowment's panel review system as a means of ensuring competence and integrity in grant decision, and he states that the Endowment will review their processes to be sure they are effective and maintain the highest artistic integrity and quality.

However, shortly after receiving Mr. Southern's response, I

became aware of yet another example of the competence, integrity, and quality of the Endowment's panel review system. It is a federally supported exhibit entitled: "Robert Maplethorpe: The Perfect Moment." The Corcoran Gallery of Art had planned to open the show here in Washington on July 1, 1989, but abruptly canceled it citing the danger the exhibit poses to future Federal funding for the arts. The Washington Project for the Arts subsequently agreed to make their facilities available and opened the show on July 21, 1989.

Offensive Photos

The National Endowment, the Corcoran, and others in the arts community felt the Mapplethorpe exhibit endangered Federal funding for the arts because the patently offensive collection of homo-erotic pornography and sexually explicit nudes of children was put together with the help of a $30,000 grant from the Endowment. The Exhibit was assembled by the University of Pennsylvania's Institute for Contemporary Art as a retrospective look at Mr. Mapplethorpe's work after his recent death from AIDS. It has already appeared in Philadelphia and Chicago with the Endowment's official endorsement.

I have a catalog of the show and Senators need to see it to believe it. However, the catalog is only a survey, not a complete inventory, of what was in the Endowment's show. If Senators are interested, I have a list and description of the photographs appearing in the show but not the catalog because even the catalog's publishers knew they were too vulgar to be included—as sick as that book is.

Pornography

Vanity Fair magazine ran an article on another collection of Mapplethorpe's works which appears at the Whitney Museum of Modern Art in New York. This collection included many of the photographs currently in the NEA funded exhibit. There are unspeakable portrayals which I cannot describe on the floor of the Senate.

This pornography is sick. But Mapplethorpe's sick art does not seem to be an isolated incident. Yet another artist exhibited some of this sickening obscenity in my own State. The Duke Museum of Art at Duke University had a show deceptively titled "Morality Tales: History Painting in the 1980's." One painting, entitled "First Sex," depicts a nude woman on her back, legs open, knees up, and a little boy leaning against her leg looking into her face while two sexually aroused older boys wait in the background. Another work shows a man urinating on a boy lying in a gutter. Other, more despicable, works were included as well.

I could go on and on about the sick art that has been displayed around the country. These shows are outrageous. And, like Serrano's blasphemy, the most outrageous thing is that some of the shows, like Mapplethorpe's, are financed with our tax dollars. Again, I invite Senators to see what taxpayers got for $30,000.

Deceptive Descriptions

How did the Endowment's vaunted panel review system approve a grant for this pornography? It was approved because the panel only received a description, provided by the Endowment's staff, which read as follows:

> To support a mid-career summary of the work of photographer Robert Mapplethorpe. Although all aspects of the artist's work—the still-lifes, nudes, and portraits—will be included, the exhibition will focus on Mapplethorpe's unique pieces where photographic images interact with richly textured fabrics within carefully designed frames.

What a useless and misleading description. No legitimate panel of experts would know from this description that the collection included explicit homo-erotic pornography and child obscenity. Yet none of the descriptions for other projects funded by the Endowment at the time were any better. Indeed, Mr. Jack Neusner—who sat on the panel approving the Mapplethorpe exhibit—was mystified as to how he had approved a show of this character. He knows now that he was misled.

Protecting the Taxpayer

If a democratic society cannot find a way to protect a tax-paying Christian heterosexual from finding that he is engaged in subsidizing blasphemous acts of homoeroticism, then democracy simply isn't working.

William F. Buckley Jr., *Conservative Chronicle*, August 9, 1989.

There is a fundamental difference between Government censorship—the preemption of publication or production—and governmental refusal to pay for such publication and production.

There have been instances where public outrage has forced artists to remove works from public display. For instance, shortly after Mayor Harold Washington's death, a work portraying him as a transvestite was forcibly removed from a show in Chicago. Another work on display at Richmond's airport was voluntarily removed after the night crew complained about a racial epithet which had been inscribed on it. There was little real protest from the arts community in these instances.

At a minimum, we need to prohibit the Endowment from using Federal dollars to fund filth like Mr. Serrano's and Mr. Mapplethorpe's. If it does not violate criminal statutes and the private sector is willing to pay for it, fine! However, if Federal funds are used, then Congress needs to ensure the sensitivities of all groups—regardless of race, creed, sex, national origin, handicap, or age—are respected.

An Insult to Taxpayers

Federal funding for sadomasochism, homoeroticism, and child pornography is an insult to taxpayers. Americans for the most part are moral, decent people and they have a right not to be denigrated, offended, or mocked with their own tax dollars. My amendment would protect that right.

If Senators want the Federal Government funding pornography, sadomasochism, or art for pedophiles, they should vote against my amendment. However, if they think most voters and taxpayers are offended by Federal support for such art, they should vote for my amendment.

"The distinction between censorship and determining the distribution of taxpayers' dollars on moral grounds eludes me."

Restricting Art Funding Is Censorship

Robert Brustein

The National Endowment for the Arts is a federal agency which has been criticized for funding artists whose work may be considered offensive. In the following viewpoint, Robert Brustein argues that public tastes should not dictate what the NEA supports. Placing restrictions on who the NEA can fund infringes on artists' constitutionally protected right of free expression, he maintains, and amounts to censorship. Brustein is the theater critic for the weekly magazine *The New Republic.* He has directed a national theater company and has served on the National Endowment of the Arts' theater panel.

As you read, consider the following questions:

1. What is the hidden target of Senator Jesse Helms's attack on art funding, according to Brustein?
2. Why does the author quote the legislation that created the National Endowment of the Arts?
3. How does the author use his experience on the Endowment's review panel to support his argument?

Robert Brustein, "The First Amendment and the NEA," *The New Republic,* September 11, 1989. Reprinted by permission of *The New Republic,* © 1989, The New Republic, Inc.

One of the troubling things underlying the flap over the National Endowment for the Arts is the belief that "no artist has a First Amendment right to a government subsidy." This is an assumption not just of moral absolutists on the right; it is being expressed by many liberals. . . . A cartoon by Jules Feiffer shows a wild-haired, scraggle-bearded artist raging against society, then concluding his tirade with the words "FUND ME." And Garry Trudeau's Mike Doonesbury covers his eyes when his wife, J.J., demands government subsidy for her "urinal art." Even among those who think the commonwealth will survive the works of Robert Mapplethorpe or Andres Serrano, some are questioning the judgment of the institutions that initially displayed them because they used government funds. It would seem that federal subsidy completely changes the ground rules governing freedom of artistic expression.

An Unrecognized Threat

While some organs of the press—notably *The New York Times*, which has covered the controversy superbly—recognize analogies between restraints on artistic freedom and on freedom of speech, I do not think the censorship threat is being properly appreciated, largely because it has been clouded by charges of obscenity and blasphemy. A consensus in Congress, and probably in society at large, seems convinced that the NEA should not be allowed to fund art that the majority finds unpalatable. Jesse Helms affirms that "if someone wants to write nasty things on the men's room wall, the taxpayers do not provide the crayon," while a letter signed by 27 senators and written on Alfonse D'Amato's stationery says, "This matter does not involve freedom of expression. It does involve whether taxpayers' money should be forced to support such trash."

In a cogently argued article in *The American Scholar*, Richard A. Posner reminds us that "nowadays there is no objective method of determining what is art and what is offensive. . . . Even if everyone to whom judges are willing to listen agrees that a work has no artistic value, we know from historical experience that it may." I am not in a position to judge whether Serrano's "Piss Christ" or Mapplethorpe's homoerotic photographs represent art or pornography. Along with most of their outraged critics, I haven't seen the exhibits. But even if posterity were to prove these works worthless, civil libertarians would be obliged to defend them, on the principle that if you are not prepared to protect bad speech, you are in a poor position to protect the good. . . .

It is modern art itself—not just a crucifix dipped in urine—

that represents the hidden target of the conservative backlash. Hilton Kramer is too sophisticated a critic to second Helms's fundamentalist religious prohibitions, and he is a well-known defender of high modernism, but his own position is not all that different. Opposed to government intervention in the arts through systematic programs of censorship, he nevertheless equates these with government intervention through systematic programs of support—citing such "antisocial" NEA-funded work as Richard Serra's *Tilted Arc*. What should the federal money support instead? Those artworks that Kramer calls "the highest achievements of our civilization." Invoking the same pious language, Samuel Lipman asks the NEA to reject "the latest fancies to hit the art market" and champion instead "the great art of the past, its representation in the present and its transmission to the future." (Compare Helms, pointing with pride to the paintings of pastoral North Carolina scenes on his walls: "I like beautiful things, not modern art.")

Steve Artley. Reprinted by permission of Artley Cartoons.

All this takes place in a rather grim historical context. Totalitarianism's campaign against "degenerate modern art," and its insistence that art be "the handmaiden of sublimity and beauty, and thus promote whatever is natural and healthy," is well known. The memory of it is still fresh. At this late date, we should be wary of the attack on the new and the "offensive." Conservatives would reply, of course, that the United States, unlike Nazi Germany or Stalinist Russia or Khomeini's Iran, is not calling for the suppression of offensive art, only its exclusion from federal funding. But the distinction between censorship and determining the distribution of taxpayers' dollars on moral grounds eludes me. It derives from the pernicious American tradition of letting the marketplace—rather than a Commissar of Culture or a Minister of Propaganda—function as the censor of the arts.

In short, the moral question of censorship is ultimately less threatening than the related political question with which I began: whether the federal government should be funding unpopular modern art at all. This issue was directly confronted in the original enabling legislation of the Endowment, which was created precisely to prevent politicians from voting directly on artists or projects. An unequivocal paragraph stated: "No department, agency, officer, or employee of the United States shall exercise any direction, supervision, or control over the policy, determination, personnel, or curriculum, or the administration or operation of any school or other nonfederal agency, institution, organization, or association." The NEA was thus intended as a buffer between Congress and the arts, with the legislators responsible for approving the budget and professional peer panels responsible for approving grants. Congress was never empowered to be a watchdog on the Endowment as it is, say, on HUD [Department of Housing and Urban Development] or the Pentagon. It was charged rather with guaranteeing the integrity of the grantmaking procedure, however controversial. The decisions of the panels were rarely, if ever, overruled; and only 20 grants out of more than 85,000 were even questioned.

Forgetting Free Speech

Today Congress seems to have forgotten that the original resolution of the Endowment committed the federal government "to help create and sustain not only a climate encouraging freedom of thought, imagination, and inquiry, but also the material conditions facilitating the release of this creative talent." Contrary to current thinking, this placed the Endowment squarely under the protection of the First Amendment, guaranteeing free artistic expression on the same grounds as freedom of speech and freedom of the press. Of course some of these expressions were bound to enrage the majority. That is what we mean by dissent. But it is the very function of the First Amendment to defend unpopular minority opinion against the tyranny of majority constraint.

This fundamental purpose was soon undermined by know-nothing cries of "elitism." If there is anything on which both right and left agree, it is the need for "populist" sovereignty of the majority over the arts. But popular taste has always been perfectly well represented by the market—by Broadway shows, best-selling books, platinum records, rock concerts, Hollywood movies. The National Endowment, by contrast, was designed as a countermarket strategy, not only to "create the material conditions facilitating the release of creative talent," but in the hope that by subsidizing cultural offerings at affordable prices, "the people," in Chekhov's words, "could be brought up to the level of Gogol rather than bringing Gogol down to the level of the people."

Paying for Intolerance

The U.S. Senate's vote to bar federal support of "obscene or indecent" artwork is the most serious and radical assault on freedom of expression to occur in this country since the days of Joe McCarthy and "blacklists."

We can understand that sometimes some people may find a particular work of art offensive. Yet there is a great difference between criticizing a work as reprehensible and censoring it. . . .

Without an atmosphere of tolerance, the artistic imagination is forced underground. Those societies that have absolutely no tolerance for expressions outside the narrow bounds of a particular ideology pay for their lack of dialogue. The result in such intolerant societies: disappearances, gulags and massacres in public squares.

John Farrell and Max Benavidez, *Los Angeles Times*, August 7, 1989.

Critics like Kramer try to meet this argument by trying to discredit the credentials of the professional panelists. "Professional opinion in the art world," he writes, "can no longer be expected to make wise decisions on these matters. . . . There is in the professional art world a sentimental attachment to the idea that art is at its best when it is most extreme and disruptive." It is certainly true that some artists like to flout prevailing codes of conduct. But even the high modernism that Kramer reveres was "extreme and disruptive," as good art often is. And the professional panel system, for all its flaws remains the best we have. It is clearly preferable to the punitive grant procedures being prepared by our elected officials.

The Peer Panels

I was invited to participate on these panels a number of times, as a drama critic and as director of a professional theater company. I joined other critics, directors, playwrights, theater artists, state council members, union leaders, and related figures, and was consistently amazed at the quality and objectivity of their judgments. Naturally I had a stake in these meetings. Like others on the panel, my own theater was an annual candidate for funding, and grants were always preceded by evaluations. But like the others, I was obliged to leave the room when my theater was being discussed, and neither the grant amount nor the evaluation ration was disclosed until we were later officially informed.

To the charges that peer panels are old-boy networks rewarding like-minded colleagues and excluding outsiders, or simply funding "the latest fancies to hit the art market," I can only reply that this was never my experience. The theater panels on which I served were composed of a great variety of people, drawn from many aspects of the profession. There was usually heated disagreement around the table. Often I disagreed with other panelists. But what always impressed me was their capacity to accept arguments and fund theaters, that were fundamentally different in aesthetic from their own. Our judgements were made not only on the basis of personal knowledge and the quality of grant applications, but on the basis of the reports of anonymous on-site observers. And most astonishing was the panel's capacity to evaluate, almost invariably correctly, the intrinsic worth of the applicant theater, rather than its extrinsic reputation among audiences and critics. It was not at all unusual to see the grant of an establishment theater reduced because it had gotten *too* fashionable, while a little-known experimental theater was rewarded for taking risks.

In sum, these were self-interested, passionate theater people judging others in a disinterested, dispassionate manner. They gave me heart about the capacity of normally egoistic professionals to perform a selfless civic duty. I can't say if the professional panels in Opera/Music Theater, Dance, Literature, Art, and the other divisions of the Endowment function in the same manner, but I suspect they do. At any rate, the peer system remains far superior to the system proposed by the Congressional School of Criticism, if only for understanding what most legislators do not understand: that "in proportion as freedom is diminished," to cite the language of the NEA resolution, "so is the prospect of artistic achievement."

Supporting Art

In the past 25 years, the National Endowment, however small its subsidies (the Endowment accounts for less than five percent of the budget of a normal-sized institution), has helped to support a great surge of artistic achievement in this country. Its original declaration of purpose was one of a few hopeful signs that America was coming of cultural age, an unusual legislative response to the Bowlders and Mrs. Grundys and Senator Claghorns who invariably oppose anything creative and daring. These figures are once again in the ascendant. But people of goodwill, rather than joining the moralistic brigade, must recognize that if you inhibit artistic expression, however controversial, you threaten the rights of us all. They must recognize that only government—in a time when other funding has grown increasingly restrictive and programmatic—can guarantee free and innovative art. And that means acknowledging that, yes, every artist has a First Amendment right to subsidy.

Distinguishing Between Fact and Opinion

This activity is designed to help develop the basic reading and thinking skill of distinguishing between fact and opinion. Consider the following statement as an example: "The National Endowment for the Arts provides federal funds to artists." This statement is a fact which could be easily verified by checking a description of the Endowment in the *United States Government Manual.* But consider this statement: "The National Endowment for the Arts funds obscenity and pornography." This statement is clearly an opinion. Many people would disagree with this judgment on the projects the Endowment funds.

When investigating controversial issues it is important that one be able to distinguish between statements of fact and statements of opinion. It is also important to recognize that not all statements of fact are true. They may appear to be true, but some are based on inaccurate or false information. For this activity, however, we are concerned with understanding the difference between those statements which appear to be factual and those which appear to be based primarily on opinion.

Most of the following statements are taken from the viewpoints in this chapter. Consider each statement carefully. *Mark O for any statement you believe is an opinion or interpretation of facts. Mark F for any statement you believe is a fact. Mark I for any you believe are impossible to judge.* If you are doing this activity as a member of a class or group, compare your answers with those of other class or group members. Be able to defend your answers. You may discover that others will come to different conclusions than you. Listening to the reasons others present for their answers may give you valuable insights in distinguishing between fact and opinion.

O = opinion
F = fact
I = impossible to judge

49

1. Currently, there are twenty thousand members of the Ku Klux Klan.

2. The "free speech" of the dominant class will never be the "free speech" of the oppressed class.

3. The Ku Klux Klan must not be allowed freedom of speech.

4. The Ku Klux Klan advocates white supremacy.

5. Some artists like to flout prevailing codes of conduct.

6. Some art, music, and writing should be banned to protect society.

7. Some minority college students want all forms of expression that offend them censored.

8. Artwork which features children and has sexual themes is sick.

9. Artwork is clearly protected by the First Amendment.

10. Many rock albums contain sexually explicit material.

11. Sexism and bigotry do not have a legitimate place in music.

12. Many people argue that the federally funded National Endowment for the Arts should not be used to support obscene or indecent materials.

13. All art of every kind should be completely free from censorship and artists' freedom of speech should be respected.

14. Congress has the power to censor the artists of the United States.

15. The National Endowment for the Arts awarded fifteen thousand dollars to one of the artists whose art provoked controversy about federal funding for art.

16. Both Democrats and Republicans have argued "no artist has a First Amendment right to a government subsidy."

17. The National Endowment for the Arts falls under the protection of the First Amendment.

18. A "chilling effect" will inevitably befall the whole popular music community as a result of the boycotts of unorthodox music.

19. Putting an end to taxpayer funding of objectionable art is not censorship.

20. Freedom of speech is a right that belongs to everyone, even those who advocate the overthrow of the government and advocate violence.

21. In 1969 the American Civil Liberties Union defended the Ku Klux Klan's right to free speech.

22. Once people allow obscene rock music and obscene art to be censored, society is only a few steps away from censoring all music, art, and literature.

Periodical Bibliography

The following articles have been selected to supplement the diverse views presented in this chapter.

Jeff Bounds	"Heavy Meddle," *Mother Jones*, January 1990.
William F. Buckley Jr.	"Irradiations of Subtle Light and Kink," *Los Angeles Times*, May 8, 1990.
Raymond L. Fischer	"Sex, Drugs, and TV," *USA Today*, March 1990.
James Gardner	"False Witness," *National Review*, January 22, 1990.
Michael Gartner	"If Corporations Are Silenced in Political Debate, Who's Next?" *The Wall Street Journal*, April 5, 1990.
Tipper Gore	"Curbing the Sexploitation Industry," *The New York Times*, March 14, 1988.
Nat Hentoff	"First Amendment Racketeers," *The Progressive*, February 1990.
Robert Hughes	"Whose Art Is It, Anyway?" *Time*, June 4, 1990.
Carol Iannone	"From 'Lolita' to 'Piss Christ,'" *Commentary*, January 1990.
Morton A. Kaplan	"The Limits of Artistic Tolerance," *The World & I*, April 1990.
Garrison Keillor	"Thanks for Attacking the NEA," *The New York Times*, April 4, 1990.
Charles Krauthammer	"We All Believe in Censorship," *Los Angeles Times*, April 29, 1990.
John Leo	"Rock 'n' Roll's Hatemongering," *U.S. News & World Report*, March 19, 1990.
Los Angeles Times	"Censorship in Cincinnati: Art, However Vulgar, Must Not Be Policed This Way," April 10, 1990.
Tom Matthews	"Fine Art or Foul?" *Newsweek*, July 2, 1990.
Richard N. Ostling	"No Sympathy for the Devil," *Time*, March 19, 1990.
Lois Therrien	"Nightmare on Video Street, Part 1: The Legislators," *Business Week*, September 11, 1989.
U.S. News & World Report	"Should Dirty Lyrics Be Against the Law?" June 25, 1990.
Tom Wicker	"After Lyrics, What?" *The New York Times*, February 5, 1990.
Jon Wiener	"Free Speech for Campus Bigots?" *The Nation*, February 26, 1990.

Should the News Media Be Regulated?

CENSORSHIP

Chapter Preface

Although the First Amendment to the U.S. Constitution guarantees freedom of the press, critics complain that journalists sometimes go too far in their pursuit of a story. In the race to beat competitors, critics say, journalists jump to conclusions or accept facts they have not verified. Most journalists acknowledge that they face competitive pressures, in addition to constraints of limited time and space. But their job, they say, is to present the fairest, most accurate and complete picture possible so that the public can make informed decisions.

One possible solution to the conflict between freedom of the press and complaints about media unfairness involves the court system. If someone believes that a journalist has distorted the truth or told damaging lies, that person or company can sue the journalist for libel. Libel suits are intended to prevent irresponsible journalists from publishing untruthful stories. But some journalists argue that the threat and expense of libel suits can deter journalists from aggressive investigative reporting and critical commentary. Critics of libel laws believe that these laws inhibit the press and constitute a form of censorship.

Two noted Supreme Court rulings have examined libel law. In 1964, the Supreme Court ruled in the landmark case *New York Times v. Sullivan* that it was not enough for the information to be false and for a person (or company) to *feel* maligned. It must be proved that the journalist wrote or broadcast material that he or she *knew* was false or had not bothered to verify. This ruling offered strong protection to investigative reporters and other journalists who may have been inhibited from writing important stories out of fear of being sued. A 1990 ruling, however, sided against journalists. In *Milkovich v. Lorain Journal*, the Supreme Court decided that newspaper columns and editorials may be held libelous, even when they are only expressing opinions, if they "imply an assertion of objective fact" that can be proved false. This ruling left columnists, reporters, and even editorial cartoonists newly vulnerable to libel suits. Many journalists fear that the ruling could stifle freedom of expression.

Both Supreme Court rulings raise general questions on the behavior and ethics of journalists and freedom of the press. The viewpoints in the following chapter debate whether there should be limits to freedom of the press.

"We are approaching a time when shifts in our law seriously may dilute the protection of the press and thereby weaken the fabric of this society."

Freedom of the Press Must Be Unlimited

Mario M. Cuomo

Mario M. Cuomo has been the Democratic Governor of New York since 1982. He has gained national prominence for being pro-choice in the abortion debate, for opposing the death penalty, and for strongly advocating a free press. In the following viewpoint, Cuomo argues that the press deserves absolute protection. To restrict the media in any way, he contends, could interfere with its legitimate function of watching the government and keeping the people informed.

As you read, consider the following questions:

1. What developments lead Cuomo to believe the free press is in danger?
2. What practices have undermined public confidence in the press, according to the author?
3. How does Cuomo suggest changing the coverage of important issues?

Mario M. Cuomo, "Preserving Freedom of the Press," *USA Today,* January 1988. Reprinted with permission from *USA Today* magazine, January copyright 1988 by the Society for the Advancement of Education.

The more I learn about government and especially about democracy, the more deeply convinced I become that one of our greatest strengths as a people is our right to full and free expression. No people have benefited more from the gift of free speech and a free press. Never before in history has the gift been so generously given or so fully used. From the very launching of our nation, these freedoms were regarded as essential protections against official repression.

When the geniuses who designed this wonderful ship of state came to draw the blueprints, they remembered Britain and other lands which had discouraged criticism of government and public officials, declaring it defamatory and seditious. The Founding Fathers considered that to be one of the worst parts of British tyranny. They were convinced that much of the struggle for American freedom would be the struggle over a free press. So, they were careful to provide that the right of free expression, through a free press, would be preserved in their new nation, especially insofar as the press dealt with government and public officials. They declared that right of free expression in the First Amendment to the Constitution and wrote it in the simplest, least ambiguous language they could fashion: "Congress shall make no law respecting an establishment of religion, or prohibiting the free exercise thereof, or abridging the freedom of speech or of the press. . . ."

Having provided for the right of free speech for the whole citizenry, they went further and provided separately for "freedom of . . . the press"; as broadly as possible, not tentatively, not embroidered with nuances, not shrouded and bound up in conditions, but plainly and purely.

Gambling on Liberty

The Founding Fathers knew precisely what they were dealing with. The press of their time was not only guilty of bad taste and inaccuracy, it was partisan, reckless, sometimes vicious, and, indeed, the Founding Fathers were themselves often at the point end of the press sword.

In view of that experience, they might have written amendments that never mentioned freedom of the press, or they might have tried to protect against an imperfect press like the one they dealt with—with conditions, qualifications, requirements, and penalties—but they did not. They knew the dangers. They knew that broad freedoms inevitably would be accompanied by some abuse and even harm to innocent people. Knowing all the odds, they chose to gamble on liberty.

The gamble has made us all rich. Over all, the press has been a force for good—educating our people, guarding our freedom, watching our government—challenging it, goading it, revealing it, forcing it into the open. Teapot Dome, the Pentagon Papers, Watergate, the revelations of corruption in New York City —these are all examples of disclosures that might never have occurred were it not for our free press. The press' insistence on forcing the White House to begin to tell the truth about the Iranian arms transaction is a dramatic reminder of how the press works incessantly to assure our liberty by guaranteeing our awareness. Less dramatically, the work of revelation by the press goes on day after day at all levels of government, all over the nation.

By Wright for The Miami News

"Americans have grown so much happier since we eliminated the free press."

Don Wright/*The Miami News*. Reprinted with permission.

Surely, the preservation of this extraordinary strength is worth our eternal vigilance. That is why I believe it is appropriate to consider the matter of freedom of the press now, at this moment. It appears to me—and to others as well—that we are approaching a time when shifts in our law seriously may dilute the protection of the press and thereby weaken the fabric of this society.

Our Constitution is not self-executing; it must be interpreted and applied by the Supreme Court. In effect, no matter how plain the language of the great document may appear to the rest of us, the Constitution will say what the Supreme Court says it says. The dimensions of the right to a free press are therefore in the care and at the mercy of the Supreme Court.

In recent decades, the Court has dealt often with the First Amendment and most of the time has expanded its reach, culminating in the landmark protection of the press in the case of *New York Times v. Sullivan* in 1964. *Sullivan* said that, notwithstanding the fact that the press was inaccurate, even negligent, and the inaccuracy substantially damaged a public figure, there would be no liability on the part of the press. Only if the press were guilty of actual malice—that is, a deliberate falsification or conduct that evinced a reckless disregard—could there be a recovery.

This protection obviously was designed to free the press from the chilling—maybe paralyzing—effect of huge damage awards as a consequence of inaccuracy in trying to report the truth. Some believed this was too much protection; they called it a license to defame, an invitation to dangerous, harmful carelessness. However, some—I among them—thought it was good and necessary policy, good and necessary law; that gamble the Founders took was still a good one.

Changing Interpretations

Supreme Court law, however, is not static or permanent; it changes. In 1985, Justice Byron R. White, who joined the majority in *Sullivan,* announced that he had become convinced the Court had struck "an improvident balance" in 1964. He urged that a better approach would be to return much less protective common-law standards of liability. In a 1986 case, Justice William H. Rehnquist indicated that he too would like to revisit Sullivan with an eye to the possibility of overruling it. . . .

Conservatives generally seem to sense this is a good time to strike. Some recently have proposed making simple "negligence" the standard for responsibility for injurious inaccuracy. What would it do to a small newspaper, magazine, or station to be subjected to a multi-million-dollar verdict, because a jury discovered its reporter did not make what the jury considered to be a reasonable search, perhaps in the library, perhaps through clips, perhaps seeking out witnesses, perhaps checking their stories, checking out their references, going to experts?

There is considerable other evidence to suggest that the courts are moving gradually, but consistently, away from *Sullivan* and toward less protection for the press. Floyd Abrams, a noted attorney and expert on the First Amendment, says the *Sullivan* principles are now under "sustained attack."

One more point about the Supreme Court: putting aside its

somewhat esoteric legal jurisdiction, the truth is that the Court is a living institution. Its nine members are subject to the same public events that affect and instruct you and me. Their decisions to some extent reflect changing circumstances in the world around them or changing ideas about what is reasonable or wise.

This means that, when trying to predict a change in First Amendment rulings, the quality of the press as perceived by the public is a relevant factor. In the *Federalist Papers,* Alexander Hamilton asked: "What is the liberty of the press? . . . Its security, whatever fine declarations may be inserted in any constitution respecting it, must altogether depend on public opinion and on the general spirit of the people and the government."

This is still true today. A press regarded by the public as reckless invites the attention of the Supreme Court and tempts it to perform corrective judicial surgery. That is what Mr. Dooley meant when he said, "Th' Supreme Coort follows th' iliction returns."

Dedicated to Fairness

Americans' dissatisfaction with newspeople seems to have grown, even as journalism has paid increasing attention to its behavior and ethical standards. At the professional seminars, workshops and conferences on journalism ethics that I have participated in, the dedication to fairness and responsible behavior is obvious. So is a tenacious commitment to the function of the press as a watchdog over government. . . . With a persistent current of feeling in the United States that somehow the press should be given its comeuppance, there is a clear and present danger to the venerable and cherished notion that only with a free press can a free people receive the uncensored information it needs to make its choices.

Doug Ramsey, *Los Angeles Times*, March 26, 1988.

This raises a number of questions: What is the public perception of the press today? Is it regarded as less than perfect? If so, how specifically?

Official Criticism

It might be worth noting here that, in earlier times, many of our leading public officials were among the press' harshest critics. Today, the press is apt to refer to a public official who criticizes the media as "Nixonian." If, however, presidential labels are appropriate, the media might just as fairly call its critics "Washingtonian," "Jeffersonian," "Lincolnian," "Taftian,"

"Wilsonian," "Rooseveltian," "Kennedyesque," or "Johnsonian."

For example, George Washington called the press "infamous scribblers." Thomas Jefferson wrote: "Even the least informed of the people have learnt that nothing in a newspaper is to be believed."

Theodore Roosevelt added action to his vitriol. He had Joseph Pulitzer and his *New York World* indicted for criminal libel after the newspaper charged corruption in connection with the digging of the Panama Canal.

William Howard Taft found one paper so bad as to be "intolerable." He told his assistant not to show him *The New York Times.* "I don't think reading the *Times* will do me any good and would only be provocative in me of . . . anger and contemptuous feeling."

Woodrow Wilson lost his conciliatory disposition in dealing with the press. He said, "The real trouble is that the newspapers get the real facts but do not find them to their taste and do not use them as given them, and in some of the newspaper offices, news is deliberately invented.". . .

The Best Evidence

The truth is that criticism of the press by its natural targets—public officials, governors, presidents—however illustrious, is not necessarily good evidence of the press' imperfection. Indeed, it can be argued that it is the best evidence of the press' effectiveness.

The press' job is to find the whole truth, especially that part of it which is forgotten, ignored, deliberately concealed, or distorted by public officials. The better the press does its job, the more likely future generations will be reading colorful condemnations of reporters and commentators by today's politicians, and the more likely that the historical record will be truthful and accurate.

I think I understand this as a public official myself. Although I believe I have been treated very well by the press overall, from time to time I have had occasion to make my own criticisms of some members of the press and their coverage in particular cases. The response has revealed that politicians are not the only ones who are sensitive.

Of much more concern to the press than criticism from me and other public officials should be the criticism that comes from candid, thoughtful members of the press itself. Recently, it has been harsh indeed. What is worse is that the public at large appears to agree.

Harper's Magazine observed in 1985 that, when the *Westmoreland* case hit the headlines, a "flood" of commentary from the press ensued. Editorial writers noted that the press was "widely

maligned, criticized, abused, and worst of all, 'distrusted.'"
They pointed to numerous polls and "the public's conspicuous
failure to be outraged when reporters were barred from
Grenada." *Harper's* continued, "Though Americans ritually in-
tone their devotion to the 'freedom of the press,' they delight in
repeating another prized national dictum: 'Don't believe what
you read in the papers.'"

Obnoxious But Necessary

No one denies that the press can be annoying and intrusive. The
American press, among the least restricted in the world, has so
often abused its powers (planting spies in bushes outside the
home of Gary Hart comes quickly to mind) that many citizens
like to see it slammed. But for all of its faults, the press is still
one of the greatest weapons in the arsenal of freedom. The South
Africans try to keep out journalists and cameras because they
know that one day, the press will help to dismantle apartheid.
Mikhail Gorbachev knows that he cannot modernize the Soviet
Union unless he opens it to the West, including Western journalists: and as he does, gulags will become a relic of the past.
Nowhere in the world will butchers like Idi Amin be safe if the
press can be there, watching and writing.

It may seem that censorship and intimidation are aimed at the
press: in fact, they are targeted on the public, seeking to blind us
all to the truths we need to see and know.

David R. Gergen, *U.S. News & World Report,* April 11, 1988.

The press itself attributes much of this public disfavor to its
own curable defects. Thus, "pack journalism" is a frequently
heard complaint, citing the press' dependence on one another,
forging a uniform point of view so as to avoid embarrassing differences, written as though every statement previously made
by any reporter is indisputable, and the clannish locking of
arms against critics from the outside. As Hodding Carter said in
1985, " . . . We are very, very good at pitching and very, very
bad at catching. . . . The press appears to be paranoid when facing criticism itself.". . .

Tom Wicker adds a larger and more substantive complaint.
He feels the media generally is too prone to promote what it believes is easiest for people to accept and in the process fails to
cover significant issues adequately.

The criticism that is set out here easily could be offset with
generous accolades from sources equally credible. That is not
the point. No one is more eager than I to proclaim how successfully the press has done its job over the last couple of hundred

years, or how much better government might do its job. Still, we must recognize the fact that this nation currently is debating—in the place where we make the rules, the Court—whether or not to limit the freedom of the press despite its good record of 200 years.

The possibility of limitation is a real one. I believe it requires that we admit the media's confessions of imperfection and what appears to be a disconcertingly serious loss of public favor that could encourage restrictions of First Amendment rights.

The first thing we must do is sound the alert and make it clear that we are facing a real threat of restriction of the constitutional freedom of the press. That is not easy. The drift of the Supreme Court does not get reported in the morning headlines. It is an elusive subject to which we must direct attention. Then, we must hope—and we can not be sure it will work—that the reaction will affect, for the better, both the press and the courts. . . .

Freedom and Responsibility

Let me offer you what I believe is an opportunity for all the media to make a contribution to the forming of public policy in this nation: Cover the public issues more thoroughly. Cover campaigns even more extensively. Cover state and local government more deeply, not just press events created by candidates or public officials. . . .

The press is about finding the truth and telling it to the people. In pursuit of that, I am making a case for the broadest possible freedom of the press. However, with that great gift comes great responsibility. The press—print and electronic—has the power to inform, but that implies the power to distort. The press can lead our society toward a more mature and discriminating understanding of the process by which we choose our leaders, make our rules, and construct our values, or it can encourage people to despise our systems and avoid participating in them. The press can teach our children a taste for violence, encourage a fascination with perversity and inflicted pain, or it can show them a beauty they have not known. The press can make us wiser, fuller, surer, and sweeter than we are.

One of the miracles of this democracy is that all of us—both the press and the public—are free to make the choices. We must work to keep it that way, to keep the miracle alive.

"As the media grow in power . . . they increasingly indulge in what many people consider irresponsible or unethical practices."

Freedom of the Press Must Be Limited

John C. Merrill

John C. Merrill is a former newspaper reporter and editor who has also taught journalism. He is the author of the book *Freedom, Ethics, and the Press: Toward a Dialectical Journalism.* In the following viewpoint, Merrill argues that the power of the press must be limited because journalists are unethical. Reporters invoke the constitutional guarantee of freedom of the press to cover their excesses, according to Merrill. He contends that the press should be more responsible by being less critical of the government and by recognizing that there are some things the public does not need to know.

As you read, consider the following questions:

1. How do reporters justify their unethical activities, according to Merrill?
2. How does the author believe journalists manage the news?
3. What examples of unethical press behavior does Merrill cite?

John C. Merrill, "Needed: An Ethical Press," *The World & I.* This article appeared in the February 1988 issue of, and is reprinted with permission from, *The World & I,* a publication of *The Washington Times Corporation,* copyright © 1988.

Journalists in the United States who enjoy bashing everything and everybody in sight are beginning to get growing amounts of their own medicine. The spotlight of criticism is being focused on them and the media they serve.

As the media grow in power and as they cling to their self-designation as a "watchdog on government" and other self-enhancing labels, they increasingly indulge in what many people consider irresponsible or unethical practices. In their mad rush to meet deadlines and what they see as their prime responsibility "to let the people know," American journalists have been pushing ethics out of the picture and enthroning expediency and self-interest. Many critics would contend that "ethical journalism" in today's world is really oxymoronic.

Whether ethics and journalism are contradictory terms or not, it must be said that a considerable degree of unethical activity exists in the press. And often this activity is poorly reported, if at all, because of the press's natural self-interest and its capacity for controlling the news and having the last word.

Certainly the American media must be commended for their alertness to governmental and social immorality and questionable activities. Such media attention does, no doubt, help to keep society "honest" and "careful"—at least to a certain degree. But the media also need to look to their own houses; they themselves must have a greater resolve to be ethical—if for no other reason than to improve their negative image among a skeptical public. . . .

The Press as "Watchdog"

The "adversarial relationship" between press and government is an important consideration for the press. It may well be a myth, as some say, but it is a very important one to journalists. It is a responsibility, in the press's own journalistic dogma, that forces the news establishment of the country to act as a watchdog on government. Many of the ethical problems of the press spring from the assumption that the press must be a check on government, be a critic of government, keep the government honest, and so on. This prompts the press to dig and probe, snipe and snoop; it causes the press to speculate, and to deal in innuendo in its attempt to unearth corruption in high places and to explain the misdeeds of others.

This concept is responsible for the press's accentuating the negative in government matters, seldom revealing positive activities or trends. Of course, the press could stress the positive, defend government positions, and have a partnership relationship with the government; it has no constitutional mandate to do otherwise. Only its own self-assigned duty has generated this adversarial relationship to government.

Many of the press's modern critics see such a self-assigned duty as another instance of press arrogance that often pushes the journalists into unethical areas where damage is done to the whole social fabric, and where many good potential public servants are dissuaded from participation in the governmental arena due to the persistent and prying minions of the press.

This "watchdog" attitude of the press fosters—or creates—the idea that government is necessarily and inherently evil and must be checked. And, in this game, the press has set itself up as the institution that must keep the government honest. Today, as an increasing number of voices are asking who checks the checker, the press falls back on its constitutional freedom guarantee, and when all the rhetoric is done, the answer from the press is essentially this: *Nobody checks the checker.* The press is free and autonomous.

Such a perspective is filled with danger, especially when significant numbers of journalists are unconcerned with ethics. And there is no real evidence to show that journalists are any less evil and need less careful scrutiny than government employees. But, say the journalists, the press is "free" and this is paramount in the United States.

Confusion over Freedom

One reason the press is confused about ethics is that it is confused about its freedom, which it sees as endangered if it puts too much emphasis on its "responsibilities." Talk of responsibility leads to obligations and duties, say the press people, and therefore tends to restrict press freedom. So the journalists always get back to stressing *press freedom* and deemphasizing *press responsibility.* The result is that this deep antipathy to the concept of "social responsibility" keeps journalists from giving much continuing and serious thought to ethics.

What journalists should do is recognize that the concept of "press freedom" can just as easily include the freedom to be positive as negative, and that it can include the freedom of the press to be an ally or apologist for government as well as an adversary. In fact, when the press convinces itself that it is an adversary or watchdog vis-à-vis government, it thereby restricts its own freedom by accepting a very limited role. This "adversary dogma," interestingly, is not even consistent with libertarian theory, and it would seem that journalists who talk about "press freedom" would cease being tied to this "adversary role."

A Know-It-All Press

Press people say that their negative approach to news is natural, and that the people want such news. Anyway, how can the people put their house in order if they do not know that it is out of order? The fact is that journalists, by and large, see themselves as a kind of permanent, relentless opposition to government. They must watch government carefully; they must protect the people from government crimes and excesses. But does every grin and every act of every politician contribute anything important to the public understanding? What about news balance? It means little if the journalist is mainly concerned about pouring out every scrap of information. Where is the balanced overview that tries to correct distortions resulting from all these bits and pieces of disjointed "news"? It is not to be found, for the press is dedicated to its specious formula of accentuating the negative and watchdogging ("hounding"?) the government. . . .

Never, however, does it seem that the press asks itself this basic question: Where does the press get this directive? The answer, of course, is that it has no such mandate, except that which it constantly whispers in its own ears. Maybe the press should remember that, after all, the people at least elect government officials (or some of them); the people never elect an editor, an anchorperson, a news director, a publisher, or a reporter.

The People's "Right to Know"

The other journalistic shibboleth that impinges on press ethics and seems so dear to the heart of media people is "the people's right to know." In any discussion about press ethics or press responsibility, this sacred tenet is dragged out to support almost any journalistic tactic. After all, the story goes, the people have a right to know this or that and we, the journalists, must see to it that they do. This "right to know" concept is fraught with semantic and logical implications, and is one that causes many anxious moments for journalists (and government officials, too) who think seriously about ethics.

Do Journalists Represent the Public?

Many media people, obviously not comfortable with the right granted them in the First Amendment, feel they must justify their activities vis-à-vis government by appealing to a people's right to know. This justification goes something like this: We're not really getting this information for ourselves; we're getting it for the people who have a right to know it. Therefore, you people in government are obligated to give it to us because we are representatives of the people. (Isn't this rather strange? Many of us thought that government officials were the representatives of the people, and the journalists were private-sector, profit-making employees of capitalistic enterprises and not representatives of anybody except publishers and other media owners and managers.)

A Flawed View

The reporter's work should be like a pane of glass, flawlessly clear and unspotted, through which the reader might view the important events of the day. Today, the practice of "personal" journalism in news reporting has persistently sacrificed objectivity for entertainment and the personal gratification—and presumably the greater popularity—of the reporter. The pane of glass is dirtied and distorted. Too often we see and read, not what happened or what was said, but the personal views of the fourth estate.

John Silber, *The World & I*, February 1988.

Perhaps more fundamental is this question: Where do the people get this "right to know"? Much has been written on this subject, but little has been resolved. Perhaps one can infer such a "right" from the free-press clause of the Bill of Rights. It would certainly have to be inferred, for nowhere is such a right specified. Some persons, admitting the lack of a constitutional right to know, insist that it is a "natural" right. At any rate, if there is such a right to know, then the press needs to rethink its own position, for it is abridging this "right" every single day. And it is abridging it in the name of editorial self-determination or "press freedom."

Journalists constantly decide what they will and will not publish; they arbitrarily determine what the public will or will not know. They call this reporting and editing, of course. Certainly they do not call it news management—they reserve that term for governmental activities. But it really is news management; in fact, news management is what journalism is all about. Journalists know this, of course, but talk about and advocate a "people's right to know."

Such concepts as the "watchdog function" of the press (adversarial role) and the "people's right to know," well entrenched in the traditional dogma of American journalism, evidence a considerable confusion in the minds of journalists about the nature of press freedom. And this leads to difficulty in developing any kind of consistent journalistic ethics. Little wonder there is so much ethical confusion—in fact, a kind of ethical vacuum—in American journalism. The basic philosophical foundation stones are not very solid and the mortar holding them together is rapidly turning to powder.

The press looks at ethics from a vested-interest and relativistic perspective, shying away from any absolutes and relegating ethics to particular times, circumstances, and problems. Journalists, by and large, conceive of ethics as prudential actions in certain circumstances that will achieve some preconceived plan of theirs—such as getting information from a source. What they often do is to engage in trying to attain their ends and then justifying or rationalizing the means they use. The philosopher Immanuel Kant would not have considered this ethics at all. Journalism conferences show that, almost without exception, participants shy away from absolutes and the Kantian emphasis on "duty to principle," preferring instead to embrace relativistic and personal morality where any option they choose can be justified as the ethical one.

There seems to be no will today for the press to break through self-serving platitudes and gain any real insight into the ethical issues that beg to be dealt with. No common standards exist for normative press ethics. Absolutes are shunned, and everything beyond a strictly personal or individualized ethics is seen as endangering diversity and, by extension, journalistic freedom.

A Competitive Profession

Ethical decisions confront the journalist at every turn. Most often the journalist looks on his decision making as "professional" or institutional and deals with it as such—rather than approaching it from a truly ethical perspective. "It's newsworthy; so we'll print it." This is an example of considering journalism from a pragmatic or professional perspective instead of going to the ethical level. "If we don't print it, some other medium will," journalists often say. "It's the policy of our newspaper to do it, so we do it," the standard excuse goes. Competition, not ethics, too often determines editorial decisions.

This journalistic reflex action is understandable for several reasons. Beyond the fact that American journalists are highly institutionalized, routinized creatures of habit, they are part of a highly competitive, capitalistic enterprise; as such they are largely concerned with doing what "works" best. Secondly, they are suspicious of "social ethics" or any group-imposed rules or system of restraints that might cause them to lose their sense of identity and freedom. And lastly, and probably most important of all, journalists know very little and appear uninterested in learning about philosophical ethics. In other words, they appear not to have what Kant would call the "will to be ethical." Journalistic pragmatism has taken precedence over journalistic ethics. Too often journalists, engulfed as they are in the daily routine of habit, tradition and pragmatism, leave the business of morality—personal and social—to theologians and academics.

Journalistic Self-Restraint

All members of the media must sooner or later engage in self-restraint or they run the risk, because of the power and pervasiveness of their teaching, of destroying the society on which their livelihood and profession depend.

If we heedlessly trash the minds, indeed the very souls, of our children; if through reiterated models of violence and the false promise of endless instant gratification, we produce generations incapable of self-discipline and restraint; if we encourage the development of insatiable men and women who put the pursuit of pleasure above the pursuit of happiness; if by shortening the attention span, we create persons incapable of complex analysis and responsible judgment; if we distort events of the day, garble the words of our leaders, simplify the character of nations, positing a false equivalence between democratic and totalitarian nations—there can be only one result. A dictatorship may survive by virtue of the strength of one man and an army loyal to him, but the survival of democracy depends upon the moral virtue and reasoning power of its people. If the media fail to assume responsibility for their immense power to educate free men and women, how will democracy survive the onslaught of false and counterfeit values?

John Silber, *The World & I*, February 1988.

The press, for its part, is so protective of its traditional idea of individualism and pluralism that it resists anything that might result in standardization or conformity—even codes of ethics and news councils are often suspect. Such a situation is probably still basically in place, but evidence exists that things are changing, that journalists are becoming more serious about ethics and are merging their concern for pragmatism with a recognition that such a concern is not contradictory to ethics. Perhaps this long-time dedication to pragmatism is the very machine that will move the press toward a higher morality. Now they may be seeing that "ethics is the best policy" for long-term success. . . .

Across the country people are beginning to talk about the use of anonymous sources, inaccurate quotes, unbalanced stories, biased and false statements in news stories, shocking and even gruesome photographs, gossip masquerading as news, political bias in the news, and a large number of other questionable practices. Press people themselves are becoming more conscious of ethical problems: Do we print the name of the rape victim? What about the name of the accused rapist? Do we really believe in full-disclosure reporting—in the people's right to know? Or do we place ethics above such full-disclosure reporting? What really are our responsibilities, and to whom are they owed? Do the ends (such as getting the story) really justify the means? Any means, which means? Such questions, and many others, are presently being taken seriously by journalists.

Doing the Right Thing

It may be that the time has not yet come for a journalistic revolution in ethics. The day of the Kantian "will to be ethical" may still be over the horizon, but there are indications that ethical consciousness is rising in the press and considerable soul-searching about the right thing to do is now mingling with concern about such traditional shibboleths as the people's right to know and the press as a watchdog on government.

Many journalists are recognizing at long last that their calling is a public trust as well as a business and that the press is a powerful ethical force in society, relegating to them an important responsibility. The thought has finally struck home that maybe, just maybe, the people have just as much a right not to know as to know certain things, and that the press can point out positive and helpful facts about government as well as negative and harmful ones.

"The fairness doctrine . . . is definitely not a restriction of the First Amendment, but rather an enhancement."

Broadcasting Should Be Regulated

The Spotlight

The Spotlight is a newspaper whose self–described mission is to report the news that would be "hushed up or distorted by the controlled press." In the following viewpoint, the editors of *The Spotlight* argue that the Fairness Doctrine, which was discontinued by the Federal Communications Commission in 1987, should be reinstated. The Fairness Doctrine was a requirement that broadcasters give equal time to opposite sides of controversial issues. The authors of this viewpoint contend that the Doctrine is necessary because without it only special interest groups have access to the media. All views, including those of *The Spotlight*, must be assured a voice in the major media, they write.

As you read, consider the following questions:

1. How is the liberal media inconsistent, according to *The Spotlight*?
2. What programs do the authors cite as normally exempt from the Fairness Doctrine?
3. What will happen if the government does not regulate broadcasting, according to the authors?

"Put Fairness Doctrine Back to Work Again," *The Spotlight*, October 22, 1989. Reprinted with permission of *The Spotlight*, 300 Independence Ave. SE, Washington, DC 20003.

It's very odd how the most vocal advocates of government interference into the private sector suddenly become very "libertarian" when it is their particular field of activity which the government threatens to regulate.

The Liberal Media

The liberal Establishment media, for instance, routinely plumps for government regulation of the marketplace, schools, health care, buying and selling of real estate, etc.

When it comes to mandating the racial makeup of the private work force, the provision of day care for employees' children, deciding just what type of child care should be available to employees, or mandating the employer to give time off to employees to care for sick relatives or to have children, the media always throws its considerable clout behind such moves. But all of its mouthpieces routinely shout, "Get the government off our backs," whenever the fairness doctrine is discussed.

The fairness doctrine, which until the Reagan administration was considered to have the force of law, simply states that: "A broadcast licensee shall afford reasonable opportunity for the discussion of conflicting views on issues of public importance."

This was considered too intrusive to the free flow of dollars—whoops, make that "ideas"—by the *laissez faire* Reagan administration.

The Fairness Doctrine

The fairness doctrine was established to ensure that the publicly owned airwaves would not be used by the private interests operating them to advance their own private political agendas. Until its repeal in August of 1987, it had been a mainstay of broadcast policy for over 50 years. Its origins dated back to before the Communications Act of 1934.

Under the 1934 act, the Federal Communications Commission (FCC) was to ensure that broadcasters serve the public interest, convenience and necessity. In 1934, the FCC determined that a licensee must make his facilities available for the community on various issues of public importance. In 1959, Congress gave statutory approval to the fairness doctrine through amendments to the 1934 act.

The FCC has historically exempted news programs, political debates and newsmaker interviews such as *Meet the Press*. It has been most often applied to advertising and broadcasts espousing a political view or promoting a specific public policy position.

The application of the doctrine evolved through a series of FCC administrative judgments and court decisions. Then, in 1985, the U.S. Court of Appeals ruled that the doctrine was not a statutory obligation imposed by Congress on broadcasters, but rather a commission policy that could be altered or eliminated at any time.

The History

The FCC, seizing the opportunity to put its libertarian principles into action, formally revoked the doctrine in 1987, a move that was cheered by the National Association of Broadcasters, who had charged that the doctrine was a violation of their First Amendment free speech rights. Since that time, there have been several attempts in Congress to codify—that is, enact into law—the provisions of the fairness doctrine.

Rep. John Dingell (D–Mich.) has been in the forefront of this drive. He has succeeded twice in winning congressional approval of the measure. Once it was vetoed by the president; the second time it was killed in conference committee when threatened with another presidential veto.

On October 3 of 1989 the House approved the measure yet again, this time as part of the budget reconciliation package. The vote was 261-162. Some comments from the debate are instructive. Said Dingell: "It is only fair that when broadcasters own that wonderful right to use the money machine which they are given by the FCC, that they should use it in the public interest. This is what is at stake here. . . ."

Testing Human Nature

Rep. William Dannemeyer (R-Calif.) expressed puzzlement over his fellow conservatives' opposition to the measure. "One of the things that I have puzzled about in my mind is . . . how do we achieve an ability to respond to a contrary point of view without it? I have never heard a rational argument of how we get a recalcitrant radio station to give an opportunity for another point of view without this doctrine.

"To leave to the tender mercies of those who manage a radio station by placing on their tender conscience whether or not they will respond in time to give the other point of view is a test of one's credulity as to the nature of human nature itself.

"But the point I want to get across is, what is the harm of having this in our law? What is the harm of having a law which says that if the owners of a radio station want to give us a bias on a particular point of view that the people on the other side have an opportunity of having their views heard?"

No Chill

To rebut the arguments of opponents that the doctrine would cast a "chill" on the First Amendment by causing broadcasters to avoid controversial subjects and issues altogether, Rep. Al Swift (D-Wash.) said: "The fairness doctrine . . . was the law of this land for decades, and none of the horror stories that the opponents of the fairness doctrine will tell you will occur if it is restored occurred when it was in place. It worked. It served a useful purpose.

"It did so without transgressing the rights of broadcasters, and it was repealed as a part of some kind of an ideological mantra [by an] erstwhile and not lamented Federal Communications Commission that is no longer whinnying with us.". . .

The doctrine addresses a vital aspect of freedom of speech that the Constitution does not address.

The First Amendment simply prevents the government from abridging freedom of speech. It says nothing about private institutions. What is important to realize about the modern media is that it has usurped the role of the sovereign.

Today, in this country, instead of the government manipulating the media, it is most often the other way around. The media tells the government and politicians what to do and say.

The Media's Power

The media's unprecedented power derives from its ability to mold public opinion through selective and biased coverage of world events. This new arrangement of powers renders freedom of speech a dead letter.

The media functions as judge and jury. When smeared or ignored by the media, its victims have no recourse, except, in the case of broadcast coverage, through the fairness doctrine. Doing away with the doctrine will not hurt the Republicans or the Democrats, the liberals or the conservatives, but only the odd man out—populists, for instance.

Under the present setup the so-called free marketplace of ideas is a joke. Only the organized pressure groups have access to the media, which actively discriminates against populist ideas.

The libertarian-conservative ideology dictates that government remove itself from the private sector altogether, which leads to the formation of monopolies where a few big fish set the tune and the small fry sing along in unison—an apt description of the media today.

These monopolies and oligopolies set the public agenda, dictate to the public the positions that are acceptable, and ignore or smear those who don't go along with the prevailing orthodoxy.

The fairness doctrine is the one tool available to the non-conformist to respond to smears or lack of coverage by the broadcast media. It definitely is not a restriction of the First Amendment, but rather an enhancement.

"Support for the Fairness Doctrine is support for the government deciding what the public should be watching or listening to."

Broadcasting Should Not Be Regulated

John Fund

The Fairness Doctrine was a Federal Communications Commission rule that required broadcasters to air both sides of controversial issues. Since the FCC discarded the requirement in 1987, there has been an ongoing effort to make the Doctrine into law. In the following viewpoint, John Fund argues that reinstating the Fairness Doctrine would actually inhibit the coverage of controversial issues. Broadcasters would face such harsh fines if their coverage was thought to be biased, he contends, that they would avoid anything that was contentious. Fund is an editorial writer for *The Wall Street Journal*.

As you read, consider the following questions:

1. How does the Fairness Doctrine benefit incumbents, according to Fund?
2. Why does the author believe it can no longer be argued that opportunities to broadcast opinion are scarce?
3. Why do some people object to eliminating the licensing of broadcasters, according to Fund?

John Fund, "Fairness Flimflam." Reprinted with permission, from the February 1988 issue of *Reason* magazine. Copyright 1988 by the Reason Foundation, 2716 Ocean Park Blvd., Suite 1062, Santa Monica, CA 90405.

"How could anyone be against something called the Fairness Doctrine," says Sen. Ernest Hollings (D-S.C.), chairman of the Senate Commerce Committee. The senator is the leading backer of an attempt in Congress to overturn the 1987 decision by the Federal Communications Commission to repeal the doctrine. Broadcasters, said the FCC, would no longer be required to give equal time to all sides of controversial topics.

Inhibiting Free Speech

The senator touts the 38-year-old Fairness Doctrine as a way of letting diverse viewpoints be heard. Actually, it inhibits free speech by discouraging broadcasters from ever taking up controversial issues.

Hollings is so eager to keep broadcasters under the federal fairness thumb that in November 1987 he rushed through a bill writing the Fairness Doctrine into law. His tactics included calling a committee meeting on two hours' notice, changing the hearing room three times, and allowing almost no witnesses.

To make the measure especially palatable, Hollings married his Fairness Doctrine bill to a 2 percent tax on the sale of all commercial radio and television stations. The tax would raise some $300 million a year, and after 1990 the money would go to subsidize public television. Broadcasters who violated the Fairness Doctrine would have to pony up an additional 1 percent fine when their stations were sold—an easy way to deep-six controversial programming at most stations.

Benefiting Incumbents

Why are Hollings and so many of his colleagues eager to pump life into the Fairness Doctrine? Because they are prime beneficiaries of its constraints on broadcasters. Hollings himself credits the doctrine with providing the media exposure he needed to win his first statewide race.

The doctrine is just one of a host of benefits Congress has written into law to give incumbents more TV and radio air time. These include equal-time laws that ensure that a challenger won't receive more coverage and a requirement that political ads be sold at special low rates. . . .

A constitutional challenge to the doctrine may find favor with the Supreme Court. In the 1969 *Red Lion* case, the Court upheld the Fairness Doctrine on the grounds that there was a natural "scarcity" of outlets for diverse viewpoints.

At the time, such a view was plausible. There were only the three big networks. Now there are almost too many to count —even a simple cable-television system has 25 channels. To call the current environment one of "scarcity" is a little like thinking there aren't enough game shows on TV. In a 1984 decision, the high court hinted agreement and said it might be willing to examine the Fairness Doctrine in light of the new technological landscape.

A Source of Revenue

The explosion of the myth of scarcity in broadcasting has led to a new attitude toward the electromagnetic spectrum. Slowly but surely, the government has begun to look at it as a source of revenue. Hollings's bill, while wrongheaded, is a sign of this change. More importantly, the FCC has asked for authority to take public bids on new band rights for satellite and mobile-radio services—six megahertz of the spectrum, or about as much as a single TV channel takes up. This spectrum space is conservatively estimated to be worth $800 million over a two-year period.

"EVICT HIM? ABSOLUTELY NOT! HE'S THERE FOR THEIR BENEFIT!"

John Trever/*Albuquerque Journal*. Reprinted with permission.

Talk of privatizing the airwaves—and thereby eliminating the licensing process from which government control of broadcast content springs—drives supporters of the Fairness Doctrine into a near frenzy. They are a curious coalition, ranging from Phyllis Schlafly and the National Rifle Association on the right to antinuclear activists and Ralph Nader on the left. All have something in common: They are very visible yet still never think they get enough attention from the media. They would get even less if the spectrum were privatized.

But the key special-interest group in support of the status quo is Congress. Bill Monroe, former host of NBC's "Meet the Press," says that what really concerns members of Congress is that broadcasters might not adequately cover them and their causes. Sens. Claiborne Pell (D-R.I.) and David Boren (D-Okla.) propose requiring free air time for the two major parties during the last two months before an election.

But if people don't want to watch political coverage, this can hardly be described as programming "in the public interest," the supposed aim of broadcast regulation. Support for the Fairness Doctrine is support for the government deciding what the public should be watching or listening to. That kind of elitism is unwise in times of calm and downright dangerous in times of crisis. If the Constitution is clear on any point, it is that free speech isn't free if it can be dictated by bureaucrats.

"If damaging articles or broadcasts turn out to be false, the [libeled] person should have the ability to recover damages."

Libel Laws Should Be Strengthened

Michael Ledeen

In the following viewpoint, Michael Ledeen argues that the mass media are so powerful that they can gravely damage people's reputations and lives. Ledeen believes that this fact justifies strengthening libel laws. A person who is the victim of false allegations in the news media should be able to recover damages, he contends. Ledeen is a senior fellow in international affairs at the Center for Strategic and International Studies, a Washington, D.C. think tank. He is a columnist for the conservative monthly magazine *The American Spectator* and the author of the book *Perilous Statecraft: An Insider's Account of the Iran-Contra Affair.*

As you read, consider the following questions:

1. What does Ledeen call the New McCarthyism?
2. When should the media be able to publish allegations, according to the author?
3. Why does Ledeen argue that reporters should be required to give background information for readers?

Michael Ledeen, "The New McCarthyism," *The American Spectator*, October 1988. Reprinted with permission.

The great evil of McCarthyism was the political witchhunt, in which innocent people were smeared and ruined on the basis of rumor and innuendo rather than solid evidence of wrongdoing. With the defeat of McCarthy and the triumph of liberal democracy in the mid-fifties, such things were supposed to have been driven from American political life. Wrong. McCarthyism thrives in Washington, D.C., a city in which, once you have been attacked in the media, you are widely held guilty until proven innocent, in which guilt by association is commonplace, and where political witchhunts are now so frequent as to escape comment. The inquisitioners, now as in the fifties, generally come from the Congress, but the organizers of the witchhunts, the leaders of the lynch mob, the Red Queens of this murderous pack of cards, come from the media.

The Victims

The stories of the victims of the new McCarthyism now fill a good-sized volume: from Raymond Donovan to Hamilton Jordan to Robert L. Green (the former president of the University of the District of Columbia, who was hounded out of town on the basis of charges that were found to be false), from James Beggs to Anne Burford, Les Lenkowsky and Bert Lance, people are damaged—even ruined—on the basis of unsubstantiated, anonymous allegations. From the moment the allegations are published, the curtain falls. Clients run away, job opportunities vanish, friends are hard to find, telephone calls don't get answered, children are subjected to ridicule even by their teachers, wives develop homicidal tendencies. Even if they are eventually "cleared," it is often too late for them to resume their lives at anything like the level at which they functioned prior to the scandals. When Raymond Donovan asked where he could get his reputation restored, he was only telling half the story. For many victims of the new McCarthyism, the ability to find work and earn money is also very much at stake.

Like the original version, the new McCarthyism is wrong, vicious, and un-American. It is a warning sign, a symptom of the possible degeneration of democracy into mob rule. This dangerous process is catalyzed by the media and fueled by the lawyers and investigators that make up such a large part of the population of the nation's capital. It has already produced a terrifying result: the most fundamental principle of our legal system—a person is innocent until proven guilty—has been driven out of town on a rail. I wonder if there is any real hope of bringing it back until the cycle has run its full course.

"Innocent until proven guilty" is something precious, and a real rarity on this planet. In those parts of Europe where Napoleonic law still rules, the burden of proof is on the accused, not the accusers. And in most of the rest of the world, the same basic principle applies. We and the British, along with those countries that go by British tradition, maintain the opposite approach, firm in our conviction that it is better for some of the guilty to go unpunished than for the innocent to be sent to prison.

"...WE DEFAMED SHARON. WE PRINTED FALSE INFORMATION. WE WERE CARELESS AND NEGLIGENT. BUT, HEY, IT WAS ALL AN HONEST MISTAKE. CHEERS, GENTLEMEN! ANOTHER TRIUMPH FOR THE FIRST AMENDMENT!"

Reprinted with permission: Tribune Media Services.

Yet today, the ruination of a person in public life takes place long before (and often without) any finding of guilt. It is generally sufficient for the odor of scandal to attach itself to a person for the process of ostracism and decline to begin. And while the odor comes from many places—the investigators, colleagues, enemies, "informed sources"—it invariably arrives through the media. Some publications seem to make it a point of honor to slander public figures. The *St. Louis Post-Dispatch*, for example, ran an editorial about the 1988 Pentagon scandal which included the following "thoughts":

> A strong-willed manager like former Navy Secretary John Lehman and his cohorts could ride rough-shod over Congress and the other armed services. It is also not surprising that the current bribery investigation centers on many of these same people.

81

John Lehman has been named in article after article as a potential target of some investigation or other. His picture has been on the front pages. His name has been pronounced in close proximity to other words like "bribery," "illegal," and "scandal." The disgraceful *Post-Dispatch* speaks of "many of these same people," yet names only Lehman. Yet John Lehman has been accused of nothing, and, so far as I can tell, no evidence of any wrongdoing on his part has been introduced by anyone. . . .

Waiting to Publish

If one is truly to be held innocent until proven guilty, then unsubstantiated allegations should not be published. The media should be required to wait until wrongdoing has been established, or, as the Founding Fathers wished, until an indictment has been handed down by a grand jury (that is the reason why grand jury proceedings are supposed to be secret, in order to protect the good names of innocent persons). To be sure, a good prosecutor can, as the saying goes, get a grand jury to indict a ham sandwich, but waiting for indictments is a lot better than the present situation, in which a prosecutor can indict someone in the media, and doesn't have to bother with the rather slower tempo of due process.

Requiring that wrongdoing has been established before writing about it would do wonders to calm the currently superheated atmosphere in which media and government officials operate, but it has some serious problems. For starters, such a requirement would violate the First Amendment, and, by depriving the press of its important investigatory role, would undoubtedly encourage favoritism among prosecutors and judges. One wants good investigative journalism, for it is sometimes the only way to uncover wrongdoing. But one also wants to avoid besmirching innocent parties.

A Compromise

So we have two important principles of American life in conflict. A satisfactory compromise must be found. In order to work, that compromise will have to provide satisfactory answers to two questions: Can we devise a reasonable set of rules that will safeguard the media's right to free expression and also the individual's right against mischievous and damaging attacks from the press? Is there some method of accountability that can be enforced on those who flagrantly violate those rules?

We can certainly make a set of rules that would, if observed, restore some sense of calm and orderliness to our political life. The main requirement is that, if the media are going to publish or broadcast damaging information about a person, the information should be true. If damaging articles or broadcasts turn out to be false, the person should have the ability to recover damages. That is the reasoning behind antidefamation laws. Yet the current interpretation of libel requires that a plaintiff establish not only that the offending articles or broadcasts were false and damaging, but that they were created, in full knowledge that they were false, precisely to damage him. This is just too much to ask. In the rest of the world, the only defense against a libel suit is . . . truth. If the publication or broadcast is found to be false and damaging, then the plaintiff wins. We must move closer to this position.

The Wrong Road

Many of us think that U.S. courts took the wrong road and should restore the earlier balance between the rights of the press and one's right to protect his reputation. We ought to get back to the old and simple rule that if someone publishes a falsehood about you, he's liable—simply and certainly—for adverse results. That will tend to increase freedom and not, as our courts have implied, diminish it.

Herb Schmertz, *Conservative Chronicle*, January 20, 1988.

At the same time, one does not have to insist that only "truth" can save the media from paying damages. I would favor, for example, permitting the media to defend themselves by demonstrating that they were misled by one or more sources. But in that case, the sources should automatically become the defendants in the suit (and the media could not refuse to identify the sources, while using the sources to protect themselves from libel accusation). I believe this would stop many of the false stories.

Second, the set of rules should require that we make an effort to put stories about individuals in some sort of overall context. For example, in stories about defense contractors allegedly involved in illegal or even unethical behavior, it would help readers—and probably temper the often excessive zeal of the reporters—to describe the ethical standards of the industry at large. What is generally accepted as proper behavior, and what is universally frowned upon? One fact that took quite a while to emerge from the coverage of this very big story is that more and more American companies are refusing to do business with the United States government because of the seemingly infinite levels of bureaucracy, green-eyeshade types, and the inevitable barristers, that consume time and energy in any contractual relationship with the Department of Defense. The country can ill afford a situation in which only those who can't make it in the open market will agree to do work for the government. So context is very important indeed, and should be given in any of these stories.

Time for Enforcement

That leaves us with the question of accountability and enforcement. . . . The media folks don't like it at all, but the clock is ticking on their free ride with the American public. It is time to enforce professional standards in the media, a need as obvious to concerned citizens as it is distasteful to the media practitioners.

"Libel suits . . . are having an insidious effect upon our access to news."

Libel Laws Should Not Be Strengthened

Lois G. Forer

Lois G. Forer is a trial court judge in Philadelphia, Pennsylvania. She is the author of *Criminals and Victims* and *Money and Justice*. The following viewpoint is excerpted from her book *A Chilling Effect: The Mounting Threat of Libel and Invasion of Privacy Actions to the First Amendment*. In it, she argues that libel suits are so expensive that they lead the press to censor themselves rather than risk litigations. In addition, the high costs of such suits can drive smaller publications out of business, thus suppressing the diverse opinions they represent. Forer concludes that current libel laws amount to censoring the press.

As you read, consider the following questions:

1. Why is self-censorship particularly dangerous, according to Forer?
2. Why are editorial decisions to refuse or cancel certain articles or books threatening, in the author's opinion?
3. Why does Forer believe the number of libel suits is increasing?

Excerpted, with permission, from *A Chilling Effect: The Mounting Threat of Libel and Invasion of Privacy Actions to the First Amendment* by Lois G. Forer. New York: W.W. Norton & Company, 1987. Reprinted with permission.

For Americans unrestricted access to the spoken and printed word is of vital importance. We consider the right to speak and to hear, to write and to read an inherent and essential aspect of our unalienable freedoms guaranteed by the Constitution. Libel suits, however, are having an insidious effect upon our access to news, information, and entertainment. This chilling effect is both dangerous and contrary to our First Amendment rights.

The dangerous effects of libel suits require examination and discussion. They cannot be sloughed off by the general public as legal issues to be relegated to lawyers and judges. Restriction of information, literature, and entertainment is incompatible with a free society.

A "Wimpy" Press?

When government imposes limitations on expression, the danger is clear and is resisted. Such actions by government officials are bitterly litigated. But when the restrictions are the result of economic coercion and self-censorship, there is little opportunity for the public to protest. No one can compel the press to publish information that is kept secret. Readers and viewers cannot require editors to publish and the electronic media to air programs they have suppressed in order to avoid litigation.

There is no accurate measure of this growing caution. But a number of developments portend more than a mere "blanding" of the press. TV personality Phil Donahue devoted a program to press fears of litigation. He asked, "Is the press becoming wimpy?" In response, Gene Roberts, executive editor of the *Philadelphia Inquirer*, stated: ". . . There are so many libel suits that letters to the editor, your letters to the editor, are not being run by some newspapers because you are being sued and the paper is being sued by politicians because they don't want you to make criticisms of them.". . .

Catastrophic Costs

Although the national networks and large newspapers are extremely wealthy, many magazines, book publishers, local papers, and radio stations have modest assets. For such defendants, the cost of defending a libel suit, much less paying a judgment of $100,000 or more, is catastrophic. Defense of a libel suit entails more than simply retaining high-priced expert counsel. The editor and staff have to spend hours of time preparing documents, attending depositions, and obtaining both defensive and offensive evidence. For a small enterprise, this use of management and staff time is a real hardship. During the past ten years, many smaller publications and radio stations have severely curtailed investigative reporting and publication of controversial pieces.

The national media and magazines will probably continue

fearlessly to report international and national news and activities in metropolitan areas. But in a country as geographically large and diverse as the United States, many significant state and local activities cannot adequately be reported by the national media. The people in smaller communities must rely on local sources for information. Many periodicals like *The Nation, The New Republic, The Atlantic* and *Dissent*, with a national but small readership, make a significant contribution by publishing stories about events and ideas that are not covered by the giant weeklies and monthlies. Diversity of opinion is a desirable end in itself. Small publications also provide an outlet for new, unknown commentators and authors of fiction and nonfiction. Any substantial diminution of the number of publications seriously restricts the opportunities for expression to the detriment of the entire public.

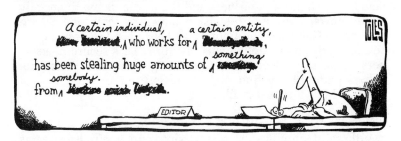

No defendants can ignore the costs of litigation, particularly when their insurance is cancelled or the deductible amount is so high that the media and publishers become, in effect, self-insurers. CNA Insurance Co. ceased writing insurance for the media as of December 31, 1985. Other companies have also stopped writing insurance for publishers and the media. Even when the publisher has insurance coverage, the author may have to expend large sums to compel the insurance carrier to defend a libel action.

Self–Censorship

In the 1970s, defense of a typical libel suit brought to trial cost $20,000. In 1985, the average defense of a libel suit that goes to trial is estimated at $150,000. Some lawyers give a figure of $250,000. Inevitably these facts affect editorial policy.

It is now a common practice for newspapers, as well as publishers of magazines and books and the electronic media, to have their material examined by lawyers before release. This vetting may be deemed defensive journalism. It is intended to save defendants the expense of future litigation. But it is a costly and essentially nonproductive practice. Defensive journalism, like defensive medicine, is not good for either the reader or the patient. When doctors practice defensive medicine, patients are subjected to unnecessary tests and invasive procedures, all of which are costly and often painful. These procedures are followed not for the purpose of benefiting the patient but of protecting the doctor. When defensive journalism is practiced, readers and viewers are given sanitized print and electronic material, not for their benefit but to save the authors, publishers, and producers the expense of litigation and the possibility of substantial damage awards. Floyd Abrams, attorney for many media defendants, points out that, "The ultimate way to avoid the risk is not to write the story."

There are no reliable statistics on the extent of this kind of defensive action by publishers and the media. Some financially strong newspapers and television networks may take a hard line, refuse to settle, and fight every lawsuit in the hope of discouraging or outlasting litigious plaintiffs. Less secure newspapers, radio and television stations, magazines, and book publishers undoubtedly find that discretion is the better part of valor and that survival is all.

Stifling Expression

Authors of unpublished manuscripts and unaired programs have no legal right to compel publication or production of their works. Readers and viewers can write letters of protest when comic strips, columns, and radio and TV programs are cancelled or withdrawn. But they have no legal right to compel publication or production of such works. To date, no one has advanced any credible legal theories that would permit them to bring such suits. When editors and media personnel decide, for any reason, to refuse or to cancel publications and programs, those decisions cannot be contested. The public will probably never know about manuscripts consigned to the wastebasket to avoid lawsuits. Such expressions of opinion or creative works that are quietly and privately stifled have no right to life. No member of the public has standing to sue on their behalf.

Editors and publishers frequently insist on changes to avoid possible litigation. The unhappy author is then faced with a Hobson's choice of acceding to the alteration of the manuscript or rejection. If such softening of comments or opinions was ordered by the government, as happens in many countries, it would be held to be unconstitutional censorship. When practiced by publishers and broadcasters, it is deemed to be editorial discretion from which there is no appeal. . . .

The insatiable demand of the print and electronic media for material has increased the number of references to living persons, thus giving rise to many more potential libel suits. With recent technological developments that enable news to be transmitted almost instantaneously and the rapid growth of the electronic media, the public demand for information and entertainment has risen exponentially. Before transatlantic cables, governments and the public had to wait weeks and months to learn the outcome of battle. Today, the entire world watches the bombs falling. News is reported both in the press and on the air while events are occurring. Radio stations air "all news all the time."

The Costs of Libel

Some notion of the economic pressures on the press as a result of libel suits is revealed by this alarming fact. During a forty-six day period, eight defamation suits were filed against the *Philadelphia Inquirer*. Most of these cases arose out of reporting news. The *Inquirer* is not the *National Enquirer*. It does not engage in sensationalism or irresponsible charges. There is no reason to believe that the *Philadelphia Inquirer* is exceptional or that other daily papers are not sued with the same frequency. The cost of defending a libel suit is estimated at $200,000. If the case is appealed all the way to the U.S. Supreme Court, the cost may be doubled. If the case is remanded, the second trial is almost as costly as the first one. In addition to legal fees and out-of-pocket expenses, the preparation of the defense takes the time and energies of reporters, editors, and managing personnel. To defend against such charges at the rate of fifty a year is a not inconsiderable burden even for a very wealthy paper or radio or television stations.

Lois G. Forer, *A Chilling Effect*, 1987.

The legal equating of oral and written expression with property is of very recent origin. But it, too, is an essential component in the analysis of the conflict between damage claims and First Amendment rights. The concept of property underlies much of Anglo-American law. Right to property was also a significant element of John Locke's philosophy that strongly influenced the American founding fathers. An early draft of the Declaration of Independence proclaimed that among the unalienable rights with which all men are endowed are "life, liberty, and property." The Fifth and Fourteenth Amendments to the Constitution provide that "no one shall be deprived of life, liberty or property without due process of law."

For centuries, British and American civil courts were concerned primarily with property rights. Loss of real and personal property and damage to property was compensated with money, the fair value of what was taken or damaged. Gradually it was recognized that loss of bodily parts and functions resulted not only in pain but also in economic loss, the ability to work. Such injuries became compensable in money damages. In the twentieth century, pain, suffering, and loss of life's pleasures were also recognized as compensable losses. Damage to reputation has for centuries under English law been awarded compensation. In the past few decades, seclusion, peace of mind, and privacy have been accorded limited recognition as legal rights. The remedy for infringement of all these rights is monetary damages.

Differences of Opinion

A large element of news involves individuals and their activities. People want to know which government officials made a particular decision and which individuals opposed it. People are interested in the identity of generals, civilian officials, captains of industry, and movers and shakers in all fields of human endeavor. They also want to know more than the names and positions of newsmakers. They are interested in learning about the lives and characters of the persons making decisions that affect society. Publications like *People* magazine and the *National Enquirer* cater to this natural interest in the lives of people in the news. As more news is reported and presented more fully, inevitably more individuals are mentioned by name, described, and commented upon in all publications.

Moreover, people are not satisfied with the bare bones of facts. They want "in depth" reporting that is more informative. Books, news magazines, and weekly and special documentaries on the air attempt to meet this demand for more information and explanations about a world that is increasingly complex and bewildering to the average person.

Anything more than a summary account of facts ineluctably involves judgment and opinion. Decisions as to items included and excluded, what is to be stressed and what is to be mentioned only briefly are made by the author. The subject may well disagree. Such differences of opinion as to fairness and accuracy lead to litigation. . . .

A Confusing Law

Blaming victims for their misfortunes is a common phenomenon. Many suggest that the media have invited litigation by their obtrusive and irresponsible behavior. Although there are instances of such conduct by publishers of books and magazines, as well as the news media, this is only a partial and limited cause of libel litigation. Defamation suits have been brought against many other types of defendants. Employees and former employees have brought libel suits against their employers because of unfavorable references or failure to give references. Libel actions have also been brought against credit organizations like Dun & Bradstreet for giving customers erroneous information about the plaintiff. Students have sued teachers and teachers have sued students for defamation. All such lawsuits are an inevitable response to the uncertainty and confused state of the law of defamation. . . .

Chilling Press Freedom

I suggest that the price paid by society for punitive damage awards under present standards is too high. Investigative journalism is unduly chilled by the fear and unpredictability of multi-million dollar punitive damage awards, and this, in turn, causes the public to suffer a serious reduction in the amount of information available about its public officials. Accordingly, the courts and legislatures should control the award of punitive damages through the imposition of heavier burdens on libel plaintiffs, limitations on the size of awards, and increased use of summary judgment.

Arlin M. Adams, *Vital Speeches of the Day*, June 1, 1987.

Rationalization of the law governing rights of subjects and authors is designed to promote several important societal goals. It should provide rules that lead to more just and sensible decisions. Subjects who have been harmed by the carelessness of authors should receive redress. Authors should not be compelled to pay enormous sums to subjects who have not suffered any provable harm. Rationalization should clarify the law and thus reduce the amount of litigation. Subjects who know they are unlikely to prevail will probably not sue. Authors who know they are probably liable will usually settle. Clarity of the law would also protect the public interest. If authors were not influenced by the fear of litigation and the inability to predict their liability, they would undoubtedly be less timid in their publications and broadcasts.

a critical thinking activity

Recognizing Stereotypes

A stereotype is an oversimplified or exaggerated description of people or things. Stereotyping can be favorable. Most stereotyping, however, tends to be highly uncomplimentary and, at times, degrading.

Stereotyping grows out of our prejudices. When we stereotype someone, we are prejudging him or her. Consider the following example: Mr. Martin was once interviewed by a journalist. He felt badgered by the journalist's questions and concluded that all journalists have obnoxious, overly aggressive personalities. He has used this one experience to make a generalization about all journalists, a diverse group of people. The possibility that many journalists are pleasant, compassionate human beings who care deeply about the people they interview never occurs to Mr. Martin. He has prejudged all journalists and will not recognize any possibility that is not consistent with his belief.

Part I

The following statements relate to the subject matter in this chapter. Consider each statement carefully. *Mark S for any statement that is an example of stereotyping. Mark N for any statement that is not an example of stereotyping. Mark U if you are undecided about the statement.*

If you are doing this activity as a member of a class or group, compare your answers with those of other class or group members.

S = *stereotype*
N = *not a stereotype*
U = *undecided*

92

1. Journalists are not interested in presenting the public's views, just their own.

2. Never talk to reporters! They always twist what you say into a statement that will get you into deep trouble.

3. *The New York Times* has the most reporters of any New York newspaper.

4. An apt description of the media today is a monopoly where a few big fish set the tune and the small fry sing along in unison.

5. The media are the backbone of American liberty—and always will be.

6. The Fairness Doctrine insures that both sides of an issue get publicized.

7. The media should never be subject to libel suits.

8. Journalists are committed to defending the American people's right to know what goes on in government.

9. If it weren't for investigative reporters, politicians (who, we all know, are crooks) would get away with murder.

10. News reporters have a tough job trying to unearth the truth behind government policymaking.

11. The public deserves the most accurate news reporting available.

12. Newspaper reporters are just doing their jobs. It's the TV reporters who are after all the dirt they can dredge up on people.

13. Anyone who believes in unlimited free speech is a true American and worthy of trust.

14. Censorship of the media is a growing cancer in the American body politic.

15. People who want to censor the media also like to paint swastikas on synagogues.

16. A reporter who invades a citizen's privacy should be sued for libel.

Part II

Based on the insights gained from this activity, discuss these questions in class:

1. Why do people stereotype one another?

2. What are some examples of positive stereotypes?

3. What harm can stereotypes cause?

4. What stereotypes currently affect members of your class?

Periodical Bibliography

The following articles have been selected to supplement the diverse views presented in this chapter.

David Aikman	"The Press Is Missing the Scoop of the Century," *Christianity Today*, March 4, 1988.
Jorge Amador	"Fairness Doctrine, R.I.P.," *The Freeman*, June 1989. Available from The Foundation for Economic Education, Irvington-on-Hudson, NY 10533.
Richard Bernstein	"'Just Kidding'—But at Whose Expense?" *The New York Times*, April 8, 1990.
John Chamberlain	"Uncovering the Liberal Bias of the Media," *Conservative Chronicle*, May 18, 1988. Available from *Conservative Chronicle*, Box 11297, Des Moines, IA 50340-1297.
Marc Cooper and Lawrence C. Soley	"All the Right Sources," *Mother Jones*, February/March 1990.
Tim W. Ferguson	"Toward a Shield Law—From the Press," *The Wall Street Journal*, June 29, 1989.
Raymond L. Fisher	"The FCC and the Fairness Doctrine," *USA Today*, May 1988.
Jeff Kamen and Robert H. Kupperman	"When Terrorists Strike . . . The Lessons TV Must Learn," *TV Guide*, September 23-29, 1989.
Michael Ledeen	"Deadly Reminders," *The American Spectator*, April 1988.
Janet Malcolm	"The Morality of Journalism," *The New York Review of Books*, March 1, 1990.
Eleanor Randolph	"Policing the Press or Censoring It?" *The Washington Post National Weekly Edition*, January 30-February 5, 1989.
Herb Schmertz	"Britannia's Rule on Defamation Is Right One," *Conservative Chronicle*, January 20, 1988. Available from *Conservative Chronicle*, Box 11297, Des Moines, IA 50340-1297.
Rodney A. Smolla	"Why Does Libel Law Need Reform?" *Society*, July/August 1989.
Laurence Zuckerman	"Knocking on Death's Door," *Time*, February 27, 1989.
Mortimer B. Zuckerman	"TV's Incomplete Picture," *U.S. News & World Report*, February 1, 1988.

Does National Security Justify Censorship?

CENSORSHIP

Chapter Preface

Citing national security, the government regularly restricts public access to military information. Many journalists who view themselves as watchdogs on the government oppose these restrictions and consider them a form of unnecessary censorship. Most journalists would agree that there are some legitimate reasons for government (including military) secrecy. The difficulty comes in distinguishing between those times when secrecy is legitimate and when it is not. And who gets to decide? Usually, the person with access to the information decides and his or her view may not be in the public interest.

In defending the public's right to know about military matters, journalists point to the example of the "Pentagon Papers," classified information on the Vietnam War that was leaked to the press. The publication of this information (opposed by President Richard Nixon but permitted by a U.S. Supreme Court decision) helped mobilize public opposition to the war. Some people think publication of the Pentagon Papers also might have speeded the war's end.

On the other hand, many government officials say that the lives of government employees and the security of the U.S. as a whole are reasons to restrict media access to sensitive information. The Central Intelligence Agency (CIA) has long argued that some information, if made public, can be harmful. For example, the CIA points to the assassination of a CIA agent in Athens, Greece in 1975. The agent was killed less than a month after a newspaper had published his name and the fact that he worked for the CIA. The agency concluded that it was the publication of his name and title that led to the agent's death. This case, and others like it, has led the CIA, other government agencies, and many private citizens to conclude that freedom of the press should be restricted. Reporters should not be allowed to print information that could threaten the lives of government employees or damage national security, these critics believe.

The debate over national security and the public's right to know is a debate over two concerns Americans hold dear—the security of the country and the right of free speech and a free press as guaranteed in the Constitution. It will continue to generate controversy in the years to come.

"Potential injury to the rest of society . . . has been most apparent in the media's publication of classified information."

National Security Justifies Censorship

Elmo R. Zumwalt and James G. Zumwalt

In the following viewpoint, Elmo R. Zumwalt and James G. Zumwalt argue that information which threatens national security should not be published. The First Amendment should not be interpreted as allowing journalists to publish classified materials, they contend, because the Constitution's authors could not have known how powerful, and therefore dangerous, the press would become. Elmo Zumwalt is a retired admiral and his son, James G. Zumwalt, is an attorney. They are cocontributors to the weekly *Conservative Chronicle*.

As you read, consider the following questions:

1. What are the traditional exceptions to the First Amendment, according to the Zumwalts?
2. How do the authors support their argument that reporting classified information has hurt America's foreign policy?
3. What steps do the Zumwalts believe must be taken to protect national security?

Elmo R. Zumwalt and James G. Zumwalt, "Putting Responsibility Back into Journalism," *Conservative Chronicle*, October 4, 1989. Reprinted with permission.

The press has been coming under increasing attack for its journalistic irresponsibility:

• Former presidents Gerald Ford and Jimmy Carter, at a conference on presidents and the press sponsored at the Gannett Center for Media Studies in 1989, criticized the media for doing "a lousy job" in news reporting.

• Cries of foul were raised when a major television network, reporting on the Felix Bloch espionage investigation, showed a "simulation" of the act by the senior State Department representative on its nightly news broadcast.

• Classified information, critical to US national security, was obtained by journalists who published the material without fully considering what the ramifications of such a publication would be.

A Present Danger

How have we allowed such a situation to arise and, more importantly, how should we deal with the problem in the future? While our Founding Fathers demonstrated amazing foresight in the wording of the First Amendment of the Constitution, which guarantees freedom of speech, it is very doubtful they ever envisioned the power the media would eventually come to wield in its exercise of that right. The thought of the media as a major, profit-making business is not likely one that crossed their collective mind.

Periodic constraints have been placed on freedom of speech since the Constitution was penned but, in such instances, they have been quite limited and only applied to those instances in which an obvious danger to the rest of society would arise by allowing that freedom to be exercised. That is why the exercise of one's freedom of speech does not entitle one falsely to utter the word "fire" in a crowded theater, for there would be an obvious danger to those attempting to escape in the ensuing panic.

Unfortunately, however, the danger or potential injury to the rest of society is often not so clearly obvious as in the case of the crowded theater. Yet it is there—although our courts have been reluctant to act upon it. This has been most apparent in the media's publication of classified information.

The Libyan Case

An example of this occurred during President Reagan's second term in office: A meeting was held at the White House to discuss possible actions to be taken against Libyan strongman Muhamar Quadaffi who had long been suspected of supporting terrorism around the world. A memorandum was generated from that meeting—marked classified—outlining various alternatives if Quadaffi's misconduct continued. A particular alternative was recommended which would not have required the use of US military force and, while being somewhat unorthodox, might well have terminated Quadaffi's support of terrorism without risking a single American life. The classified memo was somehow obtained by *The Washington Post* which then published it. As a result, the plan had to be scrubbed by the Reagan Administration, which then was forced to explore other options.

Kelley/Copley News Service. Reprinted with permission.

Months later, Quadaffi was linked to the bombing of a West Berlin discotheque frequented by US servicemen. Once the Libyan connection had been established, however, the only remaining option available to Mr. Reagan—due to the *Post's* disclosure—was the military one. In the ensuing attack by US bomber aircraft on military targets in Tripoli, two US aviators were lost. That loss, in the authors' opinion, was unnecessary—incurred as the direct result of irresponsible news reporting which denied us the opportunity to curb Quadaffi's terrorist activities without endangering American lives.

Corrective Steps
There are two directions in which we should be moving to address this problem—one must be undertaken by Congress while the other must be initiated by the media itself:

1) Congress must be pressed to pass an official state secrets act which would make the publication of any classified material a criminal offense. While critics of such a law say it will impinge drastically on freedom of speech, a similar law in England has had no telling effect on freedom of speech there.

2) The news reporting industry must be encouraged to police itself and to establish a "code of ethics" which would seek to set certain performance standards for the media. Such standards should address accuracy as well as substance.

Journalistic Responsibility

The journalist wields an awesome sword. With one fell swoop, he or she can topple a government, can decimate a business, can destroy a career. If properly wielded, that sword serves the public good. But, when it is unsheathed for an ulterior motive—at the expense of the public good—or having little benefit for the public good relative to the injury that will result, it does a great disservice. The journalist has a responsibility to understand the difference. To do otherwise is to take the public trust lightly.

"Virtually every government 'scandal' and controversial national security matter that arises seems replete with lessons on the evils of keeping secrets from the public."

National Security Does Not Justify Censorship

Joseph C. Spear

In the following viewpoint, reporter Joseph C. Spear contends that most classified information is so innocuous that publishing it would not threaten national security. Moreover, he argues, hiding government information from the public has often led to mistaken policies. Public debates can reveal errors in judgment such as those made during the Iran-Contra affair, he maintains. Spear is the author of *Presidents and the Press: The Nixon Legacy.*

As you read, consider the following questions:

1. How did former President Reagan change the process of classifying information, according to the author?
2. What does the author believe is the role of the press?
3. What point does Spear make in his discussion of the Pentagon Papers?

Joseph C. Spear, "An Almost Absolute Right." This article appeared in the February 1988 issue of, and is reprinted with permission from, *The World & I,* a publication of *The Washington Times Corporation,* copyright © 1988.

In a 1974 speech at Yale, the late Supreme Court Justice Potter Stewart, usually given to expansive interpretations of the First Amendment, had this to say:

> There is no constitutional right to have access to particular government information, or to require openness from the bureaucracy. The public's interest in knowing about its government is protected by the guarantee of a free press, but the protection is indirect. . . . The Constitution, in other words, establishes the content, not its resolution.

In varying degrees, these have been the sentiments of our presidents as well. Since 1951, four executive orders have been promulgated to define national security information and to establish rules for classifying it. Each edict called for less official secrecy than the one preceding it—until Ronald Reagan came on the scene.

The Reagan Legacy

Executive Order 12356, signed by the president on April 2, 1982, greatly extended the authority of government officials to classify national security information. It eliminated Jimmy Carter's 1978 requirement that "the public's interest in access to government information" be considered before stamping a document "Confidential," "Secret," or "Top Secret." Definitions of classifiable material were broadened; any doubts about level of classification are now resolved in favor of the higher level of secrecy. . . .

Clearly, many of those who govern do not believe the people have a fundamental right to know what they are up to. Is this truly in the public interest? A well-regarded security expert, Air Force official William G. Florence, offered a different opinion in testimony at a congressional hearing in 1970:

> I sincerely believe that less than one-half of one percent of the different documents which bear currently assigned classification markings actually contain [classified] information. In other words, the disclosure of information in at least 99 1/2 percent of those classified documents could not be [harmful to] the nation.

Supreme Court Justice Hugo Black was another who felt that the public interest would be better served with greater disclosure. When the government asked the courts in 1970 to proscribe publication of the bureaucratic history of the Vietnam War known as the Pentagon Papers, Black dispatched the Nixon administration with these ringing words:

> In the First Amendment the Founding Fathers gave the press the protection it must have to fulfill its essential role in our democracy. The press was to serve the governed, not the governors. The Government's power to censor the press was abolished so that the press would remain forever free to censure the

I'LL TELLS YA WHAT I THINK OF THE AMERICAN PRESS: IT STINKS!

THEY SHOULD PRINT WHAT THE GOVERNMENT TELLS 'EM, AN' STOP ASKIN' QUESTIONS. IF THEY CAN'T SAY ANYTHIN' NICE, THEN THEY OUGHT TO KEEP THEIR YAPS SHUT! JUST THINK...

...WHAT A WONDERFUL PLACE THIS WOULD BE IF OUR PRESS WUZ RUN LIKE TH' SOVIETS'.

KIRK ©1983 THE SCRANTON TIMES

Government. The press was protected so that it could bare the secrets of government and inform the people. Only a free and unrestrained press can effectively expose deception in government. And paramount among the responsibilities of a free press is the duty to prevent any part of the government from deceiving the people and sending them off to distant lands to die of foreign fevers and foreign shot and shell. In my view, far from deserving condemnation for their courageous reporting, *The New York Times*, *The Washington Post*, and other newspapers should be commended for serving the purpose that the Founding Fathers saw so clearly. In revealing the workings of government that led to the Vietnam war, the newspapers nobly did precisely that which the Founders hoped and trusted they would do.

At stake in the Pentagon Papers case was the government's right to classify information that, if published, would presumably bring the nation to its knees. At one point during legal proceedings, the court asked the government's lawyers to pin-point the most sensitive secret in the papers. After considering the matter, they selected a project code-named "Marigold." This was a 1966 attempt to negotiate with the North Vietnamese through Polish contacts. In fact, the Marigold affair had already been mentioned in news journals, and President Lyndon Johnson had devoted two pages to the operation in his memoirs, *The Vantage Point*. A president, of all people, had violated the rules. The secret was out and somehow the nation had survived.

No Real Training

And how were the Pentagon's classification experts trained to make the decision to classify the Pentagon Papers? Three years after their publication, Leslie H. Gelb, the former Defense Department official who had headed the task force that classi-fied the papers, testified that the only instruction he ever re-ceived in security matters was "a movie which had the theme, 'beware of blondes who are excessively friendly—they may be Russian spies.'"

Virtually every government "scandal" and controversial na-tional security matter that arises seems replete with lessons on the evils of keeping secrets from the public. A persuasive argu-ment can be made that Richard Nixon would have finished his term and be more honorably regarded today had he owned up to his subordinates' roles in the Watergate scandal at the begin-ning and not engaged in cover-up activities. The Iran-Contra af-fair conceivably could have been avoided had those who were centrally involved not been so obsessed with secrecy that they froze their colleagues out of the decision-making process and kept essential information from other government officials, as well as the press.

Surprising Support

Support for more openness in government has come from some surprising sources. On his last day of active duty as Reagan's press spokesman, Larry Speakes had this advice for his White House colleagues:

> Let's make good on the age-old promise of less secrecy in gov-ernment, not more. . . . When we sit in the Situation Room in the White House and launch a policy initiative, let's judge it by how it would look if it showed up in tomorrow's headlines.

And how about these words uttered in 1961 by Nixon, follow-ing President John F. Kennedy's call for journalists to censor themselves on national security matters:

> The plea of security could well become a cloak for errors, misjudgments and other failings of government. . . . The whole concept of a return to secrecy in peacetime demonstrates a pro-found misunderstanding of the role of a free press as opposed

to that of a controlled press. . . . No reporter worth his salt would deliberately publish information hurtful to national security. The record of patriotic self-restraint is a good one.

In sum, as a rule of thumb the public should demand and expect that their leaders will resolve any doubts about what government activities to keep secret in favor of disclosure.

"The mere fact that one has stolen a document in order that he may deliver it to the press . . . will not immunize him from responsibility for his criminal act."

Security Leaks to the Press Should Be Punished

Michael Ledeen

In April 1988, a Richmond, Virginia appeals court convicted Samuel Loring Morison of espionage for giving secret photographs to the British publication *Jane's Defense Weekly.* The Supreme Court later refused to review the decision, thus allowing it to stand. In the following viewpoint, Michael Ledeen concurs with the court's decision. Ledeen contends that leaks to the media can damage national security. Punishing those who reveal classified information, he argues, legitimately prevents sensitive material from being published or broadcast. Ledeen is a senior fellow in international affairs at the Center for Strategic and International Studies, a Washington, D.C. think tank. Ledeen has worked as a foreign policy consultant to the government and in 1988 published the book *Perilous State Craft: An Insider's Account of the Iran-Contra Affair.*

As you read, consider the following questions:

1. Why does the media think it is acceptable to publish classified information obtained by leaks, according to Ledeen?
2. What does Ledeen believe is the media's real objection to the court's decision?

Michael Ledeen, "Treason and Accountability," *The American Spectator,* June 1988. Reprinted with permission.

Early in April 1988, an appeals court in Richmond, Virginia, upheld the conviction of Samuel Loring Morison, for violation of the Espionage Act. Morison had given secret satellite photographs of a Soviet shipyard to *Jane's Defence Weekly*, a British publication. The photos appeared in the American media some weeks later.

Most American newspapers (including the *Washington Post* and the *New York Times*) are worried, deeply worried, about the precedent set by this case, for Morison is the first American ever convicted for turning over classified information to the media. Heretofore, "espionage" was restricted to handing state secrets *directly* to the enemy. The media say—and they are undoubtedly right—that if the decision stands, it will have a chilling effect on the way they do business. Thus, lots of newspapers filed briefs asking the appeals court to overturn Morison's conviction. The basis for the media concern is not the law itself, but that it has, for the first time, been applied to a "journalist." But it seems clear enough that journalists are covered by the law, which makes it a crime for anyone to provide secret information, which he has reason to believe would harm the national defense, to "unauthorized persons." That phrase about "unauthorized persons" is almost never quoted in the newspapers, because it makes it clear that journalists, just like any other citizen, are covered by the Act.

Threatening the Press?

That Morison is guilty of espionage, as defined by the law, is hard to doubt. The issue is whether it is a good law, and whether the decision of the appeals court threatens freedom of the press. My own view is that, while I'm nervous about the implications of the decision, the participation of the media in Morison's appeal is one of the worst decisions they have made in a long time. For years now, whenever people like me have warned that it will not do for the press to publish all manner of classified information, the media's response has been (with lots of modulation): "That's not our problem. It's the government's problem. Let them take steps to stop the leaks at the source, but let them leave us alone to publish what we think is responsible."

That is precisely what has happened in the Morison case. The government did not take the press to court. The fact that Morison was moonlighting as a free-lancer for *Jane's* is interesting, but irrelevant. His crime was, as a government employee, to pass information damaging to the national defense (it told a great deal about the capabilities of our spy satellites) to unauthorized persons at *Jane's*. And, of course, from *Jane's* to, *inter alia*, the Soviet Union. But that last move isn't even crucial, for

Morison could have been charged with espionage if he had given the photographs to some friend of his.

The problem, according to the media brief (as reported by Stuart Taylor, Jr. in the April 10, 1988 *New York Times*), is that the decision "will affect, and perhaps dramatically alter, the way in which government officials deal with the press, the way in which the press gathers and reports the news, and the way in which the public learns about its government."

To which Judge Donald Stuart Russell implicitly replied in his decision: "The mere fact that one has stolen a document in order that he may deliver it to the press . . . will not immunize him from responsibility for his criminal act. To use the First Amendment for such a purpose would be to convert the First Amendment into a warrant for thievery."

Shattering Consequences

Information leaks about military plans, strategies, and the strengths and deployment of forces provide invaluable intelligence leads to foreign adversaries and inevitably cause the failure of military objectives or operations. Disclosure of information relating to weapons design and research and to the details of nuclear technology can have shattering consequences by placing such information in the hands of unfriendly adventurers. Leaks of information regarding our advanced technology of lasers, kinetics, and computers can easily erase strategic advantages of inestimable value.

Martin L.C. Feldman, *The Heritage Lectures: Why the First Amendment Is Not Incompatible with National Security Interest*, 1987.

The judge is right and the media brief was wrong. And what *really* worries the media—as opposed to all the philosophical talk about "how the public learns about its government"—is that . . . this decision . . . may frighten some leakers away, and it may lead editors to think twice about publishing certain kinds of national security revelations. That is the sum total of it.

Legitimate Concerns

The media don't like that because they want to decide what should be published and what should be secret—they don't want anyone else horning in on their act. As the ACLU's [American Civil Liberties Union] Morton Halperin put it, "There's nothing in the statute that distinguishes between government officials and the press, and under the court's legal interpretation it could be used against the press."

Exactly right. If citizens are forbidden to reveal damaging information to unauthorized persons, then no class of citizens is exempt. Journalists are just like the rest of us. I believe that most informed people of good will agree that there are certain kinds of information that should not be published or broadcast, for precisely the same concern that led to the passage of the Espionage Act. There are two serious questions at stake here: Who defines what is damaging to national security? And how can the media and the government reach a working relationship in which reasonable decisions on publication or broadcast of potentially sensitive information are made, and there is a mechanism for enforcement (that is, penalties for those who break the rules)?

There isn't room here to cover all the angles, but here are a few thoughts to keep you going for a month:

• There is going to have to be some kind of mixed government/media/legal panel to give advice (or actually make decisions?) on whether a given story is publishable or not. Both sides will hate it, because the media want to decide these things themselves, and the government thinks only it should decide when things are "properly classified." The comparison that comes to mind is the Ratings Board for the Motion Picture Association, except that the media board will have to have some enforcement capability.

Justifiable Censorship

• It will be argued that this is censorship. It is. But we have it already. There is a law that forbids publication of information about "Signals Intelligence." It has never been applied, so nobody knows whether it would stand up in court, how sweeping its scope really is, or anything else about it. Yet any journalist who writes about intelligence could very easily be prosecuted under the law. We need some Supreme Court decisions, and with the Morison case on the books, the government should quickly charge some journalist with a violation of the SIGINT law and get a ruling. It may be that these laws need some changes, but at present the media are acting like ostriches, hoping no one will notice them since they have put their heads in the sand.

• Journalism today is the only profession with no procedure for enforcing accountability. Lawyers, doctors, even college professors have to respond to professional boards that evaluate their qualifications and their standards of performance. Why should journalists be different?

"Any effort to impose criminal sanctions for breaches of government secrecy must confront the reality that the 'leak' is an important instrument of communication."

Security Leaks to the Press Should Not Be Punished

CBS, Inc., *The Washington Post*, et al.

Samuel Loring Morison was a government worker who was convicted in 1988 as a spy for leaking a photo the military had classified. His conviction had far-reaching implications for the mass media. The following viewpoint is excerpted from a friends-of-the-court brief filed during Morison's trial by numerous media organizations. They contend that leaks to the press perform a vital function in exposing incompetence or abuse of power. Punishing those who reveal classified information would in effect cover up such abuses, they maintain. The media organizations included fifteen publishers, four broadcasting companies, and twelve associations and organizations involved in reporting on the government.

As you read, consider the following questions:

1. What will be the effects of the Morison case on the way the media do business, according to the authors?
2. Why do the authors believe senior government officials leak information to the press?
3. Why do the authors contend that leaking information is not the same as espionage?

CBS, Inc., *The Washington Post*, et al., a legal brief filed in the case of *United States v. Samuel Loring Morison* and published in the May 1988 issue of *First Principles* under the title "Framing Leakers as Spies After *Morison*." Reprinted with permission of the Center for National Security Studies, Washington, D.C.

The issue on this appeal is not whether the government can enforce the espionage laws against those who provide national security secrets to agents of foreign powers. In recent, highly publicized cases, the government has done just that, securing stiff sentences for those who have spied against their own country. Nor is the issue here whether the government may discipline those who disclose sensitive national security matters to the press and the public at large. Samuel Morison was terminated by the Navy for his actions, and no one questions his termination in this case. The issue in this case is not even whether Samuel Morison's conduct could be subject to criminal sanctions under a properly drawn statute. Rather, the issue is whether the espionage and conversion statutes under which Morison was convicted—which have never been applied successfully to the dissemination of information to the press and public—were intended to proscribe such conduct, and, if so, whether they can survive constitutional scrutiny.

Broad Implications

This issue has implications far beyond this case. Its resolution will affect, and perhaps dramatically alter, the way in which government officials deal with the press, the way in which the press gathers and reports the news, and the way in which the public learns about its government. For Samuel Morison, as unique and unsympathetic as his case may be in some respects, is in other ways not unlike countless government officials who, on a daily basis, decide to disclose to the public government "secrets," sometimes classified and sometimes not. For the press and the public, these officials play an important information role: they are the "sources" for much of what we learn about government. To others, these officials have different names: they are "leakers" who breach their obligation of secrecy, perhaps to advance their own personal interest; they are "whistleblowers" who expose hidden corruption; they are "sources close to the President" or "senior State Department officials" who selectively release information to further Administration policies; sometimes they are named officials who disclose a secret to provide a point, to justify a decision, or to secure political advantage.

The motives of those who disclose publicly what has been kept secret may be honorable or dishonorable, and the immediate effects of publication may be harmful or beneficial—or these matters may be fairly open to debate. But the overall effect of public disclosures concerning the affairs of government is to enhance the people's ability to understand their government and to control their own destiny.

111

"Somebody around here has been putting out accurate information"

© 1972 by Herblock in *The Washington Post*. Reprinted with permission.

Any effort to impose criminal sanctions for breaches of government secrecy must confront the reality that the "leak" is an important instrument of communication that is employed on a daily basis by officials at every level of government. Admiral Stansfield Turner, former Director of Central Intelligence, has explained:

> [T]he White House staff tends to leak when doing so may help the President politically. The Pentagon leaks, primarily to sell its programs to the Congress and the public. The State Department

leaks when it's being forced into a policy move that its people dislike. The CIA leaks when some of its people want to influence policy but know that's a role they're not allowed to play openly. The Congress is most likely to leak when the issue has political ramifications domestically.

A recent survey of current and former senior federal officials revealed that 42 percent of them had deliberately leaked information to the press. As Howard Simons, Curator of the Nieman Foundation at Harvard University and a former Managing Editor of *The Washington Post*, has explained:

> If you live and work as a journalist in Washington long enough, several things about national security and the press become self-evident. . . .
>
> The first thing that you learn is that it is impossible, not just improbable, but impossible to do your job without bumping into a secret.

Presidents and others from time to time have decried the pervasiveness of press leaks within the executive and legislative branches of government. And in extreme cases there have been investigations to determine the sources of unauthorized disclosures. But until now, attempts to punish leakers have been through disciplinary measures, not criminal sanctions: no one has been convicted of a crime for disclosing information to the press or the public. This is due not simply to prosecutorial restraint. It reflects the judgments of Congress, which has steadfastly refused to make the mere act of leaking classified information a crime, and the Framers of our Constitution, who adopted the First Amendment "to protect the free discussion of governmental affairs," [as the Supreme Court found in *Mills v. Alabama*].

Limiting Government Power

This nation has never thought it necessary or appropriate to enact an "official secrets act" of the sort that exists in Great Britain. Indeed, in our democratic system in which the people are sovereign, there are limits upon the government's power to enforce a system of official secrecy, and limits as well upon the government's power to punish press leaks through criminal sanctions. In fact, the Supreme Court has stated:

> Truth may not be the subject of either civil or criminal sanctions where discussion of public affairs is concerned. . . . For Speech concerning public affairs is more than self-expression; it is the essence of self-government.

If there is an exception to these principles in the area of national security, then it must be narrowly tailored and carefully defined.

The espionage statute under which Samuel Morison was convicted was never intended to be applied to the simple dissemi-

113

nation of information to the press—much less to the publication of information by the press. As a result, the statute is not worded to reflect the concerns that must be addressed if those activities are to be made criminal. The extension of such a broadly phrased statute to cover press leaks threatens not only those in government who view such disclosures as an important means of public communication, but also those members of the press and the public who have come to depend upon such disclosures for much of what they learn about government.

Not Espionage

Whatever one might think of government officials who release confidential or secret information to the press, it seems clear that leaking is not the same as espionage, and it is not the same as theft. Unlike the betrayal of one's country to a foreign power, and unlike the theft of the government's property, the leaking of government information to the press can proceed from honorable motives. More importantly, press leaks can and do benefit the public—by exposing incompetence, illegality or abuse of power, or simply by keeping the public informed about the affairs of government.

Congress has been sensitive to the valuable informative role of press leaks, and has repeatedly rejected proposals to criminalize the mere public disclosure of classified or defense-related information. Samuel Morison's conviction for espionage and theft, will overrule these careful judgments of Congress. It will restrict an important source of public information about the operations of government and the conduct of public officials. And it will expose journalists and government officials alike to the threat of criminal prosecution for activity which, no matter how offensive to those in power, has never before been viewed as criminal.

Evaluating Censorship and National Security Concerns

In a democratic country there is a continual conflict between rights of individuals and the needs of the nation. One especially difficult area is that of national security. On one hand, Americans believe in complete openness and free access to the workings of the government. On the other hand, certain matters, if made public, could threaten the country's safety.

One example of this conflict came to light in 1979 when a college student wrote an article telling how to build an atomic bomb. He based his article on information he found in his college library. Subsequently, a furor arose when the article was published in a nationally distributed magazine. Alarmed officials said that publishing such information in a widely available source would make the atomic bomb possible for nations which had not previously had it and also would make it possible for terrorists and criminals to use the bomb. The editors of the magazine said that since the information was already publicly available, there was no reason not to publish it. Who was right—the magazine or its critics? Which was more important—free speech or national security?

In this activity, you will have a chance to examine your values in the area of censorship and national security.

Step 1

Below is a list of events that could occur. For each one, indicate whether you think it should be kept secret or should be public information. *If secret, put an S beside the event; if public, put a P.*

____ a writer offers a magazine a story called "How to Build a Neutron Bomb in Your Basement"

____ a convicted terrorist writes to the Freedom of Information Act office requesting all information the government has collected about her

____ a government official holds a press conference about a "secret payload" on a satellite but requests that the reporters not print the information

115

_____ a reporter bribes a military official and finds out that secret maneuvers are going to take place on a small Caribbean island

_____ a person who was involved in a peaceful demonstration against an arms-building plant writes to the FOIA office requesting her files

_____ a paper detailing new methods of secret surveillance (spying) is going to be presented at a scientific conference

_____ a paper describing research about the effects of certain gases on humans is going to be presented at a scientific conference

_____ a newspaper has obtained a list of all U.S. military officials, some undercover, in a Central American country

_____ a newspaper has obtained a list of all activities, both open and undercover, that the U.S. armed forces participated in during World War II

_____ a newspaper has obtained a list of all activities, both open and undercover, that the U.S. armed forces participated in during the past six years and up to the present

_____ a former Central Intelligence Agency official writes a novel based very closely on the secret activities he has been involved in

_____ an African refugee is willing to give an interview detailing the secret methods U.S. military personnel have taught his people to use against communists

_____ a low-level clerk in the Defense Department who files non-secret papers, answers telephones, etc., has been asked to sign a lifetime secrecy agreement

_____ a magazine has obtained a secret government report indicating that a strategic nuclear reactor does not meet safety standards and if not repaired within a short time may endanger the lives of the people who work there and who live nearby

_____ a radical newspaper has obtained a list of access codes for U.S. military computers

If you are a member of a class, discuss your answers in a small group. If you are doing this activity alone, you may want to ask someone to discuss it with you. This may lead to valuable insights about your own values regarding the First Amendment and national security. It may also expose you to significant ideas you had not thought of when you made your initial evaluation of these events.

Step 2

What criteria did you use to determine whether information should be public or secret? Below is a list of possible factors. Look the list over and add any other factors that influenced you in Step 1.

Now rank these factors: number 1 for most important, 2 for next in importance, and so on until all of the factors are ranked.

____ Free access to information is essential in a democracy.

____ National security is essential to any country.

____ Criminals do not have the same rights as other citizens.

____ Some government "secrets" are not really very important to our security.

____ Free exchange of information aids development of science and technology.

____ Lives should not be threatened by exposing secret information in the name of free speech.

____ Lives should not be threatened by withholding information in the name of national security.

____ The rights of individuals should be safeguarded no matter what the price.

____ The good of the nation must be considered above all other factors.

____ Other factors:

If you are working in a class, compare your rankings with others in the class. Try to reach a group consensus.

Also consider whether your values coincide with the interests of the nation at large.

Step 3

Reflect on the events described in Step 1 and on your own values as considered in Step 2.

Then, write a brief statement outlining policy for dealing with the censorship/national security conflict. What should be the determining factors editors or government officials use when deciding whether information affecting national security should be kept secret or made public?

Periodical Bibliography

The following articles have been selected to supplement the diverse views presented in this chapter.

Laurence I. Barrett	"Neo-Plumbers on the Attack," *Time,* September 11, 1989.
William P. Barrett	"Does the FBI Have a File on You?" *Forbes,* October 3, 1988.
Johan Carlisle	"Anatomy of a Disinformation Campaign," *Propaganda Review,* Winter 1988. Available from Media Alliance, Fort Mason Center, Building D, San Francisco, CA 94123.
Donna A. Demac	"When Governments Gag the Word," *Los Angeles Times,* July 10, 1988.
Terry Eastland	"Gray Matter," *The American Spectator,* September 1989.
Terry Eastland	"No Runs, No Drips, No Errors," *The American Spectator,* November 1989.
Terry Eastland	"Welcome to the Major Leaks," *The American Spectator,* February 1989.
David R. Gergen	"Shooting the Messenger," *U.S. News & World Report,* April 11, 1988.
Stephen J. Hedges	"The Ethics Police and Political Leaks," *U.S. News & World Report,* June 12, 1989.
Ed Magnuson	"Return of the Watergate Doctrine," *Time,* February 19, 1990.
Nat Hentoff	"How We Got an Official Secrets Act," *The Progressive,* March 1989.
Jackie Mason	"America, Land of the Unfree," *The New York Times,* March 23, 1990.
National Review	"Executive Cowardice," March 5, 1990.
Eve Pell	"The Backbone of Hidden Government," *The Nation,* June 19, 1989.
Elizabeth R. Rindskopf	"Dealing with 'Links,'" *The World & I,* February 1988.
John Shattuck and Muriel Morisey Spence	"The Dangers of Information Control," *Technology Review,* April 1988.
Diane Sherwood	"Federal Information: Who Should Get It, Who Shouldn't?" *The World & I,* January 1990.
Philip Weiss	"The Quiet Coup," *Harper's Magazine,* September 1989.
World Press Review	"New Freedom—and New Threats," February 1990.

Is School and Library Censorship Justified?

CENSORSHIP

Chapter Preface

Should schoolchildren and the general public be protected from offensive or subversive materials, or should such materials be available in public schools and libraries? This question has probably been debated as long as schools and libraries have existed. Many people feel that since selection has to be made anyway, teachers and librarians have a responsibility to select only the most uplifting materials. Others believe that in a democracy, where traditionally all ideas are debated, a wide range of materials from all points of view should be available to the public. Many also believe that schools, where young people are under the intellectual guidance of responsible adults, are the perfect place to expose them to dissenting opinions.

Both the general content and the perspective of school and library materials is at issue. The viewpoints in this chapter debate whether the views of particular segments of society should, for the general good, be allowed to dominate materials acquired with taxpayers' money.

"There is not necessarily any contradiction or hypocrisy between . . . freedoms of speech . . . and systematic standards of selection within the narrow confines of the school or public library."

Library Censorship Is Justified

Will Manley

In the following viewpoint, Will Manley argues that all librarians censor by choosing what books the library will buy, and that they should not be ashamed to admit it. Manley cites deviant sexual material as one of the things he would censor. He argues that such censorship does not contradict the First Amendment, since it in no way restricts the rights of others to print such material. Manley is director of the Tempe, Arizona Public Library.

As you read, consider the following questions:

1. Why does Manley believe the censorship debate is unnecessary?
2. Why is the concept of intellectual freedom hypocritical, according to the author?
3. How does public opinion affect library censorship, according to Manley?

Will Manley, "Facing the Public," *Wilson Library Bulletin*, February 1987. Reprinted with permission.

Lately I've been finding myself in stocks. I wish it were the Dow Jones variety, but it's not. It's the scaffolding variety. You are all familiar with that medieval instrument of torture in which your head and hands are clamped tight and you're placed on a wooden scaffolding and exposed to public ridicule. Generally you get a lot of garbage thrown at you.

Actually that description of my punishment is more metaphorical than real. I've simply been on the wrong end of a number of intellectual freedom debates. As far as I know, I'm the only person in the library profession who publicly espouses the cause of censorship, which makes me somewhat of an aberrant or as a zoologist might say "the only one left in captivity." Consequently I'm the masochist who gets dragged out to argue against the professional masses in intellectual freedom debates. So far I haven't won over any converts that I know of, although there was a busboy (the guy who puts out the pitcher of water on the speaker's podium) who smiled at me as though he thought I did pretty well. It turned out, though, that he spoke Samoan and had only a halting understanding of English.

Still an Issue?

Why we even gather together in our state and regional library conferences to discuss the subject of intellectual freedom and censorship is beyond me. With regards to this issue, I honestly didn't realize there was an issue anymore.

Just look around you. We are awash in a sea of freedom of expression. Subject areas that were once taboo are now routinely discussed on daytime television talk shows. Language that was once considered scandalous now constitutes a legitimate form of communication. Innovative and inventive juxtapositions of naked human bodies once considered obscene are now used as the visual backdrop for magazine advertisements alluring you to buy a certain kind of cologne. Pornographic movies that just a few years ago you could only obtain by surreptitiously placing an order to some obscure house of sin in Denmark or Sweden are now conveniently checked out over the counter at the corner video rental store to happily married middle-aged couples. In fact, they might get a Disney movie for the kids at the same time.

So why are we still talking about intellectual freedom? The game is up, the battle is over, and the war has been won. The grave threats to intellectual freedom that were supposed to be so alarming when Ronald Reagan and his spiritual advisor Jerry Falwell took office have proven to be impotent. . . .

So what is there left to discuss? In our society there really are no serious and effective censors left to condemn. In a sense, it's kind of like a football game where the champions of intellectual freedom are beating the forces of censorship 78 to 0 and they are not letting up. They're still passing on first down and they refuse to send in the second-stringers. What remains to be conquered? What is there left to talk about?

There is still this sticky little problem with public and school libraries. Here there are yet some limits to intellectual freedom. This makes us uncomfortable because the one thing that librarians have been quite proud of over the years is our unwavering support of intellectual freedom. It's a highly ironic oddity that our libraries are still a bastion of censorship in the freest society in the history of Western Civilization.

Offensive Materials

Certain books should be banned. Some books, particularly the ones with sexually explicit material, are being pulled from school libraries. Young children just shouldn't be exposed to this kind of material because it's too radical. This material is offensive, particularly in the lower grade levels.

Wally Klunk, quoted in *USA Today*, November 16, 1984.

But the biggest problem is that we are not willing to admit that we are censors despite the fact that study after study has shown that institutional censorship is widely practiced in American schools and public libraries. Since there is such a stigma involved with being a censor, no one has the courage to overcome peer pressure and admit that yes, we practice censorship systematically and regularly in our libraries. One would rather be called a rapist than a censor. It is the biggest insult that you can throw at a librarian, worse than "ring around the collar," "the heartbreak of psoriasis," or "yellow wax build-up."

That's why intellectual freedom has become a giant case of hypocrisy in libraryland. On the one hand, we pose as firm defenders of intellectual freedom in society and, yet, on the other hand, we are systematic censors in our libraries. More than anything we need to expel this inner tension. We need to end the guilt trip. We need to see that there is not necessarily any contradiction or hypocrisy between preaching an extreme adherence to the intellectual freedoms of speech, press, religion, and assembly in a Democratic society as expressed in the First Amendment and constructing and adhering to clear and systematic standards of selection within the narrow confines of the school or public library.

When I say "clear and systematic standards of selection" I do not mean the usual caveats of book acquisition that they teach

123

you in library school. I am not referring to such mundane considerations as quality of bindings, datedness of the material, reputation of the author, etc. I am talking about setting standards of censorship. I define library censorship to mean the decision not to acquire a book on the basis of (a) the subject matter in the book or (b) the mode of expression by which the subject matter is conveyed.

In using the first criterion, therefore, I could very reasonably set up a standard by which the library would not buy books instructing readers how to kill other human beings without leaving evidence. Or I could, using the second criterion, set up a standard in which the library would not buy books on human sexuality that have overly graphic illustrations of sodomy or bestiality. In both cases I have censored. But in both cases I have also acted in a responsible, defensible manner in which I have not abandoned my principles of intellectual freedom.

How can I have my cake and eat it too? Simple. While on the one hand I would advocate that, consistent with the principles of intellectual freedom, there should be no restrictions on the publication of materials on murder and sodomy, on the other hand I am justified to say that they are not appropriate for public library or school library collections.

By blocking access to these materials in the library I am not blocking access to these materials in the private sector. If a person wants to spend money printing books instructing people how to murder other people without leaving any evidence he or she should have that right. If another wants to open up a business selling books that have graphic representations of human beings engaging in sexual activities with elephants, he or she too should have that right. After all, the First Amendment says that "Congress shall make no law . . . abridging the freedom of speech, or of the press." There are no "ifs," "ands," or "buts." It seems fairly pure and simple. An individual should be able to use a printing press for whatever he or she desires with certain obvious exceptions like printing twenty-dollar bills or blueprints of our confidential military technology.

Practical Considerations

That does not mean, however, that public or school libraries are under some moral or legal constraint to acquire whatever that person prints. The public library has to draw the line of censorship. The public demands it. Too often when librarians get on their soapbox and preach a message of intellectual freedom extremism they forget about some basic practical considerations.

The most basic of these concerns is the matter of public relations. Why wave a red flag in front of a bull. Ordering one book that crosses over the line of what is appropriate in a particular community can wipe out years of excellent public relations. Most library administrators and book selectors understand this point almost intuitively. Take, for example, that benchmark book *Show Me*. All the librarians I've talked to say they would not hesitate to put the book in a public library collection. But what is the reality? Check your terminal. Few libraries have *Show Me*.

What does that mean? It means quite simply that there is a huge gap between our professional rhetoric and professional reality. It also proves that most librarians have not learned to be comfortable with being a defender of extreme intellectual freedom in the private sector and being a censor in the public sector. There is a large difference between the two sectors and yes, Doctor Freud, it's okay to be a radical in the one sector and a reactionary in the other.

"The new censorship represents not a piecemeal but a wholesale assault on the very nature of public education."

Library Censorship Is Not Justified

Peter Scales

In the following viewpoint, Peter Scales contends that censoring public or school libraries threatens the quality of education. Student cannot learn to make independent judgments, he argues, unless they are exposed to numerous ideas, no matter how controversial. Scales is executive director of Family Connection, a family service agency in Anchorage, Alaska. He has written extensively on child development and family relations.

As you read, consider the following questions:

1. How has censorship affected libraries in the past, according to Scales?
2. Why does the author believe sexual material is censored?
3. What does Scales believe parents who object to books should do?

Peter Scales, "Sex, Psychology, and Censorship." This article first appeared in *The Humanist* issue of July/August 1987 and is reprinted by permission.

In 1986, we in Anchorage, Alaska, noted the passing of an important anniversary—one most of us would rather not brag about. It was ten years since the Anchorage School Board bowed to a group called People for Better Education and voted four-to-three to ban the American Heritage Dictionary. Among the words deemed offensive were *tail, ball, nut, ass,* and *bed.* More recently, we had a flap in Fairbanks over a book on homosexuality that reminded us that censorship can happen even on "the Last Frontier."

Censorship is neither new nor confined to the right wing. Plato encouraged people to burn the writing of Democritus, presumably because of his differing view of cosmology. He also felt that the young should be kept from fiction—a view which has more significance than may at first be apparent. This view has popped up frequently in our history, particularly from the period of the late 1700s through the late 1800s. Boston General Library found it necessary in 1852 to remind the public that only "good" books would be stocked and that people should first read classical biographies and history and only much later deign to expose themselves to the novel.

So distrustful were even librarians of novels that, in 1876, at the American Library Association convention, a librarian noted that his library's rules forbade any novels in the library at all. When asked what the effect would be on the unfortunate reader who happened upon a novel the librarian could only reply that he had never read one! Since the 1960s, the attempt to ban *The Adventures of Huckleberry Finn* for its alleged racism and to pressure publishers to remove references considered sexist or racist have tended to come from progressive rather than conservative groups.

Today's Censorship

Censorship today, however, is indeed different from what it was even a few years ago, and, by and large, the force for this new censorship has come from conservative groups. Sexuality—sexual words, sexuality education, material covering decisions about sexuality—is repeatedly near or at the top of the list of target for censorship. Why?

Censorship in the name of salvation is a good way to describe the intent of suppressing or banning books, articles, art, or any other forms of communication. According to S. McClelland Grant, "The demand for censorship does not come from those who wish their own morals protected . . . [the censors] want to save the rest of us." Legal scholars have observed that the "fear of books seems . . . to have affected most literate societies." So, censorship today seems to be part of a long-standing tradition. . . .

Wasserman © 1982, Los Angeles Times Syndicate. Reprinted with permission.

The new censorship represents not a piecemeal but a whole-sale assault on the very nature of public education. Is it really something to be worried about? Yes. In more than 40 percent of the cases reported, censors were successful in restricting or removing materials.

On top of that figure, we have to add the restrictions due to widespread self-censorship in which all of us engage—writers, publishers, librarians, educators—simply in an attempt to avoid confrontation with the new censors. For example, 90 percent of the nation's large-district school superintendents think helping young people make better decisions about sexuality is the number one reason for having sex education. Yet, less than 20 percent of sex education courses cover decision-making in any depth. Child sexual abuse reports have been soaring for five years across the country, yet some sexual abuse prevention programs are uneasy over using the terms *penis* or *vulva*, preferring instead to talk about red and green "flags" and things under the swimming suit. Not even the life and death reality of AIDS can always make a difference. In the February 1987 issue of *The Atlantic*, Katie Leishman reports that, even in San Francisco, it has taken two years for an AIDS pilot course to be distributed among a small group of teachers. She sums it up succinctly: "In most places, the trick will be to warn children about AIDS without teaching them about sex."

Sex is a prime target but also serves as a symbol for anything controversial. In 1959, a Ford Foundation study of California libraries showed that two-thirds refused to purchase materials if they thought they were controversial, one-third reported a permanent removal of controversial material, and one-fifth said that they "habitually" avoided controversial matters. It is an irony that this study was first offered to the California Library Association, which declined to conduct it because it felt the issue was too hot. Even a cursory glance at publications such as the American Library Association's *Newsletter on Intellectual Freedom* shows that today this same type of censorship is just as common. . . .

A comment from the most influential modern censors gives us a deeper clue about their real agenda. Mel and Norma Gabler for years have bullied the Texas school textbook selection process and have attempted to control the millions of dollars at stake in school textbook publishing each year. In one of their pamphlets, they state that "ideas will never do (children) as good as facts." This is the heart of the matter—that facts are better than values, analysis, and opinions. . . .

The Control of Sexuality

What is motivating the censors . . . and how is sexuality bound up in that dynamic? In his classic work, *The Fear of the Word*, Eli Oboler points out that two powerful strands—one of language, the other of religion—contribute to making sexual words in particular so unnerving to so many. The heritage of Christianity derived a good deal of its sexually repressive messages from Paul, who, after all, preferred celibacy even to marriage, and from St. Augustine, who [embraced] celibacy as an adult after having spent, by all accounts, a sexually active youth. The taboos associated with menstruation and the notions of uncleanliness and shame attached to such bodily functions also contributed to a deep-seated, archetypal Christian discomfort with the sexual.

Insuring Our Future

Books are written to entertain, to make people think, to excite them, to expose them to new ideas. If we strip our library shelves, we will be creating a generation of young people who are not capable of thinking and understanding either themselves, other human beings, or the world at large. Fighting censorship is a way of insuring our future as a nation.

Norma Klein, *SIECUS Report,* July 1985.

The other strand relates to religious belief as well. The beginning of John's gospel includes the passage, " . . . what God was, the Word was. . . ." Although there are several interpretations as to what "the Word" actually means in this context, one is that this signifies God's power to affect action simply by speaking, so that anyone who profanes "the Word" profanes the very "center of faith." Anthropologists have noted for many years that language seems to exist almost outside of us as a separate power given to each generation as a part of inherited culture and history. The belief that the name of a thing and the thing itself are almost the same is a key to the magical powers which peoples from primitive to modern cultures have given to words. After all, today we are warned when "strong language" may be part of a television movie. Talking about sexual things can be considered, in this primitive, magical fashion, as tantamount to doing the sexual things talked about.

It is a small step from this belief to the fear the censors have of sexuality education, words, or materials. They fear that being exposed to sexual terminology will make children engage in sexual activity. Nothing in research or common sense confirms this fear. But this is not a rational fear; it is a primitive, magical one that threatens the very core of the censor's being. Psychiatrist Judd Marmor and his colleagues studied the psychodynamics of opposition to health programs and observed the same thing. They noted that the "same groups of people [are] involved over and over again in opposition to widely diverse and disparate health programs," and they suggested that the common denominator of the opposition was a perceived threat to bodily or psychic wholeness. A key to understanding the censor's motives is understanding this magical power of words.

Ernest Jones, who was Freud's translator, offered a more psychoanalytical interpretation. Perhaps censors are so afraid of their own inability to resist the lure of temptation that, in the words of Eli Oboler, they "protect themselves on the pretext of protecting others." Research on authoritarian personalities suggests too that people who have been deprived of pleasure in their childhood, reared by rigid and demanding parents, later react strongly to any sense of others "getting away with something" and show a desire to condemn, reject, and punish.

Ultimately, though, I have to agree with George Bernard Shaw's succinct analysis that "all censorships exist to prevent anyone from challenging current conceptions and existing institutions." When the Gablers say an idea is not as good for children as a fact, what they are really saying is that, to them, ideas are threatening precisely because they are open-ended, imaginative, full of possibilities and uncertainties, and ambiguous. Perhaps this is why "fiction" and "trash" have so often in our history been considered synonymous. Fiction tells us about fantasies, possibilities, and changes from the existing ways. Perhaps, too, this is the most threatening aspect of sexuality —which is the ultimate well-spring of possibility, of creation, of change, of challenge to authority. . . .

Defining Censorship

Burton Joseph, my former colleague on the board of the Freedom to Read Foundation, has said that "censorship is the ultimate elitism." I think he has described it well. In our democratic society, traditionally governed by the notion of a marketplace of ideas, it takes more than simple chutzpah to think that you know best what others should see or hear, what their opinions should be, or how they should think.

Even George Washington read banned books—in his case, the letters of Voltaire. They were banned in France and seemed to be a source of Washington's strength at Valley Forge.

Both of my children have read all the Judy Blume they wanted. They seem to have weathered the experience just fine! My oldest son read *The Diary of Anne Frank*. In some communities, he could not have done so—because the book has been banned.

I want my sons to worry that it is only a small step from going after Anne Frank's diary to going after Anne Frank. In an elegant phrase, the late Supreme Court Justice Potter Stewart said in his 1966 *Ginzburg* dissent that censorship reflects a "society's lack of confidence in itself." Well, I want my children to inherit a confident society which celebrates freedoms of the mind. The important result of these freedoms is that we define our personal and national values in this process of challenge and conflict, and we are encouraged to be tolerant of others whose values differ. That is the essence of democratic society.

If parents don't want their children to read something, then that is the ideal time for those parents to explain why and, in so doing, to communicate even more about their values. But I want to say to those concerned parents: "Please don't try to protect *my* children." I'm a "concerned parent," too, and I'm concerned that my children get a better grip on their values and a deeper appreciation of others through exercising their freedoms of the mind. Hopefully, they will gain a deeper respect for the very best their country has to offer in the bargain.

"If the school board or the library board does not reflect the values of the citizens in the area of its jurisdiction, the voters have the right to change the board members."

Libraries Should Reflect Majority Values

Phyllis Schlafly

Phyllis Schlafly, a conservative political activist, is best known for her campaign against the Equal Rights Amendment. She is a strong defender of traditional family and religious values. In the following viewpoint, she argues that the fact that teachers and librarians select which books to buy amounts to a kind of pre-censorship. Schlafly points out that taxpayers pay the bills for these books. Thus she believes it is essential that those who choose what books to buy be accountable to the values of those who pay the bills.

As you read, consider the following questions:

1. Why does Schlafly think that library and school materials must reflect the values of the people they serve?
2. Does Schlafly advocate eliminating all materials which may not agree with the values of the majority?

Phyllis Schlafly, "Citizens' Bill of Rights About Schools and Libraries," *The Phyllis Schlafly Report*, February 1983. Reprinted with permission.

All those who spend taxpayers' money are accountable to the public. (The "public" includes citizens, parents, private groups, and the media.) The public has a right to exercise its right of free speech on how taxpayers' funds are spent and on what standards, to second-guess the judgment of the persons doing the spending, and to remove from office those responsible for any misuse of tax funds. Public supervision and criticism may be annoying, but they must be endured by all those spending tax funds, whether they be Presidents, Congressmen, bureaucrats, military, teachers, librarians, or others.

Since parents have the primary responsibility for the education of their own children, schools should have a decent respect for the parents' beliefs and attitudes. Schools should make every possible effort to avoid offending the religious, ethical, cultural or ethnic values of school children and their parents. Since presumably all educators would agree that *Playboy* and *Penthouse* magazines are not suitable reading materials for school children, it is clear that the issue over any particular book is one of appropriateness (which is a value judgment), not the First Amendment or "academic freedom."

Make Requirements Flexible

Since thousands of good books and hundreds of important, educational books are easily available, and since a child can read only a small number of books prior to high school graduation, it is highly unreasonable and intolerant for a school or teacher to force a child to read a particular book as a precondition to graduation or to passing a course. When a book selected as course material or supplementary reading offends the religious, ethical, cultural or ethnic values of a child or his parents, an alternate book should be assigned or recommended which does not so offend. This substitution should be made without embarrassing the child.

This same respect for parental values and the assignment of alternate books should apply when the question is raised as to the assignment of a book at a particular grade level. Many books are appropriate in the upper grades which are not at all appropriate for younger children. Parental decisions about the maturity of their own children should be respected by the schools without embarrassing the child.

Public libraries should adhere to a standard like the Fairness Doctrine which governs television and radio broadcasters; i.e., they have the obligation to seek out and make available books on all sides of controversial issues of public importance. For example, libraries should present a balanced selection of book titles on sensitive current issues such as the morality of nuclear war, women's liberation, basic education, evolution/creationism, Reaganomics, and the Equal Rights Amendment.

Child pornography (i.e., the use of children in pictures, books or films to perform sex acts or to pose in lewd positions or circumstances) should be absolutely prohibited. In 1982, the U.S. Supreme Court held in *New York v. Ferber* that child pornography is not protected by the First Amendment because the prevention of sexual abuse of children is "a governmental objective of surpassing importance." Laws against child pornography, therefore, must apply equally to everyone including bookstores, theaters, schools, and libraries.

No library buys every book published. Every day in the week, librarians, teachers and school administrators are making decisions to select some books for library shelves and school classrooms while excluding (censoring) other books. These select-and-exclude decisions can be called "preemptive censorship."

Important Responsibility

The selection of reading materials is a major responsibility of school and library personnel. Most such personnel have the historical knowledge, fairness, and mature judgment which are necessary to make those decisions. However, the public always has the right to question whether any preemptive censorship is carried out on the basis of the personal political biases of the librarian or teacher, or results from a genuine attempt to give students and the public the wisdom of the ages through time-tested "great books" plus fairness on current controversies.

The public clearly has a First Amendment right to investigate, evaluate and critique the selections and the criteria. If the school board or the library board does not reflect the values of the citizens in the area of its jurisdiction, the voters have the right to change the board members through the political process. That's an important part of our free, democratic society.

"It is in the public interest for publishers and librarians to make available the widest diversity of views and expressions."

Libraries Should Reflect Diverse Views

American Library Association

The American Library Association (ALA) has long believed that it is the responsibility of libraries to furnish to the public the widest possible range of materials. A constant concern of the ALA is the pressure groups which attempt to impose their own values on library selection. The following viewpoint, taken from the ALA's "Freedom to Read" statement, reflects its views.

As you read, consider the following questions:

1. Why does the ALA believe that it is essential to provide a wide range of materials even though some may directly oppose majority values?
2. What does the ALA statement say librarians should do when faced with pressure by individuals or groups to censor materials?
3. Does this ALA statement offer any selection guidelines at all, or does it suggest that *all* materials have equal validity in a library?

The American Library Association, "Freedom to Read" statement adopted June 25, 1953; revised January 28, 1972.

The freedom to read is guaranteed by the Constitution. Those with faith in free men will stand firm on these constitutional guarantees of essential rights and will exercise the responsibilities that accompany these rights. We therefore affirm these propositions:

1. It is in the public interest for publishers and librarians to make available the widest diversity of views and expressions, including those which are unorthodox or unpopular with the majority.

Creative thought is by definition new, and what is new is different. The bearer of every new thought is a rebel until his idea is refined and tested. Totalitarian systems attempt to maintain themselves in power by the ruthless suppression of any concept which challenges the established orthodoxy. The power of a democratic system to adapt to change is vastly strengthened by the freedom of its citizens to choose widely from among conflicting opinions offered freely to them. To stifle every nonconformist idea at birth would mark the end of the democratic process. Furthermore, only through the constant activity of weighing and selecting can the democratic mind attain the strength demanded by times like these. We need to know not only what we believe but why we believe it.

2. Publishers, librarians, and booksellers do not need to endorse every idea or presentation contained in the books they make available. It would conflict with the public interest for them to establish their own political, moral, or aesthetic views as a standard for determining what books should be published or circulated.

Publishers and librarians serve the educational process by helping to make available knowledge and ideas required for the growth of the mind and the increase of learning. They do not foster education by imposing as mentors the patterns of their own thought. The people should have the freedom to read and consider a broader range of ideas than those that may be held by any single librarian or publisher or government or church. It is wrong that what one man can read should be confined to what another thinks proper.

Impersonal Evaluation of Books

3. It is contrary to the public interest for publishers or librarians to determine the acceptability of a book on the basis of the personal history or political affiliations of the author.

A book should be judged as a book. No art or literature can flourish if it is to be measured by the political views or private lives of its creators. No society of free men can flourish which draws up lists of writers to whom it will not listen, whatever they may have to say.

© 1982 *USA Today*. Reprinted with permission.

4. There is no place in our society for efforts to coerce the taste of others, to confine adults to the reading matter deemed suitable for adolescents, or to inhibit the efforts of writers to achieve artistic expression.

To some, much of modern literature is shocking. But is not much of life itself shocking? We cut off literature at the source if we prevent writers from dealing with the stuff of life. Parents and teachers have a responsibility to prepare the young to meet the diversity of experiences in life to which they will be exposed, as they have a responsibility to help them learn to think critically for themselves. These are affirmative responsibilities, not to be discharged simply by preventing them from reading works for which they are not yet prepared. In these matters taste differs, and taste cannot be legislated; nor can machinery be devised which will suit the demands of one group without limiting the freedom of others.

5. It is not in the public interest to force a reader to accept with any book the prejudgment of a label characterizing the book or author as subversive or dangerous.

The idea of labeling presupposes the existence of individuals or groups with wisdom to determine by authority what is good or bad for the citizen. It presupposes that each individual must be directed in making up his mind about the ideas he examines. But Americans do not need others to do their thinking for them.

Encroachments on Freedom

6. It is the responsibility of publishers and librarians, as guardians of the people's freedom to read, to contest encroachments upon that freedom by individuals or groups seeking to impose their own standards or tastes upon the community at large.

It is inevitable in the give and take of the democratic process that the political, the moral, or the aesthetic concepts of an individual or group will occasionally collide with those of another individual or group. In a free society each individual is free to determine for himself what he wishes to read, and each group is free to determine what it will recommend to its freely associated members. But no group has the right to take the law into its own hands, and to impose its own concept of politics or morality upon other members of a democratic society. Freedom is no freedom if it is accorded only to the accepted and the inoffensive.

7. It is the responsibility of publishers and librarians to give full meaning to the freedom to read by providing books that enrich the quality and diversity of thought and expression. By the exercise of this affirmative responsibility, bookmen can demonstrate that the answer to a bad book is a good one, the answer to a bad idea is a good one.

The freedom to read is of little consequence when expended on the trivial; it is frustrated when the reader cannot obtain matter fit for his purpose. What is needed is not only the absence of restraint, but the positive provision of opportunity for the people to read the best that has been thought and said. Books are the major channel by which the intellectual inheritance is handed down, and the principal means of its testing and growth. The defense of their freedom and integrity, and the enlargement of their service to society, requires of all bookmen the utmost of their faculties, and deserves of all citizens the fullest of their support.

"There is no reason an institution cannot. . . express its disdain for expression by faculty and students that is racially offensive."

Colleges Should Censor Racist Speech

Darryl Brown

A resurgence of racist physical and verbal attacks in the late 1980s led several colleges and universities to draft codes restricting racist speech on campus. In the following viewpoint, Darryl Brown contends that racism harms minority students, and therefore universities should take action against racist speech on campus. Racist speech does not belong on campus because it interferes with minority students' rights to be treated equally, he argues. Brown is a graduate of the University of Virginia School of Law and works as a law clerk in the U.S. District Court of Appeals.

As you read, consider the following questions:

1. What is the difference in how white students and black students define racism, according to Brown?
2. How does the author believe racism affects black students?
3. What steps can a university take to combat racism, in Brown's view?

Darryl Brown, "Racism and Race Relations in the University," *Virginia Law Review*, March 1990. Reprinted with permission.

American universities in recent years have endured a resurgence in racial tensions on their campuses, and the problem has manifested itself often in startlingly blatant racist incidents. At the same time, people of color continue to experience a racism that takes more subtle and elusive forms than in earlier eras, a racism that no longer manifests itself simply in the appearance of "white only" signs and the utterance of epithets such as "n-gger." It is a racism that is a persistent and constituent part of the social order, woven into the fabric of society and everyday life. It is a racism frequently less intentional, and very often—at least to white people—less obvious. But its victims insist that it is no less real, harmful, or in need of remedy. . . .

The Evidence and Experience of Racism

Race is particularly problematic in the context of higher education. In its most limited definition, to which many whites still subscribe, racism is an attitude held mostly by the unenlightened or uneducated, that is, an isolated position peculiar to the culture of Afrikaaners, some Southern state officials, or some working class white ethnics in the outer boroughs of New York. Given that definition, it is difficult to admit the presence of racism among society's most sophisticated and intellectually gifted.

The university is also a singularly powerful institution in the distribution of wealth. Its primary products, credentials in the form of college degrees, are limited and valuable commodities. Most students, especially those ambitious enough to compete for admission to top-ranked schools, are aware of this fact. Those who go to college make more money, on average, than those who do not; those who graduate from elite institutions probably make more than those who earn diplomas from second- and third-tier schools. White students who believe that admissions criteria based on grades, test scores, and the status of one's high school are objective, fair, and neutral indicia for college admissions resent scarce (and valuable) seats being filled by minority students admitted through affirmative action policies. Both faith in the meritocratic processes that are supposed to govern the university's intellectual task and the self-interest that intensifies competition for the university's key commodity mesh with a particular racial ideology to contribute to questioning by whites of the legitimacy of black students' presence in academia.

In addition, the current divisions in the understanding of racism on university campuses serve as an accurate paradigm for race issues in the larger, national context. Today's white students missed most of the civil rights movement and legally enforced segregation. Many feel no direct responsibility for institutionalized racism and believe that with formal legal barriers to

141

integration now dismantled, students of color stand on an equal footing with them. As with most white people generally, white students' conception of racism is constructed from the images that the civil rights movement confronted: enforced segregation, physical violence, blatant hateful epithets, and an overt, conscious denial of racial equality.

A Praiseworthy Aim

Prohibiting racially and religiously bigoted speech is praiseworthy because it seeks to elevate, not to degrade, because it draws from human experience, not from woolly dogmas or academic slogans, because it salutes reason as the backbone of freedom and tolerance.

Bruce Fein, *The Washington Times*, May 1, 1990.

With such barriers now either gone or greatly diminished, many whites tend to think that racism has largely disappeared, at least in any form that could serve as an impediment to opportunity and achievement. White students have a very hard time understanding how their predominantly white campuses can seem hostile to people of color; how their campus social life is a distinctly "white culture," even when the major institutions within it are not explicitly labeled the "white student union," "white student newspaper," or "white debating club." It does not occur to most white students that their indifference or hostility to the Martin Luther King national holiday, for example, is evidence of attitudes on racial issues that differ tremendously from their black colleagues. It does not occur to most white students that the major, campus-sponsored concerts of white music groups constitute distinctly *white* cultural events.

The hostility, or at least puzzlement, one hears among many white students toward distinctly black cultural centers, student groups, and social events arises from white students' lack of recognition that the overwhelmingly white campuses themselves are in some sense large white cultural centers—ones in which black students are likely to have difficulty feeling at home. Thus, white students' assertions that they only want all people treated the same, without the separatism of institutions such as black cultural centers, are often experienced by minority students as demands that they assimilate into white-dominated institutions and culture. That white norm extends even into the classroom.

The reports of racist incidents on college campuses recur continually in the popular press. The National Institute Against Prejudice and Violence collected reports of seventy-eight inci-

142

dents of racial violence or allegations of prejudice that occurred in the spring semester of 1988 alone, and that did not purport to be a comprehensive survey. The recurrence of old-fashioned intentional racism on campuses is the most obvious form of hostility, and a sampling demonstrates the ferocity of some such incidents, which have variously involved: graffiti containing swastikas and antiblack epithets; cross-burning; the protesting of an all-white fraternity's "White History Week" party; the shouting of racial slurs; the distribution of openly hostile leaflets; racial brawls; and black student class boycotts and protests. The comprehensive list of such incidents is much longer, and that list does not include unreported incidents, which may well be the majority.

Disagreement over Punishment

Such blatant incidents frequently meet with some form of condemnation from college administrators, even though there is often disagreement on the appropriate punishment or remedial action when (and if) the perpetrators are caught. Such events are less problematic as an interpretive matter because they usually have clear perpetrators and obvious racist intent. Whites usually accept such incidents as racist, though they often differ from African Americans in their assessment of the incidents' effect, importance, and need for remedy. As to forms of racism that are more widespread—the subtle manifestations of attitudes and preconceptions shaped by white race consciousness that materially affect institutional practices and interpersonal relations—there is even less recognition; there is disagreement over whether racism exists or has any effect at all.

The phenomenology of black students' experience with racism on white campuses leaves no doubt of the existence and effect of subtle (or unconscious) racism. One does not have to talk to many black college students before hearing stories about some suspicious official asking them to show ID's at the entrance of their own campus buildings because he suspected they did not belong there; of white students moving to a new seat when a black classmate sat too close; of black students rarely being invited to join study groups with whites; of white fraternity members handing out invitations on a campus sidewalk but not offering them to minority students. Despite formal equality and race neutrality in institutional policy as well as law, American universities are still infested with myriad, recurrent reminders of racism. . . .

The daily repetition of subtle racism and subordination in the classroom and on campus can ultimately be, for African Americans, more productive of stress, anxiety, and alienation than even blatant racist acts. The subtle institutional racism and white cultural bias that pervades the campus infringes on black students' right to equal enjoyment of their civil right to an education.

Freedom to Learn

Racial, sexual, ethnic, religious slurs implicitly rule out learning from folks of that color, gender, or faith. Stereotyped insults, or other forms of exclusionary speech, are antithetical to a learning community; they say I can't get anything from your head because it is on the wrong sort of body. Any individual within the academic community who indulges in such exclusionary attitudes violates the sense of this special community. . . .

When all is said and undone, it is important to recall that academic communities have a right to demand a seriousness of speech and community that is more sensitive than society at large.

Dennis O'Brien, *The Christian Science Monitor*, September 29, 1989.

When racially insensitive behavior occurs in the classroom or elsewhere in the university, black students are deprived of the opportunity to receive an education in an environment free of harassment, hurt, and humiliation. The perpetual lack of awareness that, for example, a "White History Week Party" or a Black Sambo caricature on a white fraternity's poster is offensive to black students is a clear indication that black perspectives are not part of the campus culture or community consciousness. Black students attend class (and take exams) often having just confronted offensive reminders of either overt racial hostility or subtle racial insensitivity—perhaps in the campus newspaper, on posters at the bus stop, the structure of classroom discussion—that serve as distractions from academic performance that white students do not endure. Institutions premised on a white norm must be continually reminded, on occasions when the white norm manifests itself too blatantly, that their lack of awareness is not harmless. Language has the power to cause injury. Language and behavior that demonstrate an obliviousness to minority communities stigmatize those communities and marginalize individuals' value as community members. As institutional practices they marginalize black concerns and perspectives and hinder black students' participation in community life because they are implicitly excluded from fully contributing to the creation of community norms, values, and ideals. . . .

The racial dynamic—arising out of occasional blatant racism, recurrent subtle remarks or unconscious behavior, and an ever-present white norm that is the foundation of institutional racism—conspires to create a cognizable injury to black students in predominantly white schools. It alters students' conditions of education just as courts have recognized racial harassment on the job alters conditions of employment. Racism adds to the stress and anxiety that diminish any person's ability and desire to excel in an academic environment, especially one leading to a professional world known to contain further racial roadblocks to career advancement and hospitable working conditions. The racial dynamic to which black students are subjected at predominantly white colleges contributes to stress that has a detrimental effect on personal well-being as well as academic performance. . . .

Possibilities for Remedial Action

The most egregious forms of racist language and behavior —the forms closest to traditional intentional racism—can be combated with traditional legal sanctions. One promising route for expansion of existing options would be legislation covering university students and. . .[imposing] liability for contributing to racially hostile environments. . . .

Another option would be sanctions, such as those proposed by Professors Richard Delgado and Mari Matsuda. Professor Delgado's proposal for a tort action imposing liability for intentional racial insults would be as feasible a tool to fight campus-based racism as it would be against racism generally. And Professor Matsuda has argued for a narrow criminal statute to punish intentionally racist speech, specifically citing the increase of malicious racial incidents on campus to demonstrate the need for such a law.

Finally, there is the option of institutional remedies for racially offensive speech and behavior, an option with which several universities are now struggling. In *Doe v. University of Michigan*, a federal district court struck down the University of Michigan's policy to combat campus racial harassment, finding that it violated the first amendment on vagueness and overbreadth grounds. The court's reasoning suggested the constitutional limits of any university policy, and thus the limited utility of such a policy for addressing the varieties of racial tension on campuses.

First, any limitation on speech that includes the threat of formal, institutional sanctions cannot be applied to speech that "disseminates ideas" or to statements that are made in the course of classroom academic discussions. The *Doe* court cited Michigan's resolution of complaints against students making offensive remarks in the classroom as examples of the policy's overbreadth and infringement on protected speech (even though the University did not apply formal sanctions in any of the three cases cited by the court). Thus, a university could not formally punish statements motivated by racism when they are purportedly part of a serious idea or theory offered in the university classroom or other formal forum. The *Doe* court implied, however, that a university might be able to sanction "conduct such as racial slurs and epithets in the classroom directed at an individual victim."

Second, the *Doe* court ruled that the Michigan policy was too vague, saying "it was simply impossible to discern . . . any conceptual distinction between protected and unprotected conduct." The court found the policy's requirements that sanctionable language "'stigmatize'" or "'victimize'" an individual, and "'involve an express or implied threat to an individual's academic efforts,'" to be unconstitutionally vague.

Thus, if *Doe* represents the interpretation of current first amendment doctrine that universities will face in combating racist conduct, it is clear that even a revised, more carefully crafted anti-racism policy could not reach more subtle forms of racism with formal sanctions, especially in the classroom. Universities, then, will have to develop two-part policies: one part to address egregious, blatant speech and conduct that is legally sanctionable under the first amendment; the other for nonsanctionable and more subtle conduct that is nevertheless offensive, i.e., behavior that will never be reached by formal adjudication but which the university needs to recognize, condemn, and discourage. . . .

Policies Against Subtle Racism

Finally, universities can make—and in some cases have made—affirmative use of their first amendment prerogatives, publicly and officially condemning offensive behavior that they are otherwise unable to sanction. Universities make decisions about the value of speech and ideas every day in their decisions to hire and tenure some faculty members rather than others, to fund some research and teaching programs rather than others. Choosing to fund, say, an early American history program instead of an African-American history program means that the university considers the former to be more valuable. But there is no reason an institution cannot similarly express its disdain for expression by faculty and students that is racially offensive.

Such an affirmative strategy to make racist expression unwelcome and uncomfortable could work in conjunction with the many other educative efforts aimed at eliminating white cultural hegemony on campus.

"Preventing or punishing speech . . . is a clear violation of the First Amendment."

Colleges Should Not Censor Racist Speech

Nat Hentoff

Nat Hentoff began writing about free speech issues in the 1960s. His columns on civil liberties have appeared in such publications as *The Progressive* and *The Village Voice*. He is the author of *The First Freedom: The Tumultuous History of Free Speech in America,* among other books. In the following viewpoint he argues that all speech, no matter how hateful, is protected by the First Amendment. Hentoff also contends that censorship of any kind is inappropriate at a college, since one of a college's main functions is to serve as a haven for free thought.

As you read, consider the following questions:

1. Why should students *not* be protected from bad ideas, according to Hentoff?
2. Why does the author believe there has been little protest against school codes that restrict racist speech and behavior?
3. Why must the First Amendment protect slurs, according to Hentoff?

Nat Hentoff, "Free Speech on Campus," *The Progressive,* May 1989. Reprinted with permission.

A flier distributed at the University of Michigan proclaimed that blacks "don't belong in classrooms, they belong hanging from trees."

At other campuses around the country, manifestations of racism are becoming commonplace. At Yale, a swastika and the words WHITE POWER! were painted on the building housing the University's Afro-American Cultural Center. At Temple University, a White Students Union has been formed with some 130 members.

Swastikas are not directed only at black students. The Nazi symbol has been spraypainted on the Jewish Student Union at Memphis State University. And on a number of campuses, women have been singled out as targets of wounding and sometimes frightening speech. At the law school of the State University of New York at Buffalo, several women students have received anonymous letters characterized by one professor as venomously sexist.

These and many more such signs of the resurgence of bigotry and know-nothingism throughout the society—as well as on campus—have to do solely with speech, including symbolic speech. There have also been physical assaults on black students and on black, white, and Asian women students, but the way to deal with physical attacks is clear: Call the police and file a criminal complaint. What is to be done, however, about speech alone—however disgusting, inflammatory, and rawly divisive that speech may be?

A Clear Violation

At more and more colleges, administrators—with the enthusiastic support of black students, women students, and liberal students—have been answering that question by preventing or punishing speech. In public universities, this is a clear violation of the First Amendment. In private colleges and universities, suppression of speech mocks the secular religion of academic freedom and free inquiry.

The Student Press Law Center in Washington, D.C.—a vital source of legal support for student editors around the country—reports, for example, that at the University of Kansas, the student host and producer of a radio news program was forbidden by school officials from interviewing a leader of the Ku Klux Klan. So much for free inquiry on that campus.

In Madison, Wisconsin, *The Capital Times* ran a story about Chancellor Sheila Kaplan of the University of Wisconsin branch at Parkside, who ordered her campus to be scoured of "some anonymously placed white supremacist hate literature." Sounding like the legendary Mayor Frank ("I am the law")

Hague of Jersey City, who booted "bad speech" out of town, Chancellor Kaplan said, "This institution is not a lamppost standing on the street corner. It doesn't belong to everyone." Who decides what speech can be heard or read by everyone? Why, the Chancellor, of course. That's what George III used to say, too. University of Wisconsin political science professor Carol Tebben thinks otherwise. She believes university administrators "are getting confused when they are acting as censors and trying to protect students from bad ideas. I don't think students need to be protected from bad ideas. I think they can determine for themselves what ideas are bad."

After all, if students are to be "protected" from bad ideas, how are they going to learn to identify and cope with them? Sending such ideas underground simply makes them stronger and more dangerous.

The Price of Freedom

Liberal voices are calling for restrictions on free speech. They are being heard on college and university campuses such as Michigan and Wisconsin, where penalties—including expulsion—can now be imposed for expressing opinions deemed derogatory to women, ethnic minorities, gays, or lesbians. Those who support these sanctions seem to be saying that bias, or at least its expression, has no place on US campuses. The "fighting words" doctrine, set forth in a 1942 Supreme Court ruling (*Chaplinsky v. New Hampshire*), is often cited as a legal basis for curtailing freedom of speech by means of anti-bias rules. . . .

Giving offense—no matter on what grounds or in what form—cannot be allowed in and of itself to justify curtailing free speech. The proper response to the repugnant act, the tasteless work of art, or the offensive remark is to rebut, to reprimand, to counsel, to educate—not to gag.

We must pay a price for the First Amendment. Part of the price is the fact that we shall be subjected to much that is ugly, tawdry, ignoble, silly, offensive, or just plain false.

Gresham Riley, *The Christian Science Monitor*, August 11, 1989.

Professor Tebben's conviction that free speech means just that has become a decidedly minority view on many campuses. At the University of Buffalo Law School, the faculty unanimously adopted a "Statement Regarding Intellectual Freedom, Tolerance, and Political Harassment." Its title implies support of intellectual freedom, but the statement warned students that once they enter "this legal community," their right to free speech must become tempered "by the responsibility to promote equality and justice."

Accordingly, swift condemnation will befall anyone who engages in "remarks directed at another's race, sex, religion, national origin, age, or sex preference." Also forbidden are "other remarks based on prejudice and group stereotype."

This ukase is so broad that enforcement has to be alarmingly subjective. Yet the University of Buffalo Law School provides no due-process procedures for a student booked for making any of these prohibited remarks. Conceivably, a student caught playing a Lenny Bruce, Richard Pryor, or Sam Kinison album in his room could be tried for aggravated insensitivity by association.

When I looked into this wholesale cleansing of bad speech at Buffalo, I found it had encountered scant opposition. One protester was David Gerald Jay, a graduate of the law school and a cooperating attorney for the New York Civil Liberties Union. Said the appalled graduate: "Content-based prohibitions constitute prior restraint and should not be tolerated."

You would think that the law professors and administration at this public university might have known that. But hardly any professors dissented, and among the students only members of the conservative Federalist Society spoke up for free speech. The fifty-strong chapter of the National Lawyers Guild was on the other side. After all, it was more important to go on record as vigorously opposing racism and sexism than to expose oneself to charges of insensitivity to these malignancies.

Pressure to Be Politically Correct

The pressures to have the "right" attitude—as proved by having the "right" language in and out of class—can be stifling. A student who opposes affirmative action, for instance, can be branded a racist.

At the University of California at Los Angeles, the student newspaper ran an editorial cartoon satirizing affirmative action. (A student stops a rooster on campus and asks how the rooster got into UCLA. "Affirmative action," is the answer.) After outraged complaints from various minority groups, the editor was suspended for violating a publications policy against running "articles that perpetuate derogatory or cultural stereotypes." The art director was also suspended.

When the opinion editor of the student newspaper at California State University at Northridge wrote an article asserting that the sanctions against the editor and art director at UCLA amounted to censorship, he was suspended too.

At New York University Law School, a student was so disturbed by the pall of orthodoxy at that prestigious institution that he wrote to the school newspaper even though, as he said, he expected his letter to make him a pariah among his fellow students.

The Watchdogs

Barry Endick described the atmosphere at NYU created by "a host of watchdog committees and a generally hostile classroom reception regarding any student comment right of center." This "can be arguably viewed as symptomatic of a prevailing spirit of academic and social intolerance of . . . any idea which is not 'politically correct.' "

He went on to say something that might well be posted on campus bulletin boards around the country, though it would probably be torn down at many of them:

"We ought to examine why students, so anxious to wield the Fourteenth Amendment, give short shrift to the First. Yes, Virginia, there are racist assholes. And you know what, the Constitution protects them, too."

Lesson Must Be Relearned

People of color, women and gays and lesbians owe their vibrant political movements in large measure to their freedom to communicate. If speech can be banned because it offends someone, how long will it be before the messages of these groups are themselves found offensive?

It is distressing that the "politically correct" view on campus these days seems to favor curtailment of speech. Oddly, defense of the First Amendment is now an anti-progressive view. Yes, speech is sometimes painful. Sometimes it is abusive. That is one of the prices of a free society. Unfortunately, this is a lesson that has to be learned over and over again. No victory endures.

Lee Dembart, *The New York Times,* May 5, 1989.

Not when they engage in violence or vandalism. But when they speak or write, racist assholes fall right into this Oliver Wendell Holmes definition—highly unpopular among bigots, liberals, radicals, feminists, sexists, and college administrators:

"If there is any principle of the Constitution that more imperatively calls for attachment than any other, it is the principle of free thought—not free only for those who agree with us, but freedom for the thought we hate."

The language sounds like a pietistic Sunday sermon, but if it ever falls wholly into disuse, . . . [no] journal of opinion—Right or Left—will survive.

Sometimes, college presidents and administrators sound as if they fully understand what Holmes was saying. For example, when *The Daily Pennsylvanian*—speaking for many at the University of Pennsylvania—urged that a speaking invitation to Louis Farrakhan be withdrawn, University President Sheldon Hackney disagreed.

"Open expression," said Hackney, "is the fundamental principle of a university." Yet consider what the same Sheldon Hackney did to the free-speech rights of a teacher at his own university. If any story distills the essence of the current decline of free speech on college campuses, it is the Ballad of Murray Dolfman.

For twenty-two years, Dolfman, a practicing lawyer in Philadelphia, had been a part-time lecturer in the Legal Studies Department of the University of Pennsylvania's Wharton School. For twenty-two years, no complaint had ever been made against him; indeed, his student course–evaluations had been outstanding. Each year students competed to get into his class.

On a November afternoon in 1984, Dolfman was lecturing about personal-service contracts. His style somewhat resembles that of Professor Charles Kingsfield in *The Paper Chase*. Dolfman insists that students he calls on be prepared—or suffer the consequences. He treats all students this way—regardless of race, creed, or sex.

The Incident

This day, Dolfman was pointing out that no one can be forced to work against his or her will—even if a contract has been signed. A court may prevent the resister from working for someone else so long as the contract is in effect but, Dolfman said, there can "be nothing that smacks of involuntary servitude."

Where does this concept come from? Dolfman looked around the room. Finally, a cautious hand was raised: "The Constitution?" "Where in the Constitution?" No hands. "The Thirteenth Amendment," said the teacher. So, what does *it* say? The students were looking everywhere but at Dolfman.

"We will lose our liberties," Dolfman often told his classes, "if we don't know what they are."

On this occasion, he told them that he and other Jews, as ex-slaves, spoke at Passover of the time when they were slaves under the Pharaohs so that they would remember every year what it was like not to be free.

"We have ex-slaves here," Dolfman continued, "who should know about the Thirteenth Amendment." He asked black students in the class if they could tell him what was in that amendment.

"I wanted them to really think about it," Dolfman told me, "and know its history. You're better equipped to fight racism if you know all about those post-Civil War amendments and civil-rights laws." The Thirteenth Amendment provides that "neither slavery nor involuntary servitude . . . shall exist within the United States."

The Reaction

The black students in his class did not know what was in that amendment, and Dolfman had them read it aloud. Later, they complained to university officials that they had been hurt and humiliated by having been referred to as ex-slaves. Moreover, they said, they had no reason to be grateful for a constitutional amendment which gave them rights which should never have been denied them—and gave them precious little else. They had not made these points in class, although Dolfman—unlike Professor Kingsfield—encourages rebuttal.

Informed of the complaint, Dolfman told the black students he had intended no offense, and he apologized if they had been offended.

That would not do—either for the black students or for the administration. Furthermore, there were mounting black-Jewish tensions on campus, and someone had to be sacrificed. Who better than a part-time Jewish teacher with no contract and no union? He was sentenced by—George Orwell would have loved this—the Committee on Academic Freedom and Responsibility.

On his way to the stocks, Dolfman told President Sheldon Hackney that if a part-time instructor "can be punished on this kind of charge, a tenured professor can eventually be booted out, then a dean, and then a president."

No Dissent

Hackney was unmoved. Dolfman was banished from the campus for what came to be a year. But first he was forced to make a public apology to the entire university and then he was compelled to attend a "sensitivity and racial awareness" session. Sort of like a Vietnamese reeducation camp.

A few conservative professors objected to the stigmatization of Murray Dolfman. I know of no student dissent. Indeed, those students most concerned with making the campus more "sensitive" to diversity exulted in Dolfman's humiliation. So did most liberals on the faculty.

If my children were still of college age and wanted to attend the University of Pennsylvania, I would tell them this story. But where else could I encourage them to go?

"The blatant prejudice of textbook authors and publishers against Christianity is clearly evident."

America's Textbooks Are Censored in Favor of the Left

William F. Jasper

The following viewpoint is by William F. Jasper, a contributor to the conservative biweekly magazine *The New American*. Jasper argues that textbooks ignore or deride the role Christianity has played and continues to play in the development of civilization. Textbook authors are biased and promote leftist beliefs, such as approval of communism or atheism, according to Jasper.

As you read, consider the following questions:

1. What religious events does the author contend should be covered in history textbooks?
2. How do textbooks demean religion, according to Jasper?
3. What do the schools offer in place of Christianity, in Jasper's opinion?

William F. Jasper, "True or False: Public School Students Learn Lies or Nothing at All," *The New American*, August 28, 1989. Reprinted with permission.

Are public school textbooks biased? Are they censored? The answer to both is yes. And the nature of the bias is clear: Religion, traditional family values, and conservative political and economic positions have been reliably excluded from children's textbooks. —Paul C. Vitz

Paul C. Vitz, Professor of Psychology at New York University, examined ninety widely used elementary social studies texts, high school history texts, and elementary readers. The purpose of his research, which was funded by the National Institute of Education, was to determine if public school textbooks are biased—specifically biased, that is, in their treatment of religion and traditional values. The 1983 Vitz study, the most comprehensive research effort of its kind, provided powerful validation of those charges frequently leveled against textbooks by parents, church organizations, and conservative and patriotic civic groups: that the textbooks present a distorted view of reality, and purposely advance a liberal/secular-humanist/feminist/collectivist agenda.

One Nation, Without God

The textbooks that Professor Vitz examined are used, he estimated, in 70 to 87 percent of the public school classrooms in the United States. Here is one of his startling findings concerning the elementary social studies texts he studied:

> None of the books covering grades 1 through 4 contain one word referring to any religious activity in contemporary American life. For example, not one word refers to any child or adult who prayed, or who went to church or temple. The same was true for the twenty grade 5 and 6 texts, as well. An occasional rare picture (without captions) in these sixty books does depict Jewish, Catholic, Amish, or vague nondenominational religious scenes. The few pictures . . . that do refer to religious activity were distributed over sixty books and roughly 15,000 pages. . . . [N]ot one word or image in any book shows any form of contemporary representative Protestantism.

Even more disturbing is the complete censorship of any mention of God or Christianity when reporting on historical events and people. "It is common in these books," for instance, says Vitz, "to treat Thanksgiving without explaining to whom the Pilgrims gave thanks. . . . Pilgrims are described entirely without any reference to religion." One social studies book, he reported, has thirty pages on the Pilgrims, including the first Thanksgiving. But there is not one single word or image that refers to religion as even a part of the Pilgrims' life. Another book refers to the Pilgrims merely as "people who make long trips."

This treatment of Christianity contrasts sharply with the fairly frequent, positive references to native American Indian religion in the texts. "The Pueblo can pray to Mother Earth—but Pilgrims can't be described as praying to God," says Vitz. "And never are Christians described as praying to Jesus, either in the United States or elsewhere."

Great Awakening, or Big Sleep?

Of the ten fifth-grade U.S. history texts Vitz examined, "not one book notes the extreme liveliness and great importance of religion in American life in general. This religious energy . . . is never noted." Further, says the professor, "There is not one reference in any of these books to such major religious events as the Salem Witch Trials; The Great Awakening of the 1740s; the great revivals of the 1830s and 1840s; the great urban Christian revivals of the 1870-90 period; the very important Holiness and Pentecostal movements around 1880-1910, the liberal and conservative Protestant split in the early twentieth century; or the Born-Again movement of the 1960s and 1970s."

A Cultural War

The cultural war begun in education by John Dewey and the secular humanists against religious belief and traditional social values has escalated. Threatened now is the transmission through the public school system of any knowledge of religion and traditional values. Those values, which are central to an understanding of American history and the American character, are either omitted or inadequately presented in most elementary and high school textbooks. . . .

Textbook publishing is big business. It feeds a large centralized school system that can ignore parents' wishes through regulations and red tape drawn up by an anonymous bureaucracy. Instead of a pluralism of legitimate and historical views, the school system represents a monopoly of liberal ideas and biases. We have, in effect, an "established school system" which consistently rejects conservative values of American life.

Mary Ellen Bork, *Reflections*, Fall 1986.

Another indication Vitz found of the biased treatment of religion in American history is "the universal tendency to omit from the lists of important historical events almost all dates referring to religion, especially in the last one hundred years." This bias extended to the study of world history, as well. A prime example is a 6th-grade history text's treatment of Joan of Arc, in which "her story is told without any reference to God, to religion, or to her being a saint. The treatment is entirely secular and seems to have been included simply because Joan of

Arc was a woman."

Even prominent liberals have taken the textbooks to task for this obvious bias. In July 1987, the American Federation of Teachers released its critical study of history as taught in most American schools. The AFT report, titled *Democracy's Untold Story: What World History Textbooks Neglect*, was written by Paul Gagnon, chairman of the history department at the University of Massachusetts in Boston. Among its findings: "The basic ideas of Judaism and Christianity, which inform every debate over right and wrong and the place of the individual in society, are all but ignored in some of these texts and only feebly suggested in the rest."

"Whatever one thinks of Christianity," observed Professor Vitz, "it has certainly been of central importance in world history, and the life of Jesus of Nazareth constitutes one of the more important events of that history. . . . Yet none of these books treats the life of Jesus as anything like the important event it proved to be. A few books give him some coverage . . . but four books (out of 10 sixth-grade texts) . . . give not a word of coverage to his life and teaching. Others give so little as to be banal. . . ."

Debunking the Bible

The blatant prejudice of textbook authors and publishers against Christianity is clearly evident not only by their selective censorship and glaring omissions, but by outright anti-Christian, anti-Biblical references. Christian missionaries, when mentioned, are rarely cast in a sympathetic light, and are often presented as venal, exploitive, and oppressive. Their positive contributions seem to be nonexistent.

One of the many noted scholars who have exposed this travesty is Professor George Hillocks Jr. of the University of Chicago, who in an article in the August 1978 issue of *School Review* ticked off a list of implicit deprecations of Christianity common to textbooks from the elementary level through college:

> Sunday School depicted as a tedious bore, a minister characterized as self-righteous, photographs of churches in obvious states of decay and collapse. The inclusion of "god," "goddamn," "Christ," and related euphemisms is interpreted as a tacit approval of breaking the third commandment. The presentation of evolution as established fact is taken as a clear denial of Biblical validity . . . denial of absolute values and, therefore, of "an ultimate cause" and a God who provides "a guarantee of human values."

The historicity of Biblical persons and events is regularly "debunked" in school textbooks. This is how the Scholastic Book

Services history text, *The Rise of The West*, treats the biblical account of Moses leading the Israelites through the parted Sea: "Moses may have led them across some shallow swamps and into the Sinai (SIGH-nigh) desert. The Hebrews called these swamps the 'Sea of Reeds' because of the tall grass that grew in them. It may be that the Sea of Reeds was later called the Red Sea by mistake."

Reflecting World Views

The schools in the Soviet Union are establishments of the Marxist-Leninist religion; the schools in the Puritan colonies were establishments of orthodox Christianity; and the public schools of America are establishments of secular humanism. The textbooks of these schools reflect their respective worldviews. The recognized hallmark of a secular humanist textbook is its supposed religious neutrality. In fact, its premise is that God does not exist.

The Blumenfeld Education Letter, February 1989.

Relegating Christ and the Bible to the realm of mythology is another common textbook ploy. *Psychology for You*, published by the Oxford Book Company (1973), provides an excellent example of this: "A great many myths deal with the idea of rebirth. Jesus, Dionysus, Odin, and many other traditional figures are represented as having died, after which they were reborn or arose from the dead."

In the same text we read that

> . . . myths may give a picture of the world as having fallen from a perfect state. The evil of the world, according to these traditions, resulted from man's failure to obey the will of God, and it is only by following the will of God that the world can be restored to its proper state. This is essentially the mythological standpoint of Christianity, Judaism, Islam, and many other religions.

Here is another example, from a social studies text [*People and Culture*], of the Bible as fable and myth: "A NEW GOD. Among all the hundreds of Middle Eastern gods, a very different kind of god emerged. This god was the God of the Hebrews. Here is a Hebrew children's story that tries to explain how people began believing in this new kind of God."

And yet another [from the book *Perspectives in United States History*]: "Anthropologists studying the human customs, religious practices, ritualism, and the priestcraft came to the conclusion that men created their own gods . . . the gods that men created answered their special needs. The God of the Judeo-Christian tradition was a god created by a desert folk.". . .

158

Traditional Christian . . . values are being undermined by the sins of omission and commission of the textbook writers. But these authors often engage in even more open and direct attempts to challenge and destroy those values. Religion, for instance, is treated as passé and irrelevant, or even as nonsensical superstition that is a hindrance to the rational and scientific advancement of the human race.

Holt, Rinehart and Winston's *Introduction to the Behavioral Sciences: An Inquiry Approach* declares dogmatically that religion is outmoded: "For a very few, religion can still provide a special sense of embracing belonging and selfhood, but for most, religion is but a Sunday meeting house and nursery school, and a recreation center, which cannot adequately define the entire person."

Students are encouraged to jettison orthodox Christianity for scientism, psychology, or smarmy New Age mysticism. In *Relationships: A Study in Human Behavior* by Ginn and Company, students are told: "God, then, would be the love we encounter when we turn to help others. Prayer would be essentially a dialogue of love. Salvation would be being loved in a community characterized by love."

Subverting America's Children

Psychology and sociology texts are particularly notorious for challenging Biblical morality and promoting unrestrained carnality and hedonism. *Behind the Mask: Our Psychological World*, by Prentice-Hall publishers, asserts: "It is thought-provoking to carry creativity training to its ultimate extreme, as at least one author has done. He suggests that if we wanted to truly induce completely creative thinking, we should teach children to question the Ten Commandments, patriotism, the two-party system, monogamy, and the laws against incest.". . .

There can be little, if any, doubt of the existence of a long-term, conscious, concerted effort to subvert, through public school curricula, the hearts and minds of American children. What is far more shocking than all of the abominations the textbook subversives can conjure up is the willingness of parents to tolerate such abominations—and to continue entrusting their children to a government school system that is betraying them at every turn.

159

"Vocal, well-organized groups pushing a sectarian agenda have been able to dominate textbook adoption procedures . . . in many communities."

America's Textbooks Are Censored in Favor of the Right

John H. Buchanan

John H. Buchanan is chairman of People for the American Way, a group dedicated to fighting what it believes is censorship on the part of the religious right. In the following viewpoint, Buchanan argues that religious groups want textbooks to reflect their own beliefs. These groups, according to Buchanan, seriously threaten objective learning in America's schools.

As you read, consider the following questions:

1. What are the real objectives of members of the religious right who seek to censor textbooks, according to Buchanan?
2. Why does the author object to the teaching of creationism?
3. Why are these censors dangerous, in Buchanan's opinion?

John H. Buchanan, "Religiously Inspired Censorship in Public Schools." Reprinted with permission, from *National Forum: The Phi Kappa Phi Journal,* vol. 1xviii, no. 1 (Winter 1988).

Of all subjects taught in public schools, English grammar and composition seem least likely to generate controversy, especially controversy of a religious nature. For many students the subjects inspire yawns rather than outrage. But in a middle school in Arizona, a textbook called *Composition and Applied Grammar: The Writing Process* came under attack for teaching situational ethics and undermining traditional values. The "offensive" chapters of the book were deleted.

In the state of Washington a high school science curriculum was the target of objections because it did not include creationism. The school district has a policy that enjoins teachers from expressing a personal opinion about a "controversial" topic like evolution and requires them to treat the two "theories" of evolution and creationism "fairly."

Religious Intolerance

In Nebraska, parents of some elementary school students objected to the school's traditional Halloween activities because they promoted witchcraft. The children were excused from the Halloween celebration.

These incidents are examples of a growing sentiment of religious intolerance across our country that finds expression in attacks on textbooks and other materials, courses, programs, and even ideas in our public schools. During the 1986-87 school year, People for the American Way documented 153 such incidents. Many of these attacks take their inspiration from the activities and literature of a network of religious-right and far-right groups that share a common political and educational agenda.

Among these are Phyllis Schlafly's Eagle Forum, Beverly La Haye's Concerned Women for America, Pat Robertson's National Legal Foundation, Mel and Norma Gabler's Educational Research Analysts, and Citizens for Excellence in Education, the activist arm of the National Association of Christian Educators. They are united by the belief that public schools should reflect their sectarian views and refrain from encouraging children to think critically and independently.

Catch Phrases

The pervasive influence of this far-right network is apparent in the recurrent use of a "language of censorship," a collection of catch-phrases that have become effective scare tactics. These terms and the ideas they embody are promoted by the far-right groups and were present in more than half of the incidents recorded in 1986-87.

"Secular humanism" is one such all-purpose objection. During the 1986-87 school year, this term was used to challenge a teacher's guide in a program for gifted children, a course designed to build confidence and self-esteem, drug-abuse prevention and sex-education courses, and health and home economics textbooks. The most infamous example was a court decision in Mobile, Alabama, that banned forty-four history, social studies, and home economics textbooks for promoting the godless "religion" of secular humanism in the Mobile County public schools. (The decision has since been overruled.) A curriculum director in Iowa has announced that evidence of "secular humanism" will be a criterion used in evaluating textbooks there. More than once we have seen a general call to "rid the schools of secular humanism," as though it were a pernicious substance, like asbestos.

Holes in the Texts

There remains the possibility that public education in America can help instill humane, democratic, cooperative and critical values in generations of young people who pass through the system. But despite the fundamentalists' anxieties, that is not the rule, and it is hardly the exception in most parts of the country today. Textbooks have been so bowdlerized because of fear of controversy that it must be enormously difficult for the zealots to find many that can logically be banned. Whole areas of history are left blank, and urgent issues of social development are mangled beyond recognition. You will look in vain for high-school texts that seriously examine the roots and rise of the labor movement, that present feminism as a significant force for change, that make the proper points about the Vietnam War and its opponents. No doubt there are public-school teachers who keep the liberal spirit alive in their classrooms, but by and large the public schools have abdicated any commitment they might have had to the humane values now under fire.

The Nation, May 30, 1987.

Though "secular humanism" has proven notoriously difficult to define, the following statement from Pat Robertson offers a glimpse into the meaning it holds for those who use it: "You're being hunted down by those who are essentially atheists, those who embrace so-called secular humanism. They hate religion, they hate Christianity, they hate the Bible because the Bible is truth and they don't like the truth." "Secular humanism" is used to object to materials that do not make explicit reference to the objector's religion, do not teach the "moral absolutes" or "traditional values" of the objector's religion, and do describe a variety of perspectives on complex social and moral issues.

"Values clarification" and "situation ethics" are frequent, often interchangeable, objections. These objections are rooted in an opposition to autonomy—that people must take responsibility for their decisions and behavior—and to any kind of classroom exchange that helps students wrestle with ambiguous or controversial topics. According to objectors, these notions clash with the fundamentalist belief that the Bible is the sole source of moral strictures.

Creationism

Leveled at decision-making skills programs and such activities as role playing or open-ended discussion, the charge of values clarification has even been brought to bear against mathematics. Texas textbook censors Mel and Norma Gabler issue this warning: "When a student reads in a math book that there are no absolutes, suddenly every value he's been taught has been destroyed. And the next thing you know, the student turns to crime and drugs." Children's folktales, Halloween activities, a fortune-telling booth at a student fund-raising fair, and a school mascot called the "Sun Devil" have provoked challenges that schools are "teaching the occult" or advancing "satanism." Library books about the supernatural and the witches in *Macbeth* have come under fire, as has an elementary school book called *Mrs. Piggle-Wiggle's Magic.*

The issue of teaching creationism—a literalist interpretation of the biblical account of the origin of the universe—is a hardy perennial. Lately, creationism has wrapped itself in the mantle of science appearing now as "creation science." Efforts to introduce the teaching of this religious belief into science classrooms are usually portrayed as simply seeking "balanced treatment": teaching evolutionism alongside creationism as equally scientific accounts. But one is an article of faith, while the other is an established scientific theory. Pope John Paul II recognized this distinction when he said, "The Bible itself speaks to us of the origin of the universe and its makeup, not in order to provide us with a scientific treatise, but in order to state the correct relationships of man with God and the universe."

Public schools are creatures of democracy, with their tradition of local control and parental involvement. Accordingly, democratic procedures in place in many school systems invite any and all voices to register their concerns about the schools. That is as it should be. But two important points must be made with respect to the type of objections described here.

The first is that, by provoking a volatile and highly ideological debate, such objections obscure legitimate questions about the *educational* merit of materials used in public schools. Parents might well ask, What is the educational rationale behind the presence of Stephen King's *Cujo* in an elementary school library? It is a fair question, given the limited resources available for educational materials in most districts, and schools ought to be prepared to respond. However, few of the challenges documented by People for the American Way raise this important issue at all.

Reasonable Language

The second point is that the political right has become skilled at couching its demands in reasonable terms that mask the sectarian agenda underlying them. Use of the term "balanced treatment" to describe the teaching of evolution alongside creationism as equally scientific accounts is one example of this practice. The Tennessee textbook trial is another. There, in Hawkins County, a group of parents went to court claiming that a reading series in use in the public schools violated their religious beliefs. In an initial decision, they were granted permission for their children to opt out of reading class and be taught at home. Supporters of the parents celebrated this decision as a triumph for "parental control" of education.

Dumbing Down

Publishers have often agreed to modify their texts to make them acceptable. For example, in a biology text approved for the 1981 school year [in Texas], the word "evolution" did not appear anywhere. Publishers say that given the large sums of money at stake, they have little choice but to engage in a process that has come to be known as the "dumbing down" of texts. As a consequence of this practice, a sizable portion of a generation of high school students in states like Texas have heard little mention of Darwin, evolution, and other "sensitive" topics.

Donna A. Demac, *Liberty Denied: The Current Rise of Censorship in America*, 1988.

Concerned Women for America, who funded the plaintiffs in this suit, also described it as an effort to enrich the curriculum. "We just want to *add* ideas to the curriculum," insists one of their spokeswomen. However, even as the judge sought to provide relief to the parents, he admitted it was clear that, from the nature of their many broad objections, no secular reading series would be satisfactory to them. The decision was overturned on appeal.

These are not issues of parental control or of curriculum enrichment; they are demands that the public schools incorporate specific sectarian doctrine into their teachings. Not only is this clearly impermissible under our tradition of church-state separation, regardless of how reasonable the demands can be made to sound, it is also a threat to the very nature of public education in this country. These objections are an attempt to constrict the curriculum—by requiring simple right-wrong answers to complex issues, by neglecting important topics because they are controversial or unpleasant, by limiting independent thought and imagination. Perhaps most dangerous of all is the lesson of intolerance that is taught by the demand to make specific religious beliefs the ideological screen through which public school instruction must pass.

Effects on Education

This ideological debate has spilled over into other areas of school life. Vocal, well-organized groups pushing a sectarian agenda have been able to dominate textbook adoption procedures and school board campaigns in many communities. The latter are high on the agenda of Citizens for Excellence in Public Education (CEPE). CEPE organizes locally to "bring public education back under the control of Christians," fielding candidates for school board elections and promising to drive secular humanism out of the schools.

People at all points along the religious and political spectrum will agree that public education needs improvement. But real and urgent issues of educational quality are left by the wayside in controversies about "secular humanism," "situation ethics," or "satanism." Public education in America is public not because it is free, but because its purpose is to prepare children for their roles as active citizens in a pluralistic democracy. That role requires a strong sense of civic and personal responsibility, solid literacy skills, the ability to think critically and independently, and tolerance for those who believe differently. These are the very goals of public education under attack by those on the right.

If there is anything that people of all religious persuasions should hold in common, it is a commitment to provide opportunities and incentives for all children born into our society to become all that they can be. We owe all children the chance to attain their full stature and to give the world whatever gifts they possess. However sincere those carrying forward their holy war against public education are, they are pitting themselves against the very things that make for excellence in education. They are therefore pitting themselves against the 89 percent of our young who look to the public schools for their chance to learn and to become the kind of mature people who can maintain a strong, free, democratic society as America enters her third century.

a critical thinking activity

Understanding Words in Context

Readers occasionally come across words they do not recognize. And frequently, because they do not know a word or words, they will not fully understand the passage being read. Obviously, the reader can look up an unfamiliar word in a dictionary. But by carefully examining the word in the context in which it is used, the word's meaning can often be determined. A careful reader may find clues to the meaning of the word in surrounding words, ideas, and attitudes.

Below are paraphrased excerpts from the viewpoints in this chapter. In each excerpt, one word is printed in italics. Try to determine the meaning of each word by reading the excerpt. Under each excerpt you will find four definitions for the italicized word. Choose the one that is closest to your understanding of the word.

Finally, use a dictionary to see how well you have understood the words in context. It will be helpful to discuss with others the clues that helped you decide on each word's meaning.

1. A racist *INVECTIVE* hurts as much as a physical blow.

   INVECTIVE means:

   a) punch   c) insult
   b) smile   d) joke

2. The university proclamation forbids remarks based on prejudice and stereotype. This *UKASE* is too broad and subjective.

   UKASE means:

   a) lesson   c) class
   b) edict   d) answer

3. A *PALL* of intolerance hung over the university, preventing the students from freely expressing themselves.

   PALL means:

   a) question   c) guarantee
   b) cover   d) blessing

166

4. The increasing amount of racial harassment led the college to use censorship to stop this *BURGEONING* problem.

   BURGEONING means:

   a) growing
   b) decreasing
   c) violent
   d) exciting

5. The bigoted students first used *VILIFICATION*, then physical violence to scare the minority students.

   VILIFICATION means:

   a) slander
   b) hospitality
   c) rowdiness
   d) diplomacy

6. According to many books, Christian missionaries were not kind people, but rather were *VENAL* oppressors who would do anything that would benefit themselves.

   VENAL means:

   a) skillful
   b) helpless
   c) corrupt
   d) stupid

7. Because many textbook writers believe all religion is medieval superstition, they often treat religion as unimportant and *PASSÉ*.

   PASSÉ means:

   a) boring
   b) damaging
   c) uplifting
   d) outmoded

8. There has been a general call to rid the schools of secular humanism, as though it were a *PERNICIOUS* substance, like toxic waste.

   PERNICIOUS means:

   a) useless
   b) deadly
   c) prevalent
   d) beneficial

9. While some people believe students should have *AUTONOMY,* others think parents and schools should control students' decisions.

   AUTONOMY means:

   a) control
   b) direction
   c) help
   d) independence

10. It takes a lot of *CHUTZPAH* to think that you know best what others should see or hear, what their opinions should be, or how they should think.

    CHUTZPAH means:

    a) gall
    b) optimism
    c) cowardice
    d) insight

11. A few years ago you could not openly buy pornographic movies. You had to *SURREPTITIOUSLY* order them from some obscure house of sin in Denmark or Sweden.

SURREPTITIOUSLY means:

a) easily
b) secretly
c) legally
d) carefully

12. A librarian who favors censorship must be a *MASOCHIST* if he enjoys the abuse he is bound to receive from other librarians.

MASOCHIST means:

a) hates books
b) enjoys debate
c) is courageous
d) enjoys suffering

Periodical Bibliography

The following articles have been selected to supplement the diverse views presented in this chapter.

Richard Bernstein	"On Campus, How Free Should Free Speech Be?" *The New York Times*, September 10, 1989.
William F. Buckley Jr.	"This is the Age of White Discrimination," *Conservative Chronicle*, August 10, 1988. Available from *Conservative Chronicle*, Box 11297, Des Moines, IA 50340-1297.
Christianity Today	"Parents Run Out of Options in Textbook Case," March 18, 1988.
Alexander Cockburn	"Their Mullahs and Ours," *Zeta Magazine*, April 1989.
Phillip Dunne	"Dissent, Dogma and Darwin's Dog," *Time*, January 15, 1990.
Raymond English	"Trials of a Textbook Writer," *National Review*, February 24, 1989.
Chester E. Finn Jr.	"The Campus: An Island of Repression in a Sea of Freedom," *Commentary*, September 1989.
J.R. Joelson	"Religious Fanatics and Censorship," *The Humanist*, May/June 1989.
David Klinghoffer	"Random Notes," *National Review*, July 14, 1989.
Alfred Krass	"Religion and the Public Schools," *The Other Side*, May/June 1989.
Jon G. Murray	"Equal Access," *American Atheist*, February 1990.
Seth Mydans	"In a Small Town, a Battle Over a Book," *The New York Times*, September 3, 1989.
Natalie Robins	"Library Follow-Up," *The Nation*, June 25, 1988.
The Wall Street Journal	"The Ivory Censor," May 9, 1990.
Wilcomb E. Washburn	"Liberalism Versus Free Speech," *National Review*, September 30, 1988.
Jonathan S. Weil	"Dealing with Censorship: Policy and Procedures," *The Education Digest*, January 1988.
George F. Will	"The Liberals Favor Censorship of Speech," *Conservative Chronicle*, November 15, 1989. Available from *Conservative Chronicle*, Box 11297, Des Moines, IA 50340-1297.

Should Pornography Be Censored?

CENSORSHIP

Chapter Preface

The problem of pornography has long been debated by civil libertarians, conservatives, feminists, and the general public. While there is a small faction which believes that pornography is not only harmless but may even be beneficial, more people believe that it is damaging to individuals and society. However, there is little agreement on what to do about it.

Traditionally, the answers to the problems of regulating pornography have been divided along political lines: liberals said it was repulsive but that it was protected by the First Amendment. Conservatives said that it was repulsive and harmful and therefore was *not* protected by the First Amendment.

The feminist debate over pornography, however, has not followed traditional political lines. The feminist movement, long equated with liberal politics, has split into two camps: those who oppose the censorship of pornography, and those who believe pornography should be censored because it harms women.

Organizations such as the Feminist Anti-Censorship Taskforce (FACT) have argued that the First Amendment demands that all speech, even pornography, be protected. They and other like-minded feminists contend that laws against pornography could be used to censor artistic works, such as Erica Jong's *Fear of Flying*. This novel contains explicit descriptions of sex which could be interpreted as pornographic.

Leading feminists on the other side of the debate, such as Andrea Dworkin and Catharine MacKinnon, argue that First Amendment concerns are outweighed by the harm pornography causes. They maintain that pornography promotes a sexist view of the world in which women exist only to be used and abused by men.

The debate within feminism is indicative of the controversy pornography poses for society. The viewpoints in this chapter debate the fundamental question of what is more harmful: pornography or censorship.

*"The notion that government may censor
expression because it may alter accepted moral
standards flies in the face of the guarantee of
free expression."*

The First Amendment Should Protect Pornography

Geoffrey R. Stone

Geoffrey R. Stone holds the honorary position of Harry Kalvern Jr. Professor of Law at the University of Chicago. He is the author of the book *Constitutional Law* and has written extensively on freedom of expression. In the following viewpoint, he argues that pornography is not proven to be harmful and therefore should not be censored. In a democratic society, he contends, adults should be free to obtain pornography.

As you read, consider the following questions:

1. What forms of expression are protected by the First Amendment even though they are thought to be of slight social value, according to Stone?
2. According to the author, what are the costs and benefits of regulating pornography?
3. Why does Stone object to police enforcement of obscenity laws?

Geoffrey R. Stone, "Repeating Past Mistakes." Published by permission of Transaction Publishers, from *Society*, vol. 24, no. 5. Copyright © 1987 by Transaction Publishers.

The Attorney General's Commission on Pornography had a unique opportunity to redirect society's regulation of obscene expression. The current state of the law is marred by overly broad, ineffective, and wasteful regulation. This was an appropriate opportunity to take a fresh look at the problem and to strike a new balance—a balance that more precisely accommodates society's interests in regulation with the individual's often competing interests in privacy, autonomy, and free expression. The commission squandered this opportunity. Instead of taking a fresh look, it blindly performed its appointed task of renewing and reaffirming past mistakes.

Suppressing the "Obscene"

The United States Supreme Court has held that federal, state, and local government officials have the power, consonant with the First Amendment, to prohibit all distribution of obscene expression. The mere existence of power, however, does not mean that its exercise is sound. . . .

The Supreme Court itself is sharply divided over the constitutional power of government officials to prohibit the distribution of obscene expression to consenting adults. In its 1973 decisions in *Miller v. California* and *Paris Adult Theatre v. Slaton*, the Court divided five-to-four on this issue. Justices William O. Douglas, William J. Brennan, Potter Stewart, and Thurgood Marshall concluded that the First Amendment strips government officials of any power to deny consenting adults the right to obtain obscene expression.

Even apart from the division of opinion in these cases, the Court's analysis of obscene expression is anomalous in terms of its overall First Amendment jurisprudence. At one time, obscene expression was merely one of several categories of expression held by the Supreme Court to be "of such slight social value as a step to truth that any benefit that may be derived from them is clearly outweighed by the social interest in order and morality." In the past quarter-century, the Court has increasingly recognized that such previously unprotected categories of expression as profanity, commercial advertising, incitement, and libel can no longer be regarded as wholly unprotected by the First Amendment. The Court has held that, although such categories of expression have only a "subordinate position in the scale of First Amendment values," they can nonetheless be restricted only if government has at least a substantial justification for the restriction. The Court has thus recognized that even low-value expression may have some First Amendment value, that government efforts to restrict low-value expression will often chill more valuable expression, and that the constitutional and institutional risks of restricting low-value expression are worth taking only if the restriction furthers at least a substantial governmental interest.

Obscene expression now stands alone. No other category of expression is currently regarded as wholly outside the protection of the First Amendment. No other category of expression may be suppressed merely because it has only "slight social value." No other category of expression may be censored without a showing that the restriction serves at least a substantial governmental interest. The current analysis of obscene expression is thus the sole remaining artifact of a now discarded jurisprudence.

The Offensive and Controversial

The regulation of offensive material, either as conduct itself or that which presumptively stimulates disapproved conduct, is contradictory to our traditional guarantees of expression which must allow protests against our moral code of the day if First Amendment speech guarantees are to mean anything. Indeed, the protections inherent in the First Amendment are inconsequential if used only to assure continued expression of the inoffensive and the noncontroversial. If the controversial, the objectionable, and the offensive, customarily thought of as things which provoke the need for censorship, are to be proscribed, then the freedom to differ becomes limited to things that do not bother much.

Dolf Zillmann and Jennings Bryant, eds., *Pornography: Research Advances & Policy Considerations*, 1989.

The current analysis of obscenity is not necessarily wrong as a matter of constitutional law. Nevertheless, the constitutional authority to act in this context hangs by the slender thread of a single vote and is very much in doubt as a matter of constitutional principle. In such circumstances, government must exercise special care in deciding whether and how to exercise its power. We should not simply assume that because it is constitutional to act it is wise to do so. The very closeness of the constitutional question is itself a compelling reason for caution.

In deciding on the appropriate regulation of obscene expression, we must consider both the costs and benefits of regulation. Laws prohibiting the distribution of obscene expression to consenting adults impose at least three types of costs. First, although the Court has held that such expression has only low First Amendment value, it may nonetheless serve a useful function both for society and the individual. That the demand for sexually explicit expression is as great as it is, suggests that such expression serves an important psychological or emotional function for many individuals. It may satisfy a need for fantasy, escape, entertainment, stimulation, or whatever. Thus, whether or not obscene expression has significant First Amendment value, it may have important value to the individual. Laws prohibiting its distribution to consenting adults may frustrate significant interests in individual privacy, dignity, autonomy, and self–fulfillment.

Defining Obscenity

The suppression of obscene expression may also have a severe chilling effect on more valuable expression. The legal concept of obscenity is vague in the extreme. As a consequence, individuals who wish to purchase or distribute sexually explicit expression will invariably censor themselves in order to avoid being ensnared in the ill-defined net of our obscenity laws. Laws prohibiting the distribution of obscene expression spill over and significantly limit the distribution of constitutionally protected expression as well.

Any serious effort to enforce laws prohibiting the distribution of obscene expression to consenting adults necessarily draws valuable police and prosecutorial resources away from other areas of law enforcement. In a world of limited resources, we must recognize that the decision to criminalize one form of behavior renders more difficult and less effective the enforcement of laws directed at other forms of behavior. It is necessary to set priorities, for the failure to enforce our laws vigorously can serve only to generate disrespect for law enforcement and bring the legal system into disrepute.

Two interests are most commonly asserted in support of laws prohibiting the distribution of obscene expression to consenting adults. First, it is said that government must suppress the distribution of such expression to consenting adults in order to prevent the erosion of moral standards. The moral fabric of a society undoubtedly affects the tone and quality of life. It is thus a legitimate subject of government concern, but as Justice Brennan recognized in his opinion in *Paris Adult Theatre*, "the State's interest in regulating morality by suppressing obscenity, while often asserted, remains essentially ill-focused and ill-defined." It rests ultimately on "unprovable . . . assumptions about human behavior, morality, sex, and religion." Perhaps more importantly, the notion that government may censor expression because it may alter accepted moral standards flies in the face of the guarantee of free expression. A democratic society must be free to determine its own moral standards through robust and wide-open debate and expression. Although government may legitimately inculcate moral values through education and related activities, it may not suppress expression that reflects or encourages an opposing morality. Such paternalism is incompatible with the most basic premises of the First Amendment.

Second, it is said that government must suppress the distribution of obscene expression to consenting adults because exposure to such expression may "cause" individuals to engage in unlawful conduct. The prevention of unlawful conduct is a legitimate governmental interest, but the correlation between exposure to obscene expression and unlawful conduct is doubtful, at best. As the President's Commission on Obscenity and Pornography found in 1970, there is "no evidence to date that exposure to explicit sexual materials plays a significant role in the causation of delinquent or criminal behavior." The Attorney General's Commission's contrary conclusion in 1986 is based more on preconception than on evidence. An issue that has long divided social scientists and other experts in the field can hardly be definitively resolved by a commission of nonexperts, most of whom were appointed because of their preexisting commitment to the suppression of obscene expression. In any event, even those who claim a connection between exposure to obscene expression and unlawful conduct claim no more than an indirect and attenuated "bad tendency." Thus, although some individuals may on some occasions commit some unlawful acts "because of" their exposure to obscene expression, the connection is indirect, speculative, and unpredictable. It is not even remotely comparable to the much more direct harm caused by such products as firearms, alcohol, and automobiles. The suppression of obscene expression is also a stunningly inefficient and overly broad way to deal with this problem, for even a modest change in law enforcement or sentencing practices would have a much more direct and substantial impact on the rate of unlawful conduct than the legalization or criminalization of obscene expression.

Laws prohibiting the distribution of obscene expression to consenting adults impose significant costs on society and frustrate potentially important privacy and autonomy interests of the individual for only marginal benefits. It is time to bring our regulation of such expression into line with our constitutional traditions, our law enforcement priorities, and our own self-interest and common sense.

Protect Children, Not Adults

The course I propose . . . would leave government free to direct its enforcement energies at the more important concerns generated by obscene expression. These fall into three related categories: the protection of juveniles, the protection of captive viewers, and the regulation of the secondary effects of obscene expression. The Court has long recognized government's interest in sheltering children from exposure to obscene expression. What I propose does not undermine this interest. Nor does it interfere with society's substantial interest in restricting child pornography, which poses significantly different issues. My proposal would not in any way prevent government from protecting individuals against the shock effect of unwanted exposure to obscene expression. Government would remain free to prohibit children from viewing movies or buying books found "obscene," and it would remain free to prohibit or otherwise regulate the exhibition of obscene expression over the airwaves. Sensible accommodations can also be devised for other media, such as cable television. Also, my proposal would not prevent government from using zoning and other regulatory devices to control the distribution of obscene expression in order to prevent the decay of neighborhoods or other secondary effects associated with the availability of obscene expression.

A Sensible Balance

By leaving consenting adults free to obtain obscene expression at their discretion, and by protecting our important interests through narrowly defined regulations, we can strike a sensible balance, protecting important societal interests while at the same time preserving our traditional respect for free expression and for the privacy and autonomy of the individual.

"The American people have a legal and constitutional right to stop the abuse of society and its individual members by the pornographers."

The First Amendment Should Not Protect Pornography

Alan E. Sears

Alan E. Sears is the legal counsel for Citizens for Decency Through Law, an anti-pornography organization in Phoenix, Arizona. He has served as executive director of the Attorney General's Commission on Pornography, which issued a report in 1986 condemning pornography. In the following viewpoint, he states that the First Amendment right to free speech is not absolute. The government may limit libelous or fraudulent speech because it is harmful, despite the First Amendment. He contends that the harms caused by pornography, including aggression against women, justify restricting it.

As you read, consider the following questions:

1. Why is restricting pornography not the same as censorship, according to Sears?
2. How does the author respond to the argument that obscenity laws are dangerously vague?
3. How would Sears regulate pornography?

Alan E. Sears, "The Legal Case for Restricting Pornography," in *Pornography: Research Advances and Policy Considerations*, Dolf Zillman and Jennings Bryant, eds. Hillsdale, NJ: Lawrence Erlbaum Associates, 1989. Reprinted with permission.

The American people have a legal and constitutional right to stop the abuse of society and its individual members by the pornographers. Seldom discussed in the debate regarding pornography and contemporary American culture are the rights of the majority of the American people who want something done about what they perceive to be a very serious social problem, the problem of pornographic environmental pollution and their right to self-determination on this issue. Most often heard are the claims of alleged First Amendment protection for criminal or otherwise harmful acts. In . . . response to this citizen concern President Ronald Reagan and Attorney General William French Smith authorized the establishment of The Attorney General's Commission on Pornography in early 1985 to study problems and issues relating to pornography.

Legal Recourse

It is the opinion of this writer that the single most important finding of the Attorney General's Commission on Pornography [Final Report of the Attorney General's Commission on Pornography, 1986], was the finding perhaps least reported and least discussed in the public debate—the finding that *the rule of law will work in our society* and that within the bounds of the law the public's major concerns regarding the pornography issue can be successfully resolved. National surveys on public opinion have found that 72% of the American people demand a crackdown by the government on the problems of pornography. More than 92% want a crackdown by the government on child pornography. With regard to some of the more severe types of "adult" pornography, as many as 73% of the American people would favor the extreme remedy of banning. Concerned citizens and community groups crossing every line of socioeconomic status, race, religion, and political philosophy are frustrated, outraged, and hostile to many of the acts of pornographers in our society, and these same citizens have a lack of faith in legal recourse against the pornographers.

Somewhere in the debate on the issues relating to control of pornography and obscenity in our society, the basic constitutional rights of the majority of concerned citizens have been forgotten. Citizens who favor economic boycotts, picketing, or even enforcement of valid federal and state laws have been labeled inappropriately as censors, sex spies, enemies of free speech, or seekers of government interference in private lives. Censorship involves the concept of *prior restraint* and the review and deletion of unacceptable material by a censor *before* publication or public display. Pickets, boycotts, and other acts of speech involving the legitimate exercise of constitutional rights to express outrage or concern are not acts of censorship.

Enforcement of constitutional laws proscribing production, distribution, and sale of obscenity or child pornography, and supporting restrictions as to time, place, or manner, are not acts of censorship. Encouragement and support for new forms of legal redress for civil and human rights violations are not acts of censorship.

© Whitman/Rothco. Reprinted with permission.

Throughout the history of this nation, public protests and citizen action have been considered essential freedoms. Without the exercise of seemingly forgotten sections of the First Amendment (in context of the pornography debate)—the right to "peaceable assembly" and the right to "petition the government for redress of grievances"—many important civil rights efforts of the past would have failed. The First Amendment to the U.S. Constitution states, "Congress shall make no law respecting an establishment of religion, or prohibiting the free exercise thereof; or abridging the freedom of speech, or of the press; or the right of the people peaceably to assemble, and to petition the Government for a redress of grievances." For example, without citizen action, Blacks and women conceivably might still not be entitled to the vote in some areas of the United States. As to arguments about "privacy rights," it must be noted that there is nothing private about the commercial exploitation of persons and their sexuality by pornographers. Any "privacy" ended when the photographer, the cameras, and the production crew entered the scene to help create and record it. Privacy did not exist in the process of editing, production, duplication, distribution, or public sale. It should be noted that the U.S. Supreme Court has ruled that as to obscene material, mere possession in a private home cannot be made a crime. However, the possession of child pornography can be made illegal. . . .

Many criminal laws have an effect on speech and the content of communication and in effect may impose some *self*-censorship. Federal narcotics conspiracy law proscribes the speech of two or more persons who wish to enter into an agreement to distribute unlawful drugs. Prohibitions of mail and wire fraud clearly limit the content of communication and require no proof of any harm to any entity or individual as a precondition for their enforcement. The right to bring civil actions involving libel and slander may arguably, but permissibly, restrain public discussion. Obscenity and child pornography laws, when properly drafted and enforced, impose no unusual limitations or burdens. Some writers urge, contrary to the conclusions of the Supreme Court, that obscenity law is too vague to provide definition.

This writer suggests that obscenity laws, though far from perfect, are more definite than many other criminal laws successfully and regularly used in the criminal justice system, such as those relating to fraud, insider trading, certain antitrust matters, insanity, and even self-defense.

The citizens of this country have a right to speak and to educate one another about perceived social harms that they believe are caused by pornography. In the same public opinion surveys that show substantial concern for law enforcement efforts in the area of obscenity and child pornography, the American people also expressed their belief that sexually explicit movies, magazines, and books (not merely those which are unlawful) encourage people to consider women as sex objects, lead to a breakdown of social morals, lead people to commit rape, and lead people to commit acts of sexual violence. . . .

Child Pornography

Many supporters of the unlimited distribution and sale of pornography would like to delete the issue of child pornography from the debate. This author calls child pornography *crime scene photographs* because material that meets the legal standard for child pornography cannot be made without the actual sexual abuse of a real child. Those who hold to the absolutist position, the position that no state action is permitted under the terms of the First Amendment, argue that crimes relating to production and the abuse of children can be enforced, but once the camera records the scene and the photograph is made (the lasting record of a child's abuse), the photograph should never be restricted from sale and profit.

This absolutist position extends to photographs of rape, depictions of sadomasochism, and torture of adult women. All acts relating to abuse in the production and all other unlawful acts should be prosecuted, but the assertion that once the material is in circulation it should be left unrestricted ignores the fact that the market itself creates a reason for child abuse and torture. The purveyors of this material in the commercial marketplace are in business for profit. If there were not a profitable market in which to distribute the material, the child abuse and torture of adults would not take place. . . .

Obscenity Is Not Protected

Given that the current definitions of obscenity and pornography are workable, some individuals would still assert that obscene and pornographic materials are protected speech under the First Amendment. The Supreme Court, however, has never agreed with that proposition. It has stated, "This much has been categorically settled by the Court, that obscene material is *unprotected* by the First Amendment."

Jerry R. Kirk, *Hard-Core: Already Illegal*, 1987.

Materials that are child pornography or obscene do not have protection as *speech* under the First Amendment. That declaration raises the question of whether some materials enjoy lesser measures of First Amendment protection without crossing the threshold of obscenity.

Incumbent in this discussion is an acknowledgment of the position that the First Amendment, by its very terms, appears to prohibit the restriction of any manner of speech, including obscenity. . . .

In pertinent part, the First Amendment provides: "Congress shall make no law . . . abridging the freedom of speech, or of the press. . . ." Critics of governmental regulation of obscene material and those facing criminal prosecution for the violation of such regulations adhere to a literal or absolutist constitutional philosophy. This theory has never commanded a majority of the Supreme Court, but individual members of the Court have espoused its principles. In *Roth v. United States* (1957),

Justices Hugo L. Black and William O. Douglas summarized their view of the First Amendment restrictions:

> The First Amendment, its prohibition in terms absolute, was designed to preclude courts as well as legislatures from weighing the values of speech against silence. The First Amendment puts free speech in the preferred position.

In developing this view, Black and Douglas integrated the theories of William B. Lockhart, Chairman of the 1968 Commission on Obscenity and Pornography, and Robert E. McClure. The Justices stated:

> To allow the State to step in and punish mere speech or publication that the judge or the jury thinks has an *undesirable* impact on thoughts but that is not shown to be a part of unlawful action is drastically to curtail the First Amendment. As recently stated by two of our outstanding authorities on obscenity, "The danger of influencing a change in the current moral standards of the community, or of shocking or offending readers, or of stimulating sex thoughts or desires apart from objective conduct, can never justify the losses to society that result from interference with literary freedom."

The absolutist view of First Amendment standards relies on the thought that unfettered speech is essential to social growth. In response to concerns regarding the effect of speech that is offensive or harmful to some, absolutists advocate more speech to serve as a balance. When there are direct harms, the absolutist posits that any regulation should be directed toward the accompanying act rather than the speech itself.

Recurrent Harms

In the case of obscene material, the absolutist must assume that the harm, if any, is with the production of the material and the immediate welfare of the performers. This view fails to acknowledge the harms that may result as the material is distributed, including a recurring trauma to the performers, harms to third persons when confronted with the obscene material, and even the correlation between consumption of obscene material and aggressive, anti-social attitudes and behavior.

Although they condemned the standard for regulating obscene material in *Roth*, Justices Douglas and Black also stated:

> The absence of dependable information on the effect of obscene literature on human conduct should make us wary. It should put us on the side of protecting society's interests in literature, except and unless it can be said that the particular publication has an impact on action that the government can control.

It is important at this point to examine the practical merits of the absolutist position. Even a cursory review of current regulatory standards quickly reveals that various forms of speech are routinely restricted. One former U.S. Circuit Court of Appeals judge focused the debate over an absolute right to freedom of speech by examining the routine restriction of other forms of expression:

> Is Congress forbidden to prohibit incitement to mutiny aboard a naval vessel engaged in action against an enemy, to prohibit shouted harangues from the visitors' gallery during its own deliberations or to provide any rules for decorum in federal courtrooms? Are the states forbidden, by the incorporation of the first amendment in the fourteenth, to punish the shouting of obscenity in the streets?

The premise of this argument is also found in libel and slander law and in many federal and state crimes that involve merely speech or communication content. Examples of such criminal laws include conspiracy, consumer fraud, mail fraud, and prohibitions against false statements. This argument [by Robert Bork] concludes that the only speech that is specifically entitled to full protection is political speech:

> We must now return to the core of the first amendment, speech that is explicitly political. I mean that criticisms of public officials and policies, proposals for the adoption or repeal of legislation or constitutional provisions and speech addressed to the conduct of any governmental unit in the country.

The advocates of an absolutist philosophy must contend with the practical, routine restrictions placed on speech. They must contend with the theory that the First Amendment was intended to protect only political speech. . . .

Regulating Pornography

Throughout the historical debate about the regulation of sexually explicit materials, the courts have engaged in a categorization of the content of the material. It is apparent that this continuum approach to regulation will continue for the immediate future and restrictions are being fashioned using obscenity as the benchmark for justifying the standards. Congress, state legislatures, and the courts should consider an objective approach that would provide the practical enforcement benefits and universally clear guidelines now used for child pornography. Sexually explicit pictures of children do not have to pass or fail any subjective test to be treated as contraband. It is time for the law to fashion an objective prohibition on all hard-core pornography that explicitly depicts certain enumerated, ultimate sexual acts in publicly distributed magazines and films. The Federal Communications Commission and federal and state enforcement agencies must also enforce existing laws against nudity and simulated sex acts on broadcast and satellite television, and laws must be amended to clearly restrict the sexually graphic content of Dial-A-Porn telephone messages and cable services. Progress was made in 1988 when Congress passed and President Reagan signed into law a prohibition of obscene and indecent telephone messages, the "Telephone Decency Act of 1987." Most nudity is not allowed on broadcast television, but is permitted by a number of cable casters. Sexual activity should be prohibited from cable in order to protect children and foster appropriate community standards, even though some forms of simulated sex may be tolerated in movie theaters where minors can be excluded. The filmed fruits of pandering and the prostitution of hard-core pornography, however, have no significant expressive qualities or ideas or value and should be totally prohibited from commercial exploitation.

Pornography Can Be Restricted

There are a myriad of regulatory devices which may be used to address the concerns about the proliferation of sexually explicit material. Some devices may have specialized applications—such as zoning or anti-display laws—whereas criminal obscenity laws may find wide application. Material that is sexually explicit but not obscene may be regulated, but it is subject to additional constitutional analysis. The restrictions currently in force against the production of sexually explicit material have withstood scrutiny and attack under the mandates of the First Amendment. These regulations have consistently been upheld in principle, and they have been continually reshaped to accommodate emerging technologies. It is critical however, that new approaches be formulated and adopted to provide remedies for uncompensated harms. . . .

It is also critical that the present "pornography ethic" that accepts the premise that the bodies of women, children and men are commodities to be exploited for profit be rejected by not only the legal system but by society as a whole.

"I live in a country where if you film any act of humiliation or torture, and if the victim is a woman, the film is both entertainment and it is protected speech."

The Feminist Case for Censoring Pornography

Andrea Dworkin

Andrea Dworkin is one of the most controversial leaders of the feminist fight against pornography. With lawyer Catharine MacKinnon she co-authored a groundbreaking ordinance that defined pornography as a civil rights violation against women. Her writings, including *Intercourse* and *Pornography: Men Possessing Women*, have been the subject of intense debate. Because of her prominence in the pornography debates, she was called to testify in 1986 before the Attorney General's Commission on Pornography. In the following viewpoint, taken from her testimony, Dworkin argues that pornography is not a free speech issue but an actual crime against women. Some women are forced to make pornography, while others are attacked by men inspired by pornography, she contends. Such violence, Dworkin believes, does not deserve constitutional protection.

As you read, consider the following questions:

1. What are Dworkin's criticisms of constitutional lawyers?
2. Whose rights does the First Amendment really protect, according to the author?
3. Why does Dworkin believe the harms of pornography are invisible?

My name is Andrea Dworkin. I am a citizen of the United States, and in this country where I live, every year millions and millions of pictures are being made of women with our legs spread. We are called beaver, we are called pussy, our genitals are tied up, they are pasted, makeup is put on them to make them pop out of a page at a male viewer. Millions and millions of pictures are made of us in postures of submission and sexual access so that our vaginas are exposed for penetration, our anuses are exposed for penetration, our throats are used as if they are genitals for penetration. In this country where I live as a citizen real rapes are on film and are being sold in the marketplace. And the major motif of pornography as a form of entertainment is that women are raped and violated and humiliated until we discover that we like it and at that point we ask for more.

In this country where I live as a citizen, women are penetrated by animals and objects for public entertainment, women are urinated on and defecated on, women and girls are used interchangeably so that grown women are made up to look like five- or six-year-old children surrounded by toys, presented in mainstream pornographic publications for anal penetration. There are magazines in which adult women are presented with their pubic areas shaved so that they resemble children.

Racist Pornography

In this country where I live, there is a trafficking in pornography that exploits mentally and physically disabled women, women who are maimed; there is amputee pornography, a trade in women who have been maimed in that way, as if that is a sexual fetish for men. In this country where I live, there is a trade in racism as a form of sexual pleasure, so that the plantation is presented as a form of sexual gratification for the black woman slave who asks please to be abused, please to be raped, please to be hurt. Black skin is presented as if it is a female genital, and all the violence and the abuse and the humiliation that is in general directed against female genitals is directed against the black skin of women in pornography.

Asian women in this country where I live are tied from trees and hung from ceilings and hung from doorways as a form of public entertainment. There is a concentration camp pornography in this country where I live, where the concentration camp and the atrocities that occurred there are presented as existing for the sexual pleasure of the victim, of the woman, who orgasms to the real abuses that occurred, not very long ago in history.

In the country where I live as a citizen, there is a pornography of the humiliation of women where every single way of humiliating a human being is taken to be a form of sexual pleasure for the viewer and for the victim; where women are covered in filth, including feces, including mud, including paint, including blood, including semen, where women are tortured for the sexual pleasure of those who watch and those who do the torture, where women are murdered for the sexual pleasure of murdering women, and this material exists because it is fun, because it is entertainment, because it is a form of pleasure, and there are those who say it is a form of freedom.

Certainly it is freedom for those who do it. Certainly it is freedom for those who use it as entertainment, but we are also asked to believe that it is freedom for those to whom it is done.

MacIntosh for the *Star Tribune*. Reprinted with permission.

Then this entertainment is taken, and it is used on other women, women who aren't in the pornography, to force those women into prostitution, to make them imitate the acts in the pornography. The women in the pornography, sixty-five to seventy percent of them we believe are victims of incest or child sexual abuse. They are poor women; they are not women who have opportunities in this society. They are frequently runaways who are picked up by pimps and exploited. They are frequently raped, the rapes are filmed, they are kept in prostitution by blackmail. The pornography is used on prostitutes by johns who expect them to replicate the sexual acts in the pornography, no matter how damaging it is.

Pornography is used in rape—to plan it, to execute it, to choreograph it, to engender the excitement to commit the act. Pornography is used in gang rape against women. We see an increase since the release of *Deep Throat* in throat rape—where women show up in emergency rooms because men believe they can penetrate, deep-thrust, to the bottom of a woman's throat. We see increasing use of all elements of pornography in battery, which is the most commonly committed violent crime in this country, including the rape of women by animals, including maiming, including heavy bondage, including outright torture.

Harassing Women

We have seen in the last eight years an increase in the use of cameras in rapes. And those rapes are filmed and then they are put on the marketplace and they are protected speech—they are real rapes.

We see a use of pornography in the harassment of women on jobs, especially in nontraditional jobs, in the harassment of women in education, to create terror and compliance in the home, which as you know is the most dangerous place for women in this society, where more violence is committed against women than anywhere else. We see pornography used to create harassment of women and children in neighborhoods that are saturated with pornography, where people come from other parts of the city and then prey on the populations of people who live in those neighborhoods, and that increases physical attack and verbal assault.

We see pornography having introduced a profit motive into rape. We see that filmed rapes are protected speech. We see the centrality of pornography in serial murders. There *are* snuff films. We see boys imitating pornography. We see the average age of rapists going down. We are beginning to see gang rapes in elementary schools committed by elementary school age boys imitating pornography.

Torture and Murder

We see sexual assault after death where frequently the pornography is the motive for the murder because the man believes that he will get a particular kind of sexual pleasure having sex with a woman after she is dead.

We see a major trade in women, we see the torture of women as a form of entertainment, and we see women also suffering the injury of objectification—that is to say we are dehumanized. We are treated as if we are subhuman, and that is a precondition for violence against us.

I live in a country where if you film any act of humiliation or torture, and if the victim is a woman, the film is both entertainment and it is protected speech. Now that tells me something about what it means to be a woman citizen in this country, and the meaning of being second class.

When your rape is entertainment, your worthlessness is absolute. You have reached the nadir of social worthlessness. The civil impact of pornography on women is staggering. It keeps us socially silent, it keeps us socially compliant, it keeps us afraid in neighborhoods; and it creates a vast hopelessness for women, a vast despair. One lives inside a nightmare of sexual abuse that is both actual and potential, and you have the great joy of knowing that your nightmare is someone else's freedom and someone else's fun.

The Role of Lawyers

Now, a great deal has happened in this country to legitimize pornography since the 1970s. There are people who are responsible for the fact that pornography is now a legitimate form of public entertainment.

Number one, the lobby of lawyers who work for the pornographers; the fact that the pornographers pay lawyers big bucks to fight for them, not just in the courts, but in public, in the public dialogue; the fact that lawyers interpret constitutional principles in light of the profit interest of the pornographers.

Male Power

Women are in pornography to be violated and taken, men to violate and take them, either on screen or by camera or pen, on behalf of the viewer. Not that sexuality in life or in media never expresses love and affection; only that love and affection are not what is sexualized in this society's actual sexual paradigm, as pornography testifies to it. Violation of the powerless, intrusion on women, is.

Catharine A. MacKinnon, *Ethics*, January 1989.

Number two, the collusion of the American Civil Liberties Union with the pornographers, which includes taking money from them. It includes using buildings that pornographers own and not paying rent, it includes using pornography in benefits to raise money. It includes not only defending them in court but also doing publicity for them, including organizing events for them, as the Hugh Hefner First Amendment Awards is organized by ACLU people for *Playboy*. It includes publishing in their magazines. It includes deriving great pride and economic benefit from working privately for the pornographers, while publicly pretending to be a disinterested advocate of civil liberties and free speech.

I want you to contrast the behavior of the ACLU in relation to the pornographers with their activities in relation to the Klan and the Nazis. The ACLU pretends to understand that they are all equally pernicious. But do ACLU people publish in the Klan newsletter? No. Do they go to Nazi social events? No. Do they go to cocktail parties at Nazi headquarters? No, they don't, at least not yet.

The Repulsion Standard

Finally, they have colluded in this sense, that they have convinced many of us that the standard for speech is what I would call a repulsion standard. That is to say we find the most repulsive person in the society and we defend him. I say we find the most powerless people in this society, and we defend *them*. That's the way we increase rights of speech in this society.

A third group that colludes to legitimize pornography are publishers and the so-called legitimate media. They pretend to believe that under this system of law there is a First Amendment that is indivisible and absolute, which it has never been.

As you know, the First Amendment protects speech that has already been expressed from state interference. That means it protects those who own media. There is no affirmative responsibility to open communications to those who are powerless in the society at large.

As a result, the owners of media, the newspapers, the TV networks, are comfortable with having women's bodies defined as the speech of pimps, because they are protecting their rights to profit as owners, and they think that that is what the First Amendment is for.

I am ashamed to say that people in my profession, writers, have also colluded with the pornographers. We provide their so-called socially redeeming value, and they wrap the tortured bodies of women in the work that we do. . . .

Finally, the ultimate colluders in the legitimizing of pornography, of course, are the consumers. In 1979 we had a $4-billion-a-year industry in this country. By 1985 it was an $8-billion-a-year industry. Those consumers include men in all walks of life: lawyers, politicians, writers, professors, owners of media, police, doctors, maybe even commissioners on presidential commissions. No one really knows, do they?

And no matter where we look, we can't find the consumers. But what we learn is the meaning of first class citizenship, and the meaning of first-class citizenship is that you can use your authority as men and as professionals to protect pornography both by developing arguments to protect it and by using real social and economic power to protect it.

191

And as a result of all of this, the harm to women remains invisible; even though we have the bodies, the harm to women remains invisible. Underlying the invisibility of this harm is an assumption that what is done to women is natural, that even if a woman is forced to do something, somehow it falls within the sphere of her natural responsibilities as a woman. When the same things are done to boys, those things are perceived as an outrage. They are called unnatural.

But if you force a woman to do something that she was born to do, then the violence to her is not perceived as a real violation of her.

In addition, the harm to women of pornography is invisible because most sexual abuse still occurs in private, even though we have this photographic documentation of it, called the pornography industry.

Women are extremely isolated, women don't have credibility, women are not believed by people who make social policy.

In addition, the harm of pornography remains invisible because women have been historically excluded from the protections of the Constitution; and as a result, the violations of our human rights, when they don't occur the same way violations to men occur, have not been recognized or taken seriously, and we do not have remedies for them under law.

Injury to Women

In addition, pornography is invisible in its harm to women because women are poorer than men and many of the women exploited in pornography are very poor, many of them are illiterate, and also because there is a great deal of female compliance with brutality, and the compliance is based on fear, it's based on powerlessness and it is based on a reaction to the very real violence of the pornographers.

Finally, the harm is invisible because of the smile, because women are made to smile, women aren't just made to do the sex acts. We are made to smile while we do them.

So you will find women penetrating themselves with swords or daggers, and you will see the smile. You will see things that cannot be done to a human being and that are done to men only in political circumstances of torture, and you will see a woman forced to smile.

And this smile will be believed, and the injury to her as a human being to her body and to her heart and to her soul, will not be believed.

Now, we have been told that we have an argument here about speech, not about women being hurt. And yet the emblem of that argument is a woman bound and gagged and we are supposed to believe that that is speech. Who is that speech for? We

192

have women being tortured and we are told that that is some-body's speech? Whose speech is it? It's the speech of a pimp, it is not the speech of a woman. The only words we hear in pornography from women are that women want to be hurt, ask to be hurt, like to be raped, get sexual pleasure from sexual vio-lence; and even when a woman is covered in filth, we are sup-posed to believe that her speech is that she likes it and she wants more of it.

The reality for women in this society is that pornography cre-ates silence for women. The pornographers silence women. Our bodies are their language. Their speech is made out of our exploitation, our subservience, our injury and our pain, and they can't say anything without hurting us, and when you pro-tect them, you protect only their right to exploit and hurt us.

Pornography is a civil rights issue for women because pornog-raphy sexualizes inequality, because it turns women into sub-human creatures.

Pornography is a civil rights issue for women because it is the systematic exploitation of a group of people because of a condi-tion of birth. Pornography creates bigotry and hostility and ag-gression towards all women, targets all women, without excep-tion.

Pornography is the suppression of us through sexual exploita-tion and abuse, so that we have no real means to achieve civil equality; and the issue here is simple, it is not complex. People are being hurt, and you can help them or you can help those who are hurting them. We need civil rights legislation, legisla-tion that recognizes pornography as a violation of the civil rights of women. . . .

Women Need Equality

I am here asking the simplest thing. I am saying hurt people need remedies, not platitudes, not laws that you know already don't work; people excluded from constitutional protections need equality. People silenced by exploitation and brutality need real speech, not to be told that when they are hung from meat hooks, that is their speech. Nobody in this country who has been working to do anything about pornography, no woman who has spoken out against it, is going to go back-wards, is going to forget what she has learned, is going to forget that she has rights that aren't being acknowledged in this coun-try. And there are lots of people in this country, I am happy to say, who want to live in a kind world, not a cruel world, and they will not accept the hatred of women as good, wholesome, American fun; they won't accept the hatred of women and the rape of women as anybody's idea of freedom. They won't ac-cept the torture of women as a civil liberty.

193

"Censorship and suppression work directly against feminist goals and are always used to limit women's rights in the name of protection."

The Feminist Case Against Censoring Pornography

Barbara Dority

In the following viewpoint, Barbara Dority objects to the antipornography stance taken by many feminists. Dority argues that not all sexually explicit material is degrading to women. Moreover, she contends, the U.S. cannot limit speech that is degrading to women unless it also wishes to limit speech that is degrading to men, blacks, Jews, and other groups. Such widespread limitations, she maintains, would seriously undermine the First Amendment. Dority is executive director of the Washington Coalition Against Censorship and cochairperson of the Northwest Feminist Anti-Censorship Taskforce.

As you read, consider the following questions:

1. What is wrong with the term "pornography," according to Dority?
2. Why does the author believe pornography does not fit the "clear and present danger" format that would exempt it from First Amendment protection?
3. How does Dority defend violent pornography?

Barbara Dority, "Feminist Moralism, 'Pornography,' and Censorship." This article first appeared in *The Humanist* issue of November/December 1989 and is reprinted by permission.

The issue of "pornography" has engendered an intense debate within the feminist movement. Will feminism, having achieved some significant gains, continue to capitulate to moralistic forces, or will it wake up and take a stand for the liberation of women in all domains, including the difficult and often contradictory domain of sexual expression?

Two separate issues are involved in this debate: first, the moralistic feminist condemnation of "pornography"; and, second, the translation of that condemnation by nearly all feminist leaders into calls for various kinds of legislation which would effectively ban "pornographic" imagery and words. Both issues are alarming.

Literal Meanings

As a feminist secular humanist and a card-carrying member of the American Civil Liberties Union, I believe the writers of the First Amendment meant every word exactly and literally: "Congress shall make no law . . . abridging the freedom of speech or of the press. . . ." No law means *no law*.

The First Amendment does not say there is to be freedom of speech and press provided they are not sexually explicit, offensive, dangerous, or degrading. The authors of the Bill of Rights had learned firsthand why it was absolutely necessary to permit all manner of ideas to be expressed in the new republic. They knew this guarantee could not be confined to the expression of ideas that are conventional or shared by the majority but must include even those ideas considered repugnant or socially undesirable.

In the words of Justice William O. Douglas: "This demands that government keep its hands off all literature. There can be no freedom of expression unless all facets of life can be portrayed, no matter how repulsive these disclosures may be to some people." Justice Douglas later added that, in addition to freedom from government intervention, all manner of literature must remain available in the marketplace of ideas or the purpose of free expression is defeated. In other words, if we protect only the right to publish and then limit availability, we are still limiting freedom of speech.

The moralistic pro-censorship mind set has remained the same throughout the history of civilization. The censors aim at protecting us from the perceived harmful effects of what we read, see, and hear. Historically, they did this to protect our souls from blasphemy or society from alien political, social, or economic ideas. Today, it is being done to protect us from explicit sexual imagery and words. The justification, however, remains the same: it is best for us and best for society.

The highly subjective term *pornography* is grossly overused and abused. A wide range of materials has been so classified by feminists and summarily condemned, boycotted, picketed, and even banned.

The definition of *pornography* from Webster is: "The depiction of erotic behavior (as in pictures or writing) intended to cause sexual excitement." The blanket condemnation of all such materials is cause for grave concern. Obviously, this would include a great deal of advertising, network television, art, film, and a vast array of magazines, books, and videos. Indeed, many feminists have condemned most mainstream advertising and film as degrading and harmful to women. Most members of the feminist movement endorse and promote Minneapolis-style "antipornography" ordinances. Many feminists are committed fulltime to these pursuits.

An Institution

By definition, all feminists are against the exploitation and subordination of women. However, pornography is only a reflection of a larger problem. Violence against women exists in countries where pornography is outlawed, such as Saudi Arabia and Iran. Even if pornography were eliminated in the United States, violent misogyny would not disappear. The hundreds of ways in which women are exploited in every facet of their lives would continue to exist. The real problem is that sexism is institutionalized. As feminists, we are naïve to think that any law that represses expression, confuses gender and sexuality, or regulates sexuality will not be used against our bookstores, art, and periodicals. The result of such tactics is to substitute one impediment for another.

Donna Turley, *Socialist Review*, May 1986.

Despite their claims to a mandate, these women do not speak for all feminists. Scores of women and men dropped out (or were forced out of the feminist movement when the Equal Rights Amendment was defeated and attention shifted to moralizing and "pornography." We will never know how many feminists were lost to activism, or never activated, as a result of this departure from our basic goals and principles.

Civil Liberties

Many of us believe that feminism and civil liberties are inextricable. We remind our sisters that history has repeatedly shown that censorship and suppression work directly against feminist goals and are always used to limit women's rights in the name of protection. If such censorship laws are passed, we would create the illusion that something is being done to end sexism and sexual violence—a harmful effect in itself.

We ask: whose definitions shall we use? Who will decide? Who will make all the necessary individual judgments? Who will distinguish "dehumanizing, objectifying, degrading" materials from "erotica"?

All Sex Isn't Sexist

Many leaders in the feminist movement assert that the message of all "pornography" even "soft-core, is that women are slaves whose bodies are for sale and available to be used and degraded. Again, this is not the only feminist view. For example, many feminists do *not* believe that *Playboy* and *Penthouse* are sexist, or that the presentation of the naked female body, whether or not in "inviting positions" is intrinsically sexist. We do not believe that sexually explicit photos and words are intrinsically exploitative, degrading, or objectifying.

Many feminist leaders tell us that "pornography" is sex discrimination and hate literature against women—a violation of women's civil rights. But the history and intent of civil rights law and case law are clear: discrimination is not what people say or write about other people; it is what people *do* to other people. Individuals cannot be persecuted, censored, or condemned for their ideas. In a free society, there are no crimes of thought—only crimes of action.

Certainly some materials are offensive and degrading to many women, and few would claim that sex discrimination and oppression of women no longer exist in our culture. But many materials are offensive and degrading to *men*, blatantly promoting not only their oppression but their brutalization. There are aspects of our culture that oppress Indians, Hispanics, Asians, and homosexuals. Anti-Semitic literature is inarguably harmful to Jews, as is racist literature to blacks. Are we going to offer men and racial, ethnic, and religious minorities a civil right to suppress speech which they find objectionable? Many feminists tell us that "pornography" *causes* sexism and violence against women. But this claim draws on simplistic behaviorist psychology and has been repeatedly discredited by reputable specialists in sexual behavior. Even the notorious Meese commission reported that no such causal link can be substantiated. Sexist and violent materials are *symptoms* of a sexist and violent society—not the causes.

No Clear Danger

The claim that certain forms of expression are dangerous and an incitement to violence has been used time after time to try to prohibit speech that some people don't like. Although some of us do not support this exception to the First Amendment, the notion of "a clear and present danger" was evolved to address this threat. For "pornography" to be suppressed under this test, we would have to demonstrate that any viewer is likely to be provoked to sexual violence immediately upon seeing it.

Anecdotal stories of sex offenders who are found to possess "pornography" are often cited. As Sol Gordon has pointed out, a large percentage of these offenders are also found to possess milk in their refrigerators. Sporadic incidents do not prove a correlation, nor does a correlation prove causation.

Hurting Women's Causes

Censoring pornography and curbing First Amendment rights without dismantling the structures which insure woman-hating will only hurt us as we battle for the liberation of all oppressed people.

Eleanor J. Bader, *The Guardian*, April 22, 1987.

Even if it is assumed that a small percentage of people are "encouraged" to engage in sexist behavior or commit violent acts after exposure to certain books or films, this still would not justify suppression. Such a "pervert's veto" would threaten a broad range of literature and film. A free society must accept the risks that come with liberty.

People receive different messages from sexually explicit material, and it is ridiculous and dangerous to conclude that a picture or an idea will have the same effect on all viewers or readers.

Charles Manson testified that he was inspired by the biblical Book of Revelation to commit multiple murders. Youths involved in interracial street fights have said that viewing *Roots* led them to commit their crimes. John Hinckley testified that he knew he had to kill Ronald Reagan after reading *Catcher in the Rye*.

Worldwide Examples

If viewing and reading sexually explicit and violent materials caused people to become sex criminals, all the members of the Meese commission would now be dangerous sexual predators. The same would be true of the many sociologists who study this material, countless persons who create, publish, and disseminate it, mental health professionals who work with sex offenders, and all the moralists—on the right and the left—who pore over these materials as they analyze them for the rest of us.

In many repressive countries—whether in Central America,

Asia, Africa, eastern Europe, or the Middle East—there is practically no "pornography." But there is a great deal of sexism and violence against women. In the Netherlands and Scandinavia, where there are almost no restrictions on sexually explicit materials, the rate of sex-related crime is much lower than in the United States. "Pornography" is virtually irrelevant to the existence of sexism and violence.

Nor does a causal relationship exist between an increase in the availability of "pornography" and inequality for women. While "pornography" has increased over the past fifty years, the rights of women have jumped dramatically.

Violence

"Violent pornography" is viewed by many as the most offensive form of expression. But it can be seen in two ways: as the depiction of consensual sadomasochism or as the depiction of actual coercion and violence against nonconsenting persons. If the latter, *the actual perpetrators of the violence or coercion* have broken the law and should be prosecuted to its full extent. However, not everyone sees the degradation of women in depictions of "violent" sexual activity. What some find degrading, others may find erotic.

Human sexual behavior is very complicated. In our society, and all over the world, consenting adults exist who like to engage in sadomasochistic activity and who do so of their own free will. They enjoy publications which depict or describe this behavior. For them, these activities are not designed to degrade or promote violence against women *or men* but, rather, to satisfy a sexual need of the participants. It is not a crime or an issue subject to moral judgment to fantasize about rape, or even for two consenting adults to choose to enact a pretend rape. It is not anyone's right to judge the private sexual fantasies, inclinations, or activities of other consenting adults.

Freedom of Sex

We are told we must especially condemn materials depicting (usually simulated) violence to prove that we are opposed to violence against women. We must, many feminists say, condemn nearly all sexually explicit materials as degrading to women and label "pornography" a principal cause of women's oppression in order to retain our credentials as feminists.

Many feminist humanist women and men refuse to do this. We believe it is possible to be feminists dedicated to equal rights and the elimination of violence against women while defending the freedom of all kinds of sexual expression. It is a tragedy that the feminist movement has been drawn into an anti-sex stance, condemning "deviant" sexual representation

199

and expression. We are horrified by the assertion of many feminists that male sexuality is inherently destructive, violent, and "pro-rape." We are appalled by the condemnation of men who enjoy "pornography" as sexist and anti-humanist or, in the case of women, by the assertion that they are "brainwashed by patriarchy."

The Correct Perspective

In *Feminism Unmodified: Discourses on Life and Law*, [feminist lawyer Catharine] MacKinnon tries to distinguish the "male morality of liberalism and obscenity law from a feminist critique of pornography." The former, she writes, would cite Judge Potter Stewart's controversial statement "I know it when I see it" (referring to how an obscenity law could be enforced) as evidence of the inherent arbitrariness and unenforceability of any such law. On the other hand, according to MacKinnon, a feminist critique of pornography would not object to the idea Stewart expressed but to the male *standpoint* from which he expressed it. Thus, *he* would not know what he sees but *she* would and so, by extension, would any feminist called upon to evaluate pornography from the standpoint of women as an oppressed class. The glaring inconsistency of this contention is that it demonstrates the arbitrary nature of censorship. For, if Stewart's "male" perspective is not correct but MacKinnon's is, what is to stop another group (say, for argument's sake, other feminists who feel they have suffered even greater oppression than MacKinnon, perhaps class and racial oppression as well) from claiming that *theirs*, not hers, is the more genuine standpoint from which to make such judgments? And, further, what is to stop some subgroup within this subgroup? The argument rapidly recedes into the realm of the absurd, leaving one more, rather than less, convinced that censorship is not the answer to the problem.

Lynn Chancer, *New Politics*, Summer 1988.

This Victorian imagery—pure women controlling the vile, lustful impulses of men and being unable to think for themselves—is a feminine stereotype we should be working against. In this analysis, women cannot ever freely choose to have sex with men or use "male-identified" imagery in their sexual fantasies or practices. Certainly they cannot freely choose to earn their living by inviting the rapacious male gaze or providing sexual services to men.

Many feminist women and men believe it is moralistic, insulting, and inaccurate to maintain that no "normal" woman rationally chooses or consensually participates in the sex industry. This moralistic position alienates not only women in the sex industry but also women who create their own sexual pleasure without regard for its "political correctness."

We believe that this moralism and the attendant calls for censorship have seriously undermined the integrity of our movement. Being a feminist means being against sexism—not sex. In *Against Sadomasochism*, feminist Ti Grace Atkinson says, "I do not know any feminist worthy of that name who, forced to choose between freedom and sex, would choose sex." This is the choice being presented to feminist women and men. In so doing, the movement betrays its principles and destroys its credibility.

Many of us insist on the right to choose *both* freedom *and* sexuality. We call upon other feminist humanists to do likewise.

Author's note: The access of minors to sexually explicit material is a complex issue which would require another article for proper examination. The Supreme Court has held that minors' access to legally "obscene" materials is not protected by the First Amendment. The Court's nebulous and subjective definition of *obscenity* raises even more definitional problems, and a vast array of materials are currently restricted on the basis of this seriously flawed definition. These restrictions, instituted to protect minors, inevitably affect the freedom of adults. Legally, the burden of preventing the exposure of children to offensive or "pornographic" materials *should* rest with parents; as a *practical* matter, parents *must* assume this responsibility.

"A great harm is inextricably bound to violent pornography, and the expressive value of violent pornography is minimal."

The Harm Pornography Causes Justifies Censorship

Deana Pollard

In the following viewpoint, Deana Pollard argues that pornography hurts women and thus the government has a legitimate interest in censoring it. Pollard contends that other forms of speech have been restricted because they promote illegal activities. Since pornography leads to rape and other forms of abuse, Pollard maintains, it also should exempted from First Amendment protection. Pollard writes for the *Vanderbilt Law Review*, a publication of the Vanderbilt University School of Law in Nashville, Tennessee.

As you read, consider the following questions:

1. How does pornography differ from political speech, according to Pollard?
2. How does the author support her claim that pornography causes violence against women?
3. Why is obscenity exempt from First Amendment protection, according to Pollard?

Deana Pollard, "Regulating Violent Pornography," *Vanderbilt Law Review,* vol. 43, no. 1, January 1990, © 1990 Vanderbilt Law Review. Reprinted with permission.

Although most people probably do not find violent sex or female subordination attractive, the fact remains that violent pornography is a form of speech. Similarly, anti-Semitism repulses most people, yet the marketplace of ideas tolerates it because it is an idea. Suppressing repugnant views would be a mistake under marketplace analysis: the marketplace is a truthfinding organism, and serves to expose truly repugnant ideas. Thus, all speech warrants initial first amendment scrutiny.

The conclusion, however, that violent pornography is speech under the first amendment does not prohibit its regulation. Legislatures can regulate speech when it falls under an exception to the first amendment. This [viewpoint] will consider two existing exceptions to first amendment protection as possible justifications for regulating violent pornography: incitement of illegal activity and obscenity. Creating a new exception for violent pornography also will be discussed.

Incitement of Illegal Activity

The Supreme Court has held that it is constitutionally permissible in certain circumstances to prohibit speech that advocates lawless action. Although this justification for suppression has been considered by the Court since the early 1900s, the Court announced its current and most exacting constitutional test for the regulation of such speech in the 1969 case of *Brandenburg v. Ohio*. Under *Brandenburg* the government may regulate the advocacy of illegal acts only "where such advocacy is directed to inciting or producing imminent lawless action and is likely to incite or produce such action." This current standard has two separate requirements: 1) the advocacy must intend to produce the lawless action, and 2) there must be a likelihood of imminent harm.

Violent pornography should fall within this exception to the first amendment because it has been shown to cause aggression toward women. If violent pornography were to be deemed a form of incitement of illegal activity, courts would apply the *Brandenburg* test in the context of violent pornography. The first *Brandenburg* requirement may appear to mandate that producers of violent pornography actively advocate the harms associated with the material, that they intentionally produced the materials for the purpose of causing the harmful acts. If the courts constitutionally required this subjective standard, it would be virtually impossible to regulate violent pornography under this exception. Most pornography producers probably are driven by an economic incentive and operate without a specific intent to harm women.

While some courts adopt this subjective standard of intent, others adopt a foreseeability standard. Under the foreseeability standard, courts would hold producers to have intended the foreseeable results of their materials. This standard is akin to the "average reasonable person" standard in tort law and allows violent pornography to fall under the exception of incitement to illegality. Because producers of violent pornography know or should know of the harm caused by violent pornography, and they still produce it, they can be held to have intended the harms caused by the pornography. Although the *Brandenburg* case more clearly presented the intent requirement, unless the Supreme Court definitively resolves the courts' split on the intent issue in favor of requiring subjective intent, the *Brandenburg* test will not impede the regulation of violent pornography on grounds that it incites crime.

Time to Act

We believe that our nation is inherently opposed to the degradation or abuse of any group of citizens. If we continue to pretend that illegal pornography is just harmless "fun," we will do so at the expense of our national ideals. If we ignore the abuse, degradation and victimization that occurs daily in the world of hardcore and child pornography, we will do so at the expense of our humanity, our conscience as a society, and most of all, at the expense of our collective desire for a country that affirms the dignity of each person.

We believe that just as all people need to stand together to fight racial discrimination, illegal drugs and other social evils, so now we must also stand together against illegal pornography. It must stop; we must and can make it stop, and the time to act is now.

Joseph Bernardin and Eileen W. Lindner, *Los Angeles Times*, November 12, 1989.

The second *Brandenburg* requirement is that there be a likelihood of imminent harm. "Likelihood" and "imminence" are inherently vague terms, and because the Court has yet to rule in favor of state regulation on this issue, it is necessary to distinguish violent pornography from cases in which the Court has not found a likelihood of imminent harm.

In *Brandenburg* the Court held unconstitutional an Ohio statute that "by its own words and as applied, purport[ed] to punish *mere advocacy* and to forbid, on pain of criminal punishment, assembly with others merely to advocate the described type of action." The appellant was a Ku Klux Klan leader who had invited a reporter to a Klan rally where derogatory statements were made about blacks and Jews. One Klan speaker said, "Personally, I believe the nigger should be returned to Africa, the Jew returned to Israel." In a separate speech another Klan member said, "We're not a revengent [sic] organization, but if our President, our Congress, our Supreme Court, continues to suppress the white, Caucasian race, it's possible that there might have to be some revengance [sic] taken." In determining whether these speeches deserved constitutional protection, the Court stated, "the mere abstract teaching . . . of the moral propriety or even moral necessity for a resort to force and violence, is not the same as preparing a group for violent action and steeling it to such action." In other words, the Court found a distinction between "mere advocacy" and incitement to crime.

Imminent Harm

Violent pornography presents a better case for a court to find incitement to imminent harm than the facts of *Brandenburg*. In *Brandenburg* the political rhetoric regarding resorting to violence is tempered by the Klan speaker's own words about taking vengeance. The language "[I]f [the government] continues . . . it is possible . . . " indicates that the threat is unlikely to occur at all, let alone imminently. Political speech is notoriously replete with emotion and false threats, but the harms associated with violent pornography have occurred many times and are virtually certain to continue. It is not necessary to show that a particular producer's film caused a particular harm in order to justify regulating violent pornography. Rather, when certain actions have a known propensity to cause harm, an actor can be held liable without a showing of actual harm. For example, speeding is known to increase the likelihood of car collisions, and drivers are punished for this dangerous behavior whether or not their particular sprees cause collisions. Violent pornography, like speeding, is intrinsically dangerous, and legislatures may regulate it on the basis of its known propensity for harm without a showing of particular harm.

The harm from violent pornography is also imminent, considering that some men read from pornographic magazines while they commit sex crimes, or force women to engage in acts they just learned about through viewing a pornographic film. The government in *Brandenburg* failed to identify actual harms likely to occur given that no scientific data exists that associates listening to Ku Klux Klan speeches with kidnapping and sending blacks to Africa or Jews to Israel. On the other hand, researchers agree that a causal effect links the viewing of violent pornography with the sex crimes that are rampant in American society. Unlike the political speeches given in *Brandenburg*, violent pornography does not merely express ideas but actually causes harm, a reality confirmed by scientific data. Therefore, the imminence of harm is more certain from violent pornography than from the political ramblings of a Ku Klux Klan leader. . . .

Obscene or Pornographic?

The Supreme Court has had considerable trouble defining obscenity and its boundaries. Since 1815 when a Pennsylvania court decided the first reported American case involving censorship of pornography, one constant has emerged. The Court has held consistently that obscenity, however it may be defined, is outside of the first amendment's protection.

Stimulating Crime

The dictionary defines pornography as "the depiction of erotic behavior intended to cause sexual excitement." Just as depiction of appetizing food will stimulate salivary glands and heighten the craving for food, erotic material will start a normal human being to think about sexual satisfaction.

Once stimulated, some will descend further into the world of hard-core, violence-suggesting material. And it should not require much common sense to conclude that some of pornography's captives would then act out their fantasies and seek satisfaction, even employing force and violence to do so.

John F. McManus, *The New American*, April 10, 1989.

Under the obscenity exception only those materials the Court deems obscene under its test for obscenity are without first amendment protection. The first amendment protects many sexually explicit and pornographic materials. If, however, sexually explicit material meets specific criteria required for the Court to deem it obscene, the first amendment does not protect the material. Currently, courts define obscenity by reference to a three prong test articulated in *Miller v. California*. The *Miller* test asks whether 1) the average person, applying contemporary community standards, would find that the work, taken as a whole, appeals to the prurient interest; 2) the work depicts or describes in a patently offensive way the sexual conduct specifically defined by applicable state law; and 3) the work, taken as a whole, lacks serious literary, artistic, political, or scientific value. By failing to meet the requirements under any one of these prongs, pornographic material will be deemed not obscene, and therefore worthy of first amendment protection.

Many materials could be banned under the obscenity exception that presently are not banned. Considering the underlying policy justifications for regulating obscenity, the Court has articulated the test for obscenity in a more restrictive fashion than the exception warrants. In light of the underlying justifications for the obscenity exception, it should encompass all violent pornography. The argument here is not that courts should deem violent pornography obscene under the *Miller* test. Rather, evaluation reveals that the same justifications for not according first amendment protection to obscenity apply with equal force to violent pornography.

Throughout the Court's history of obscenity adjudication, three primary justifications have undergirded the Court's decisions. First, obscenity is utterly without redeeming social value. . . . Second, obscenity increases the likelihood of sexual violence. . . .Third, obscenity degrades society's moral values. . . .

Violent pornography meets each of these historical policy justifications for regulating obscenity. First, although "utterly without redeeming social value" is no longer the standard, violent pornography cannot be considered more valuable than obscenity. The Court has said that obscenity lacks socially redeeming value. It does not follow that sexually explicit violence contains more social value than sexually explicit material that appeals to the prurient interest or is patently offensive.

Violent Pornography

Second, the empirical data indicates that the form of sexually explicit material which presents the greatest likelihood of causing sexual violence is violent pornography. The evidence is much weaker with regard to sexually explicit, nonviolent material. If the possibility of increased sexual violence provides a justification for regulating obscenity, it provides an even greater justification for regulating violent pornography.

Third, violent pornography degrades women far more than obscene material. As noted above, studies reveal that exposure to violent pornography leads men to develop personality traits inconsistent with a healthy family and community. Even obscenity's crass exploitation of sex seems less degrading and morally perverse than the perception of women as deserving or enjoying sexual abuse, the result of violent pornography. . . .

The fundamental reasons underlying the obscenity exception apply to violent pornography with equal or greater force than to material that excites lust or lewdness. Therefore, all violent pornography should be included within the obscenity exception.

If the Court declines to recognize that either the incitement of illegal activity or obscenity exceptions to the first amendment encompasses violent pornography, the Court could create a new exception for violent pornography. The Court most recently adopted a new exception involving pornography in *New York v. Ferber*.

A Threat to Civilization

Pornography breeds crime. It creates predatory attitudes, a ruthless spiritual cannibalism, a habitual mindset of domination and aggression among all its devotees. Consumers of pornography learn to entertain themselves by using women and then tossing them aside.

In some cases, pornography acts as a "how-to-do-it" manual for those inclined to act out their fantasies in sex crimes. It provides enormous profits to the mobsters who control its production and largely direct its wholesale distribution. And the immorality of mind and heart and soul among producer and consumer spreads out like a perverse secular sacrament into external manifestations: neighborhoods decay, legitimate businesses are driven out, long-time residents in and near the new pornography neighborhoods move out or at best hang on in fear and dismay at the increase of street crimes and the perverse influences affecting their children.

In light of this ominous record, it is not an exaggeration to say that the promoters of pornography may well do to modern Western civilization what the assaults of the Barbarians did to the ancient Roman Empire. They may ultimately bring the whole thing down.

William A. Stanmeyer, *The Seduction of Society*, 1984.

In *Ferber* the Court excepted child pornography from the protection of the first amendment. The Court provided five reasons for its decision. First, the state has a compelling interest in the physical and psychological well-being of children. Second, the distribution of child pornography is related intrinsically to the sexual abuse of children. The process of making the material sexually exploits children; the sexual exploitation is inextricable from the material itself, and the material is evidence that the harm has occurred. Third, the advertisement and sale of child pornography are economically motivated and thus are an integral part of such materials' production. Fourth, the Court considered it "unlikely that visual depictions of children performing sexual acts or lewdly exhibiting their genitals would often constitute an important and necessary part of a literary performance or scientific or educational work." Finally, it is appropriate to except an entire classification of materials from first amendment protection when "the evil to be restricted so over-whelmingly outweighs the expressive interests, if any, at stake, that no process of case-by-case adjudication is required."

The Court did not need to create a new exception in order to hold that the first amendment does not protect child pornography. The Court could have reached its conclusion that the government can suppress child pornography by using the same rationale it uses in obscenity cases. A modification of the definition of obscenity to include material appealing to the prurient interests of pedophiles would leave most child pornography unprotected by the first amendment.

Child Pornography

Instead, the Court created a new exception because it could not regulate all child pornography under the obscenity definition given that all child pornography may not be adjudged obscene. The Court created a broad new exception in order to give the government greater power to control child pornography and its inherent harms. With this action, the Court demonstrated a willingness to provide a new exception when existing first amendment exceptions could not control the harms from a particular type of material. Similarly, the Court should create a new exception covering all violent pornography because existing exceptions allow some violent pornography to escape regulation and thereby deny the government adequate leverage to control the harms violent pornography causes.

The justifications underlying the *Ferber* decision differ from the rationales behind all the other recognized first amendment exceptions. For instance, *Ferber* does not focus on the harm to society caused by the communication of the speech. Audience reaction is irrelevant to the decision. Instead, it focuses on the harm that necessarily occurs to children in the production process. Thus, the Court's decision indirectly deters the harms of child pornography. Producers and distributors of child pornography are criminally liable regardless of whether they participate in the production process. This approach deters distribution, which in turn deters production, and ultimately eliminates the market for the material. Once the market is dry, pornographers will cease to make child pornography, and consequently the harm to children during the production stage will end.

A Sensible Decision

The *Ferber* decision makes sense because of the impracticality of always preventing a harm through existing criminal law. When the criminal law is not entirely effective to prevent a particular harm, the legal definition of the crime should be expanded to cover events inextricably tied to the harm.

Particularly in a commercial context, where the market and the product are continually shaping one another, courts or legislatures appropriately can control both the market and the product through criminal sanctions because the ultimate harm is attributable to both factors. As the Court stated:

> [W]ere the statute outlawing the employment of children in these films and photographs fully effective, and [had] the constitutionality of these laws . . . not been questioned, the [f]irst [a]mendment implications would be no greater than that presented by laws against distribution: enforceable production laws would leave no child pornography to be marketed.

The *Ferber* analysis is not exactly on point when applied to violent pornography because the government theoretically could enforce perfectly the criminal laws regarding the sexual abuse of women without banning violent pornography. Pornographers might produce violent pornography without breaking criminal laws by obtaining the full consent of female participants, and by simulating the violence. By contrast, child pornography cannot be produced without harming children given that the definition of the crime includes the act of production itself, regardless of the child's consent.

The General Principle

Nonetheless, the more general principle that the Court established in *Ferber*, namely the ability of government to stop the harms inextricably linked to a particular, narrowly defined form of communication, applies to permit regulation of violent pornography. Such regulation would hinder indirectly many types of crime including assault, battery, and rape. The regulation of violent pornography on the basis of its propensity to cause aggression indirectly inhibits crimes produced by that aggression. As in *Ferber*, the regulation will affect only a narrow class of materials that are closely associated with crimes that the existing criminal law is insufficient to deter.

In sum, a great harm is inextricably bound to violent pornography, and the expressive value of violent pornography is minimal. The evil involved overwhelmingly outweighs any expressive interests, and the existing criminal law fails to deter the harm. The only realistic way to deter the crime is to eliminate the market for violent pornography. Prohibiting the production and distribution of a narrowly defined class of violent pornography provides a workable and effective deterrent against the crimes violent pornography causes.

"Harm, though a tragedy, does not settle the question of what is morally permissible."

Harm Does Not Justify Censoring Pornography

Alan Wolfe

In the following viewpoint, Alan Wolfe argues that pornography has not been proven to cause violence against women. But whether it is proven to or not, he contends, pornography still deserves protection under the First Amendment. Pornography serves human needs, he maintains, and thus must be permitted. Wolfe is a book reviewer for *The New Republic*, a weekly magazine.

As you read, consider the following questions:

1. Why are First Amendment defenses of pornography undemocratic, according to Wolfe?
2. What is the author's criticism of feminists who oppose pornography?
3. When does the public interest outweigh individual sexual freedom, in Wolfe's opinion?

Alan Wolfe, "Dirt and Democracy," *The New Republic*, February 19, 1990. Reprinted by permission of *The New Republic*, © 1990, The New Republic, Inc.

Pornography exists where sex and politics meet. Since few other activities are as fascinating as these two pleasures, it is no wonder that questions involving pornography have been with us so long.

Sex is, or at least is supposed to be, intimate, caring, invisible to others: the very definition of private. Politics is, or is supposed to be, open, debatable, a spectacle: the essence of public. A world in which sex and its representations were of no concern to others could not, by force of definition, contain pornography. A world in which politics regulated all sexual activities and their representation could not, by force of police, contain pornography either. To discuss pornography is always to discuss a matter of balance.

Liberal Politics

Our politics—the way we balance public and private things —are those of liberal democracy. As Richard Randall stresses in his comprehensive treatment of the subject, both liberalism and democracy are intimately linked to the pornographic inclination, even if that link is troubling and contradictory. Liberalism respects a private sphere within which government—that is, other people—ought not to find itself. Although the founders of liberalism might be unable to imagine their arguments for freedom of expression used in defense of the prurient, pornography could not exist without the two most fundamental props of the liberal world order: a market that efficiently responds to supply and demand, with little concern for the morality of what is traded; and a legal system that places a premium on individual rights.

Yet if liberalism is inclined to protect the pornographic, democracy is inclined to forbid it. Randall is correct to emphasize that it is the elite that seeks to defend the right of pornographic expression and the majority that seeks to curtail it. Politicians never run for office in favor of pornography. Unmoved by appeals to artistic expression, little concerned for constitutional subtleties, worried about the vulnerability of their children, Americans would gladly give up this one liberal right if they could be guaranteed that in return they would be rid of unwanted ugliness. Legislatures and city councils, responsive to democratic demands, regularly try to control pornography; courts, undemocratic in principle and liberal in practice, try to stop them.

In the past 20 years, liberalism and democracy have both expanded in scope. Pornographers have shared, surely disproportionately, in the expansion of liberal rights that has defined American judicial practice since the Warren Court. The rise of the Moral Majority and other censorial movements, on the other hand, is one of the byproducts of increasingly plebiscitary democratic urges. The result of these simultaneous developments is what Donald Downs calls a "new politics of pornography" in which few of the older images, alliances, positions, and judicial standards make sense. Three developments since around 1970 have set the stage for the new politics of pornography.

© Smith/Rothco. Reprinted with permission.

First, the form of pornography has changed beyond recognition. Any images men may have in their heads about stag films—any leftover memories of fraternity bashes of the 1950s —have nothing to do with what pornography represents now. The sex is far more explicit; today's hard core is tomorrow's R-rated movie, or, to put it another way, yesterday's illegality is today's television commercial. In addition, the "quality" has improved. As Linda Williams points out, plots have been added, full-length feature status is now the norm, and efforts at credibility have been introduced. The symbol of these changes, of course, is video; most people now watch pornography at home in living color, not in grungy inner-city arcades. And high-defi-

213

nition television, once the Japanese get around to supplying it, is next.

Second, nearly all legal efforts used by local communities to control pornography in recent years have failed. The Supreme Court's 1957 decision in *Roth v. United States*—despite its famous language banning material that "appeals to the prurient interest"—effectively opened the door to previously forbidden sexual expression: 31 obscenity convictions were reversed between 1967 and 1973. The ability of pornographers to use courts and the First Amendment to their advantage (Downs notes that in Minneapolis the MCLU [Minnesota Civil Liberties Union] offices were in a building owned by its leading pornographic client, presumably rent-free) led local police to give up even trying to win convictions. Even a town as conservative as Indianapolis was able to initiate only two obscenity cases between 1979 and 1985. During the 1970s and early 1980s, in short, pornography grew increasingly worse as the ability to regulate it declined proportionately.

Third, our awareness that pornography involves violence against women has increased. Of the three developments, this is the most controversial, because there is no absolute proof —nor will there ever be—that pornography *definitely* results in harm to women. (Based on the Danish experience with legalization, the opposite case is equally as plausible: pornography may also be an excuse for men to masturbate and be done, and thus protect women.) Still, the images contained in pornography, brutal toward all, are most brutal toward women. Pornography is, to some degree, a feminist issue. How much it is a feminist issue is the most passionately debated question in the current writing on the subject.

Matters of Balance

If questions involving pornography always involve matters of balance, the rise of a new politics of pornography has placed in doubt what ought to be balanced with what. Under the rules of the "old" politics of pornography, the right to free expression stood on one side and the ability of a community to protect itself from untoward sexuality stood on the other. Under the new politics of pornography, violence against women is defined as what we need protection against, whereas what pornography might stand for is not completely clear.

The new politics of pornography crested with the report of the Meese Commission in 1986, which concluded that pornography (including the violent kind) had increased to the point of being out of control. What was most striking about the Meese Commission was not its conclusions, but the way it reached them. For the commission focused specifically on the insult and injury to women involved in pornography, even to the extent of quoting, without attribution, Robin Morgan's fighting words: "Pornography is the theory; rape is the practice." The feminist critique of pornography had arrived.

That critique was the product of the meeting of two minds: legal theorist Catharine MacKinnon and essayist Andrea Dworkin. Dworkin expounded her ideas in *Pornography: Men Possessing Women*. In Dworkin's view, sex is power, nothing else; and all the power belongs to the man. Every man is a beast, every woman an innocent and (remarkably, for a feminist) passive victim. Pornography, like heterosexual sex in general, is merely an extreme form by which men exercise power over women.

Help Victims Without Censorship

Under the guise of eliminating obscenity, the Government is seeking to limit free speech nationwide. It is doing so through a vastly increased number of Federal prosecutions and by promising aid to state prosecutors who handle obscenity cases. . . .

Some of the obscenity prosecutors are zealots. Some with whom I have spoken describe their work as a crusade aimed at saving the "moral fiber" of the country. . . .

But prosecutors' time and the millions of dollars spent in these multi-state prosecutions would be better spent safeguarding those few women and children victimized by producers of pornographic films.

Martin Garbus, *The New York Times*, April 28, 1990.

The philosophy in Dworkin's bedroom is the philosophy of Hobbes. She tells me, for example, that I have refrained from raping my son not because I love him, but because of the fear that when he grows up, he might rape me back. Dworkin, in that sense, is really not all that interested in pornography as such; the chapter of that name in her book is four pages long, whereas the one called "Force" is 70. (Brutal treatments of gay men or animals would not, presumably, bother her.) Let Dworkin herself speak:

In the male system, women are sex: sex is the whore. The whore is porné, the lowest whore, the whore who belongs to *all* male citizens: the slut. . . . Buying her is buying pornography. Having her is having pornography. Seeing her is seeing pornography. Seeing her sex, especially her genitals, is seeing pornography. Seeing her in sex is seeing the whore in sex. Using her is using pornography. Wanting her means wanting pornography. Being her means being pornography.

215

Dworkin believes that what men do to women in pornography is *worse* than what Nazis did to Jews in concentration camps: "The Jews didn't do it to themselves and they didn't orgasm. . . . No one, not even Goebbels, said that the Jews liked it." Dworkin does Robin Morgan one better: sex is the theory and extermination the practice. Women, though, unlike the Jews in the camps, are fighting back. (Totally passive, they suddenly found a voice.) Her advice to them is: "know the bastard on top of you." Men are scared. The women they have treated pornographically all their lives are massed to castrate them, and Dworkin is wielding the biggest knife.

The Minnesota Ordinance

This kind of analysis would hardly seem the stuff of local ordinances—especially in the American Midwest. But, as Downs recounts in his illuminating history of these events, one of Dworkin's readers was Catharine MacKinnon, by all accounts a brilliant political strategist. In 1983 MacKinnon invited Dworkin to teach a class with her at the University of Minnesota School of Law. Two essential conclusions were quickly reached in the seminar: first, that pornography is not a question of free speech, because women cannot speak; and second, that pornography, because it harms women, does not extend civil liberties, it violates civil rights.

The resulting Minnesota ordinance was a first in American law. Pornography—not, as in most judicial decisions since *Roth*, the narrower notion of obscenity—was defined as discrimination against women. Finding herself depicted in what she believed to be pornographic fashion by any image—nine definitions of such depictions were given in the ordinance—any woman could lodge a complaint with the local Civil Rights Commission and, after a series of steps were followed, could win the right to a hearing. The Minnesota ordinance was eventually declared unconstitutional in 1985. Still, we may hear more from the feminist anti-pornographers. . . . Since the threat of an anti-discrimination suit is designed to stop the practice of depicting women pornographically before it occurs, the issue raised by Dworkin and MacKinnon is censorship. Is the harm to women represented in pornography so great that we are justified in using our democratic powers to stop it?

The Defense of Pornography

The first reaction to the rise of a feminist movement for censorship was to argue on empirical grounds that the harm done to women by pornography is not as great as feared. It has been said that pornography has targets other than women; that women make and enjoy pornography themselves; that no harm

216

against women from pornography can be proved. Although in a narrow and technical sense these arguments are accurate, they miss the point. . . .

When a political position has as much popularity as the desire to control pornography, we ought to give those who hold it credit for their views, not dismiss them as know-nothings, anti-intellectual philistines, or (as Randall unfortunately does) people repressing the pornographic within. When the rage of women is eloquent and dramatic, we ought not let Dworkin's absurd rhetoric deny an important point. Pornography is demeaning, women are its primary targets, and even if we cannot prove that it causes violence, it certainly offends the sensibility of some very engaged citizens.

What Men Want

Presumably we are not being told by the would-be guardians of our morals that books rape women, but this notion is not too far removed from those who seek to ban the obscene out of fear that mere thoughts or feelings presumably produced will tend to cause socially harmful deeds. Indeed, given this precedent for action, why not censor books about religion or politics for evoking mere thoughts or feelings that could also be considered socially dangerous? If the mere possibility of a linkage to misconduct would be sufficient justification for censoring the obscene, would not the same reasoning also apply to apprehensions about the social consequences of "dangerous" religious or political thought—as the contagion spreads?

William A. Linsley, *Pornography: Research Advances and Policy Considerations,* 1989.

At this point, a second line of defense against censorship enters: even though pornography demeans women, it serves positive goals that are more important. Whether or not pornography has value, one form of this argument runs, liberty clearly does. Hence pornography can be bad, but what it symbolizes—free speech—is good. Pornography, therefore, has redeeming value in spite of itself. A similar response to the Dworkin-MacKinnon position has arisen among feminists who, objecting strenuously to their depiction of the passivity of women, argue that free sex has as much value as free speech. Did it ever occur to Dworkin and others like her, these thinkers have asked, that women like sex? It was hardly the intent of the feminist movement, after all, to turn all women into Puritans. (For similar reasons, gays objected vehemently to the Minneapolis ordinance.)

Revisionist feminists—if they may be called that—also find indirect value in pornography. We have libidos. They need outlets. Free speech and free sex both make a certain toleration of pornography necessary. . . .

Little Social Value

Pornography has little redeeming social value. By artistic criteria, it is close to worthless. Heroic attempts to defend the pornographic imagination by Angela Carter and Simone de Beauvoir (in the case of Sade) or Susan Sontag (in the case of Georges Bataille and Pauline Réage) treat a rarefied aspect of the genre that has little to do with the predictability and the sheer mediocrity of much of the pornographic expression. By criteria of psychological development, moreover, pornography fails again. It infantilizes people, mostly men, locking them into a stage in which limits do not exist, all desires can be satisfied, and every complexity avoided. By the Kantian criterion of respect for persons, furthermore, pornography fails a third time, treating women as things available for the whimsical pleasures of men; pornography in that sense is also without redeeming moral value.

By civic criteria, finally, pornography flunks most severely. Although free speech gives much to pornography, pornography gives almost nothing to free speech. It does not enhance our capacity to act as citizens. It does not cause us to reflect on rights and responsibilities. It does not encourage participation in the life of the community. Pornographers are free riders on the liberties of everyone else. If a human activity with so little value is balanced against even a slight possibility that it may cause rape and mayhem, the feminist case for censorship would seem to win.

Still, for all that, the bad taste that censorship leaves in the mouth cannot be easily washed away. The question of pornography raises a host of complex moral and symbolic issues that cannot be resolved by banishing the problem's manifestations. On moral grounds, for example, the case for censorship and the case for unrestricted rights to pornography are quite similar —and similarly without nuance. Feminists like Dworkin, who would regulate all the fine details of private life, believe that there is no morality to speak of when discussing pornography; everything is power. Civil libertarians, on the other hand, ruling private behavior beyond the pale of public scrutiny, also believe that there is no morality at issue; everything is principle. The moral neutrality of both positions can hardly win a hearing among most people, who believe that pornography, which is obviously about sex, is also about morality.

Pornography raises issues about the nature of the self, moreover, that cannot be addressed either by banning pornography or by celebrating it. One of the unanticipated benefits of the feminist case for censorship has been to sharpen the sense of what we are in danger of losing if the urge to censor gets out of hand. It is not individual freedom to do or say anything one wants with little regard for the sensitivity of the community. The loss would be deeper, for pornography symbolizes fundamental human needs without which we would not be fully human. Two of them are the need to be aware of the dark side of sexuality and the need to make sense out of multiple realities. If we have learned anything about texts at all in this century, it is that the more readers, the more interpretations—that reality, in short, is never simply one unambiguous thing.

Different Meanings

Those who would censor pornography have complete epistemological confidence that they know exactly what it is. Reflecting on the experience in Minneapolis, Dworkin writes: "For women who are hurt by pornography, this law simply describes reality; it is a map of the real world.". . .

Linda Williams's book *Hard Core* is a brilliant demolition of the position that pornography represents one thing only. Arguing against the feminist case for censorship, Williams urges that we take pornography seriously, which does not mean that we like it, or that we believe it is art. . . .

Pornography cannot mean one thing, and one thing only, because genre conventions, instead of confining all reality within pre-established frames, enable multiple interpretations of reality to exist simultaneously. That is why pornography is not, as Dworkin claims, *only* about men brutalizing women. It may equally be the case that what men want to see in pornographic movies is not the naked woman, since most men, in the course of their lives, get to see that with some frequency, but the image of another man enjoying himself visibly, which most men never get to see. We do not know, of course, whether this interpretation is correct. But Williams's subtle and fascinating explications suggest that, in not knowing, we are best off allowing pornographic representations to exist. . . .

If the feminist censor's conviction that pornography reflects an unambiguous map of reality is naive, so is her conviction that, knowing the single-minded evil it represents, we can abolish it by force of law. Randall makes a convincing case that such an optimistic view of the powers of law is not justified. It is, in his view, the dark side of pornography that makes it important. Humans are the "pornographic" animal, fascinated and appalled by their sexuality. The pornography that we see out there is a reflection of the pornographic deep within our selves.

Since pornography is part of what we are, we harm only ourselves by regulating it too severely. At the same time, however, since "complete sexual freedom is a contradiction of the human condition," we will need to control our sexual impulses in some way. Neither censors nor civil libertarians, Randall argues, understand "the paradoxical, mutually supportive relationship between pornography and censorship." We will have to live with various efforts to reconcile sexuality and its control, none of which will ever solve the problem.

Human Needs

The recognition that pornography speaks to needs within the self—its need to interpret as well as its need to express itself sexually—is a much firmer guide for sorting out the new politics of pornography than the purely libertarian notion of individual freedom. For one thing, the issue is not the abstract right of shady businessmen to sell dirty pictures, or the equally abstract right of sexual pleasure-seekers to purchase them—rights that in both cases apply to minorities. Pornography is important, rather, because in speaking to the self, it is speaking to a universal: we all have an interest in the many ways in which fundamental human conflicts are represented in print and in film. . . .

Imperfect creatures growing to adulthood with sexual conflicts unresolved, many of us (surprisingly many, by most sociological accounts) need outlets for our imaginations, relying on our power to give meaning to representations of fantasies buried deep within the self, even if the pictorial representations of those fantasies involve, on the surface, harm to others. A case against censorship ought to argue not that we can discover some redeeming virtue in pornographic expression, but that we cannot. . . .

The feminist case against pornography is powerful and eloquent. But it establishes a border for the public debate, it does not resolve it. Moral philosophers long ago demonstrated convincingly that harm, though a tragedy, does not settle the question of what is morally permissible.

Distinguishing Bias from Reason

The subject of pornography often generates strong emotional responses in people. When dealing with such a highly controversial subject, many allow their feelings to dominate their powers of reason. Thus, one of the most important basic thinking skills is the ability to distinguish between statements based upon emotion and those based upon a rational consideration of the facts.

Most of the following statements are taken from the viewpoints in this chapter. Consider each statement carefully. *Mark R for any statement you believe is based on reason or a rational consideration of the facts. Mark B for any statement you believe is based on bias, prejudice, or emotion. Mark I for any statement you believe is impossible to judge.*

If you are doing this activity as a member of a class or group, compare your answers with those of other class or group members. Be able to explain your answers. You may discover that others come to different conclusions than you. Listening to the reasons others present for their answers may give you valuable insights into distinguishing between bias and reason.

R = *a statement based upon reason*
B = *a statement based upon bias*
I = *a statement impossible to judge*

1. Pornography is a systematic practice of exploitation that harms women.

2. Child pornography is banned because children are not mature enough to exercise reasoned judgment about participation in sexual activities.

3. The suppression of pornography through government intervention (censorship laws) encourages intolerance throughout society.

4. Pornography is an affront to decency; it coarsens society.

5. America is swimming in a sea of filth and violence.

6. If it is legitimate to try to understand why pornography might trigger a rare individual to commit a crime of sexual violence, it is equally appropriate to try to understand how the material might prevent one.

7. Sexual repressiveness is rooted in self-hate, self-loathing, in a Puritanical inability to enjoy the full sensuality of the body.

8. Every person's voice is protected by the Constitution because we recognize that when official censors make the choice of what we see and hear, all speech is at risk.

9. It is naive to think that we can ban pornography by law.

10. When you protect pornographers' speech, you protect their right to exploit and hurt women.

11. Current pornography laws are marred by overly broad, ineffective, and wasteful regulation.

12. Pornography depicts women being exploited by and submissive to men. This encourages men to regard women as objects to be used.

13. Lurid pornography degrades women and weakens America's moral structure.

14. The First Amendment says "Congress shall make no law . . . abridging the freedom of speech or of the press." Pornography is a form of speech and should not be censored.

15. In numerous studies, the excessive viewing of pornography is directly linked to sexual crime.

16. At no point are people coerced into purchasing pornography. No one forces protesters or anyone else to buy it.

17. Feminists should not use pornography as a political springboard to foist their image and ideology on the public.

18. Pornography is not "erotic art." It is the brutal subjugation of women for the pleasure of manipulative men.

Periodical Bibliography

The following articles have been selected to supplement the diverse views presented in this chapter.

Art News	"Obscenity: What the Supreme Court Says," October 1989.
Art News	"What Is Pornography?" October 1989.
James Bowman	"But Is It Art?" *The Spectator*, April 14, 1990.
Christianity Today	"Pornography Foes Urge Renewed Awareness," December 15, 1989.
Craig M. Collins	"Porn in the USA," *Reason,* July 1989. Available from Reason Foundation, 2716 Ocean Park Blvd., Suite 1062, Santa Monica, CA 90405.
Robert Corn-Revere	"Smut and the Phone Company," *The Wall Street Journal,* September 5, 1989.
Barbara Deane	"Wrong Number!" *Family Circle*, February 1, 1989.
Don Feder	"Supreme Court Should Disconnect Dial-a-Porn," *Conservative Chronicle,* February 22, 1989. Available from *Conservative Chronicle,* Box 11297, Des Moines, IA 50340-1297.
Laura Fraser	"Nasty Girls," *Mother Jones,* February/March 1990.
John Garvey	"A Deluge of Images," *Commonweal,* May 18, 1990.
Ted Gest	"The Drive to Make America Porn-Free," *U.S. News & World Report,* February 6, 1989.
Timothy Healey	"Government—A Good Patron but Bad Censor," *The New York Times,* September 15, 1989.
Bill Hybels	"The Sin That So Easily Entangles," *Moody Monthly,* April 1989.
Bruce E. Johansen	"The Meese Police on Porn Patrol," *The Progressive,* June 1988.
Philip Nobile	"Untruth and Consequences," *Reason,* February 1990. Available from Reason Foundation, 2716 Ocean Park Blvd., Suite 1062, Santa Monica, CA 90405.
Donald E. Olsen	"The Value of Erotica," *The Humanist,* September/October 1989.

Carole Pateman	"Sex and Power," *Ethics*, January 1990. Available from the University of Chicago Press, Journals Division, PO Box 37005, Chicago, IL 60637.
Richard A. Posner	"Art for Art's Sake," *The American Scholar*, Autumn 1989.
Henry Reske	"Kiddie Porn," *ABA Journal*, January 1990. Available from the American Bar Association, 750 N. Lake Shore Drive, Chicago, IL 60611.
Mary Ellen Ross	"Censorship or Education? Feminist Views on Pornography," *The Christian Century*, March 7, 1990.
Jennifer Steinhauer	"Prosecute Porn? It's on the Decline," *The Wall Street Journal*, December 28, 1989.
U.S. News & World Report	"Smut Is Snuffed in the Undirty Dozen," April 23, 1990.
Richard Woodbury	"A Smut Buster Battles Sin in the City," *Time*, May 29, 1989.

Organizations to Contact

The editors have compiled the following list of organizations which are concerned with the issues debated in this book. All of them have publications or information available for interested readers. The descriptions are derived from materials provided by the organizations. This list was compiled upon the date of publication. Names and phone numbers of organizations are subject to change.

Accuracy In Media (AIM)
1275 K St. NW, Suite 1150
Washington, DC 20005
(202) 371-6710

AIM is a conservative watchdog organization. It researches public complaints on errors of fact made by the news media and requests that the errors be corrected publicly. It publishes the bimonthly *AIM Report* and a weekly syndicated newspaper column.

American Civil Liberties Union (ACLU)
132 W. 43rd St.
New York, NY 10036
(212) 944-9800

The ACLU champions the rights set forth in the Declaration of Independence and the Constitution. It opposes censoring any form of speech. The ACLU publishes the quarterly newsletter, *Civil Liberties Alert* and several handbooks, public policy reports, project reports, civil liberties books, and pamphlets on the Freedom of Information Act.

American Coalition for Traditional Values (ACTV)
5801 Sixteenth St. NW
Washington, DC 20011

The Coalition is led by evangelical Christian leaders who are united to restore traditional moral and spiritual values to American schools, media institutions, and government. It supports parental input into library materials that are accessible to children and opposes pornography. The Coalition publishes the annual *ACTV Network* and the monthly *Washington Report.*

American Enterprise Institute for Public Policy Research (AEI)
115 Seventeenth St. NW
Washington, DC 20036
(202) 862-5800

AEI is a conservative think tank whose resident scholars include Jeane J. Kirkpatrick and Robert Bork. AEI studies such issues as government regulation, religion, philosophy, and legal policy. The Institute believes that the media are biased and should be closely monitored. AEI's publications include books such as *The Video Campaign: Network Coverage of the 1988 Primaries* as well as the bimonthly magazine *The American Enterprise.*

American Library Association (ALA)
50 E. Huron St.
Chicago, IL 60611
(312) 944-6780

The ALA supports intellectual freedom and freedom and free access to libraries and library materials. The ALA's affiliated offices are the Office for Intellectual Freedom, which publishes *Newsletter on Intellectual Freedom,* and Freedom to Read Foundation, which works for the legal and financial defense of intellectual freedom. The ALA publishes *Censorship, Litigation, and the Schools,* pamphlets, articles, audiovisual aids, and the annotated bibliography, "Pressure Groups and Censorship."

Americans for Decency (AFD)
PO Box 218
Staten Island, NY 10302
(718) 442-6088

The AFD's goal is to "promote decency in America." It objects to pornography, suggestive rock music lyrics, classroom sex education, and adult-oriented material on prime time television. The AFD supports boycotts of magazines and television networks that print or broadcast objectionable material. It distributes copies of articles and publishes the periodic *Celestial News: Past-Present-Future, The Truth Is News in Our Time,* and various flyers.

Christian Voice
214 Massachusetts Ave. NE, Suite 120
Washington, DC 20002
(202) 544-5202

The Voice is a major Christian lobbying organization. The organization seeks to restore traditional Christian values throughout the country. Its goals include the banning of pornography, the return of school prayer, and preventing the passage of gay rights and abortion laws. It publishes many brochures, books, the monthly *Legislative Alert,* and the annual *Congressional Report Card.*

Citizens for Decency Through Law (CDL)
2845 E. Camelback, Suite 740
Phoenix, AZ 85016
(602) 381-1322

CDL seeks to assist law enforcement agencies and legislatures in enacting and enforcing Constitutional statutes, ordinances, and regulations controlling "obscenity, pornography, and materials harmful to juveniles." It provides free legal assistance in the form of legal research, briefs, model legislation, and courtroom assistance for obscenity prosecutions and civil action. CDL also conducts seminars for police and prosecutors on search and seizure, trial tactics, evidence and proof, and appeals. It publishes the bimonthly *National Decency Report.*

Committee to Protect Journalists
16 E. 42nd St., Third Floor
New York, NY 10017
(212) 983-5355

The Committee works on behalf of journalists around the world whose human and professional rights have been violated. It believes that there is a growing effort by governments to limit the ability of foreign correspondents and local journalists to practice their profession. The Committee publishes *Update* monthly.

Eagle Forum
Box 618
Alton, IL 62002
(618) 462-5415

The Forum is a Christian group that promotes morality and traditional family values as revealed through the Bible. It opposes the depiction of sex and violence in media outlets such as television, films, magazines, and rock music lyrics. The Forum publishes the monthly *Phyllis Schlafly Report* and the periodic Eagle Forum *Newsletter*.

Freedom to Read Foundation
American Library Association
50 E. Huron St.
Chicago, IL 60611
(312) 944-6780

The Foundation supports the rights of libraries to make any work which they may legally acquire available to the public. It provides legal and financial assistance to libraries involved in censorship battles. It publishes the bimonthly *Newsletter on Intellectual Freedom*.

Fund for Free Expression
36 W. 44th St.
New York, NY 10036
(212) 840-9460

This organization is a collection of journalists, writers, editors, publishers, and concerned citizens who work to preserve intellectual freedom throughout the world. It serves as the U.S. sponsor for the British publication *Index on Censorship*, which reports on violations of free expression. The Fund conducts forums and maintains the Americas Watch Committee which monitors and promotes observance of human rights in the Western Hemisphere. It publishes *Americas Watch Report*.

The Heritage Foundation
214 Massachusetts Ave. NE
Washington, DC 20002
(202) 546-4400

The Foundation is a public policy institute dedicated to the principles of free competitive enterprise, limited government, individual liberty, and a strong national defense. It believes national security concerns justify limiting the media. It publishes a weekly bulletin, *Backgrounder*, a monthly magazine, *National Security Record*, and many other books and research papers. It has published as part of its lecture series a paper entitled *Why National Security Concerns and the First Amendment Are Not Compatible*.

The Media Institute
3017 M St. NW
Washington, DC 20007
(202) 298-7512

The Institute is a think tank that studies media issues. It conducts research on the relationship between the media and business, on new communication technologies, the First Amendment, and other media topics. Its publications include *Reporting on Risk, The Diversity Principle: Friend or Foe of the First Amendment?* and *Hispanic Media: Impact and Influence*.

Morality in Media, Inc. (MIM)
475 Riverside Dr.
New York, NY 10115
(212) 870-3222

MIM believes pornography corrupts children and degrades both men and women. It has worked since 1962 to alert citizens to the dangers of pornography and to demand that the courts enforce obscenity laws. It publishes the *Handbook on the Prosecution of Obscenity Cases.*

National Coalition Against Censorship (NCAC)
2 W. 64th St.
New York, NY 10023
(212) 724-1500

NCAC is an alliance of organizations committed to defending freedom of thought, inquiry, and expression by engaging in public education and advocacy on national and local levels. Their publications include *Censorship News* and *Report on Book Censorship Litigation in Public Schools.*

National Coalition Against Pornography (N-CAP)
800 Compton Rd., Suite 9224
Cincinnati, OH 45231-9964
(513) 521-6227

N-CAP is an organization of business, religious, and civic leaders who work to eliminate pornography. They believe that there is a link between pornography and violence. They encourage citizens to support the enforcement of obscenity laws and to close down pornography outlets in their neighborhoods. The publications they have available include *Final Report of the Attorney General's Commission on Pornography, The Mind Polluters,* and *Pornography: A Human Tragedy.*

National Coalition on Television Violence (NCTV)
PO Box 2157
Champaign, IL 61825
(217) 384-1920

NCTV calls for boycotts against advertisers of certain shows as a way to reduce violence on television. The Coalition believes violence in the media increases violence in America. It monitors the number of violent acts in television shows. It publishes *NCTV News.*

Parents' Alliance to Protect Our Children
44 E. Tacoma Ave.
Latrobe, PA 15650
(412) 459-6347

The Alliance supports traditional family values. It advocates censorship in cases where it believes these values are being undermined. The Alliance supports the inclusion of Christian teachings in textbooks and the labeling of records that contain offensive lyrics. It publishes position papers such as *Academic Censorship* and *Ratings/Labels on Recordings and Videos.*

Parents' Music Resource Center (PMRC)
1500 Arlington Blvd., Suite 300
Arlington, VA 22209
(703) 527-9466

The PMRC was founded in 1985 to encourage placing warning labels on records with lyrics that promote sex, violence, and drug use. The Center opposes censorship and instead calls for record companies to voluntarily print lyrics on the outside of record albums and to use a warning label on any album with explicit lyrics. It publishes the quarterly newsletter *The Record.* Its most visible member, Tipper Gore, has published articles on record labeling in *The New York Times, Newsweek,* and other publications.

PEN American Center
568 Broadway
New York, NY 10012
(212) 334-1660

The Center is a worldwide organization of writers, editors, and translators. Its Freedom to Write Committee organizes letter-writing campaigns on behalf of writers across the globe who are censored and/or imprisoned. It publishes the quarterly *Newsletter* and *Freedom-to-Write Bulletin.*

People for the American Way (PAW)
2000 M St., Suite 400
Washington, DC, 20036
(202) 467-4999

PAW is engaged in a mass media campaign to create a climate of tolerance and respect for diverse people, religions, and values. It distributes educational materials, leaflets, and brochures. It also publishes the quarterly *Press Clips,* a collection of newspaper articles concerning censorship.

Project Censored
Sonoma State University
Rohnert Park, CA 94928
(707) 664-2149

Project Censored publicizes stories that have been overlooked by the major media. Each year it publishes a list of the ten most important censored stories, as well as a study of sensational stories that made the news but the Project feels were not noteworthy.

Reporters Committee for Freedom of the Press (RCFP)
1735 Eye St. NW., Suite 504
Washington, DC 20006
(202) 466-6312

The Committee is devoted to protecting the rights of the press and to upholding the First Amendment. It studies how subpoenas of reporters' notes affect their ability to gather news from confidential sources. It opposes closing criminal justice proceedings to the public and press. RCFP publishes *News Media Update* biweekly, and *News Media and the Law* quarterly.

Women Against Pornography (WAP)
321 W. 47th St.
New York, NY 10036
(212) 307-5055

WAP was founded by Susan Brownmiller, the feminist author of *Against Our Will: Men, Women and Rape.* WAP works to change public attitudes toward pornography by offering tours of Times Square, New York's porn center, and by offering slide shows for adults and high school students which show how pornography brutalizes women. It makes available a packet of information concerning the effects of pornography on American society.

World Press Freedom Committee
c/o The Newspaper Center
PO Box 17407
Washington, DC 20041
(202) 648-1000

The Committee monitors freedom of the press on an international level. It has several articles on censorship available, including "A Missing Agenda" and "A Free Press Means Better Development."

Bibliography of Books

American Civil
Liberties Union
Free Trade in Ideas. Pamphlet available from the Center for National Security Studies, 122 Maryland Ave. NE, Washington, DC 20036

Stephen Arons
Compelling Belief: The Culture of American Schooling. New York: McGraw-Hill, 1983.

James Aronson
The Press and the Cold War. New York: Monthly Review Press, 1990.

C. Edwin Baker
Human Liberty and Freedom of Speech. New York: Oxford University Press, 1989.

Lee C. Bollinger
The Tolerant Society: Freedom of Speech and Extremist Speech in America. New York: Oxford University Press, 1986.

Haig A. Bosmajian, ed.
The Freedom to Publish. New York: Neal-Schuman Publishers, 1989.

Lee Burress
Battle of the Books: Literary Censorship in the Public Schools. Metuchen, NJ: Scarecrow Press, 1989.

California Senate
Select Committee on
Legislature and Youth
Hearing on Effects of Media Violence on Children. Sacramento, CA: Joint Publications, 1988.

Gail Chesler and
Julienne Dickey, eds.
Feminism and Censorship: The Current Debate. Garden City, NJ: Ultra Violet Enterprises, 1988.

Eric Clark
The Want Makers: The World Advertising Industry—How They Make You Buy. New York: Viking Press, 1988.

Donna A. Demac
Keeping America Uninformed: Government Secrecy in the 1980s. New York: Pilgrim Press, 1984.

Donna A. Demac
Liberty Denied: The Current Rise of Censorship in America. New York: PEN American Center, 1988.

Everette E. Dennis,
Donald M. Gilmore, and
Theodore L. Glasser, eds.
Media Freedom and Accountability. Westport, CT: Greenwood Press, 1989.

Donald Alexander
Downs
The New Politics of Pornography. Chicago: The University of Chicago Press, 1989.

Andrea Dworkin
Pornography: Men Possessing Women. New York: E. P. Dutton, 1989.

Everywoman
Pornography and Sexual Violence: Evidence of the Links. London: Everywoman, 1988.

Fred Fedler
Media Hoaxes. Ames, IA: Iowa State University Press, 1989.

Lois G. Forer
A Chilling Effect. New York: W.W. Norton and Co., 1987.

Warren Freedman
Freedom of Speech on Private Property. New York: Quorum Books, 1988.

Jeffrey Gale
Bullshit! The Media as Power Brokers in Presidential Elections. Palm Springs, CA: Bold Hawk Press, 1988.

230

Doris A. Graber	*Media Power in Politics.* Washington, DC: Congressional Quarterly Press, 1990.
Jonathan Green	*The Encyclopedia of Censorship.* New York: Facts on File, 1990.
Kent Greenawalt	*Speech, Crime, and the Uses of Language.* New York: Oxford University Press, 1989.
Susan Gubar and Joan Hoff	*For Adult Users Only: The Dilemma of Violent Pornography.* Bloomington, IN: Indiana University Press, 1989.
Gordon Hawkins and Franklin E. Zimring	*Pornography in a Free Society.* Cambridge, England: Cambridge University Press, 1988.
Nat Hentoff	*The First Freedom.* New York: Delacorte Press, 1988.
Richard F. Hixson	*Privacy in a Public Society.* New York: Oxford University Press, 1987.
Frank Hoffman	*Intellectual Freedom and Censorship: An Annotated Bibliography.* Metuchen, NJ: Scarecrow Press, 1989.
Sue Curry Jansen	*Censorship: The Knot That Binds Power and Knowledge.* New York: Oxford University Press, 1988.
Harry Kalven	*A Worthy Tradition: Freedom of Speech in America.* New York: Harper & Row, 1988.
Walter Kendrick	*The Secret Museum: Pornography in Modern Culture.* New York: Viking Press, 1987.
Theodore R. Kupferman	*Censorship, Secrecy, Access, and Obscenity.* Westport, CT: Meckler, 1990.
Danny Lacombe	*Ideology and Public Policy: The Case Against Pornography.* Toronto: Garamond Press, 1988.
Robert M. Liebert	*The Early Window: Effects of Television on Children and Youth.* New York: Pergamon Press, 1988.
Michael Linfield	*Freedom Under Fire: U.S.Civil Liberties in Times of War.* Boston: South End Press, 1990.
Tibor R. Machan	*Liberty & Culture: Essays on the Idea of a Free Society.* Buffalo, NY: Prometheus Books, 1989.
Ralph D. Mawdsley	*Free Expression and Censorship: Public Policy and the Law.* Topeka, KS: NOLPE, 1988.
James Moffett	*Storm in the Mountains: A Case Study of Censorship, Conflict, and Consciousness.* Carbondale, IL: Southern Illinois University Press, 1988.
Kathryn C. Montgomery	*Target: Prime Time: Advocacy Groups and the Struggle over Entertainment Television.* New York: Oxford University Press, 1989.
Edward L. Palmer	*Television and America's Children: A Crisis of Neglect.* New York: Oxford University Press, 1988.
Henry Reichman	*Censorship and Selection: Issues and Answers for Schools.* Chicago: American Library Association, 1988.
Donald J. Rogers	*Banned! Book Censorship in the Schools.* New York: Messner, 1988.
William A. Rusher	*The Coming Battle for the Media: Curbing the Power of the Media Elite.* New York: William Morrow & Co., 1988.

Nancy Signorielli and George Gerbner	*Violence and Terror in the Mass Media: An Annotated Bibliography.* Westport, CT: Greenwood Press, 1988.
Stansfield Turner	*Secrecy and Democracy: The CIA in Transition.* Boston: Houghton Mifflin Co., 1985.
Mark I. West	*Children, Culture, and Controversy.* Hamden, CT: Archon Books, 1988.
Mark I. West	*Trust Your Children.* New York: Neal-Schuman Publishers, 1988.

Index

Abrams, Floyd, 57, 88
Adams, Arlin M., 91
affirmative action, 150
AIDS, 129
Allen, Woody, 21
Allende, Hortensia, 20
American Civil Liberties Union, 22
  protects free speech, 23, 25, 26
  con, 190-191
American Federation of Teachers, 157
American Indians, 155-156
American Library Association, 127,
  129, 136
Amin, Idi, 60
anti-Semitism, 26, 203
apartheid, 60
Artley, Steve, 44
arts
  federal funding restriction
    is censorship, 35, 42-48
    con, 36-41
Asay, Chuck, 38
Asians, 187
atheists, 162
Attorney General's Commission on
  Pornography (Meese Commission),
  173, 176, 179, 214-215
Augustine, Saint, 129-30

Bataille, Georges, 218
Beggs, James, 80
Benavidez, Max, 46
Benson, Steve, 81
Bernardin, Joseph, 204
Bible, 157-158, 163
Black, Hugo L., 26, 102-103, 182-183
blacks, 148, 152-153, 180
  Klan harassment of
    must be censored, 18, 20, 204-205
    con, 23, 26
  pornography and, 187
  rap music and, 29-30
Block, Felix, 98
Blume, Judy, 131
Blumenfeld Education Letter, 158
book banning
  is appropriate, 123, 179
    con, 127, 130, 131-132, 138-139,
    162
Boren, David, 78
Bork, Mary Ellen, 156
Bork, Robert, 184
Boston General Library, 127

Brandenburg v. Ohio (1969), 23, 27,
  203, 204-206
Brennan, William J., Jr., 173, 175
broadcasting
  should be regulated, 70-74
    con, 75-78
Brown, Darryl, 140
Brustein, Robert, 42
Bryant, Jennings, 174
Buchanan, John H., 160
Buckley, William F., Jr., 40
Buffalo, University of, 149, 150
Burford, Anne, 80
Bush, George, 35
Byrd, Robert C., 37

Cahn, Edmond, 25
California Library Association, 129
Carter, Angela, 218
Carter, Hodding, 60
Carter, Jimmy, 98, 102
CBS, Inc., 110
censorship
  is appropriate for
    libraries, 121-125
      con, 126-132
    national security, 97-100
      con, 101-105
    obscene music, 28-31
      con, 32-35
    offensive art, 36-41
      con, 42-48
    racist speech, 17-21, 140-146
      con, 22-27, 147-153
  of pornography
    feminism calls for, 186-193
      con, 194-201
    First Amendment allows, 178-185
      con, 172-177
    harm justifies, 202-210
      con, 211-220
  of school textbooks
    favors conservatives, 160-165
    favors liberals, 154-159
    violates freedom of speech, 22-27
      con, 17-21
Chaplinsky v. New Hampshire (1942),
  149
Chekhov, Anton, 46
Christianity, 25, 26
  is censored out of textbooks,
    155-156, 157, 158-159
      con, 162, 165

sexual repression in, 129-130
Citizens for Excellence in Public
  Education, 161, 165
civil rights
  First Amendment and, 20, 24, 180
  pornography and, 193, 216
Clay, Andrew Dice, 31
CNA Insurance Company, 87
Cohen, Richard, 29, 30
colleges
  should censor racist speech, 140-146
    con, 147-153
Communications Act (1934), 71
Communist Party, 23
Concerned Women for America, 161,
  164
conservatives
  favor censorship, 43-44, 57, 72
  school texts favor, 160-165
    con, 154-159
Corcoran Gallery of Art, 39
Cox v. Louisiana (1956), 26-27
creationism, 161, 163, 164
crime, 18, 208, 209
Crouch, Stanley, 30
Cuomo, Mario M., 54

D'Amato, Alfonse, 43
Dannemeyer, William, 72-73
Davis, Rod, 17
de Beauvoir, Simone, 218
defamation, 83, 89, 91
defense contractors, 83-84
Demac, Donna A., 164
Dembart, Lee, 151
democracy
  cannot allow censorship, 55, 61,
    137, 175, 212
    con, 40
  public schools and, 163
Democritus, 127
Dewey, John, 156
Dewhurst, Colleen, 29
Dingell, John, 72
Dionysus, 158
Dolfman, Murray, 152-153
Donahue, Phil, 86
Donovan, Raymond, 80
Dority, Barbara, 194
Douglas, William O., 26, 173,
  182-183
Downs, Donald, 213, 216
Dred Scott v. Sandford (1857), 20
Dreyfus, Alfred, 26
due process of law, 89
Duke Museum of Art, 39
Dworkin, Andrea, 35, 186, 215-216,
  217, 218, 219

Eagle Forum, 161
Educational Research Analysts, 161
Edwards v. South Carolina (1963),
  26-27
Endick, Barry, 151
espionage
  justifies censorship, 107-108
    con, 111, 114
Espionage Act (1917), 107, 109
evolution, 157, 161, 163, 164

Fairness Doctrine, 134
  should be reinstated, 70-74
    con, 75-78
Falwell, Jerry, 122
Farrakhan, Louis, 152
Farrell, John, 46
Federal Communications
  Commission (FCC)
  and Fairness Doctrine, 71-72, 73,
    76, 77
  and pornography, 184
Federalist Papers, 58
Federalist Society, 150
Feiffer, Jules, 43
Fein, Bruce, 142
Feldman, Martin L.C., 108
feminism
  requires censoring pornography,
    186-193
    con, 194-201, 214, 215, 216,
      217-218, 219
flag burning, 29, 33, 35
Florence, William G., 102
Ford, Gerald R., 98
Ford Foundation, 129
Forer, Lois G., 85, 89
Foxx, Redd, 31
Frank, Anne, 131
free speech
  limits needed on, 17-21
    con, 22-27
  news media, 72, 98, 100
    con, 76
  when speech is racist, 140-146
    con, 147-153
  see also censorship; pornography
Fund, John, 75

Gabler, Mel and Norma, 129, 131,
  161, 163
Gagnon, Paul, 157
Gannett Center for Media Studies, 98
Garbus, Martin, 215
Gates, Henry Louis, 30
Gelb, Leslie H., 104
Gergen, David R., 60
Gibbs, Jewelle Taylor, 31

Ginn and Company, 159
Ginzburg v. United States (1966), 131
Goebbels, Joseph, 216
Gogol, Nikolai V., 46
Goldman, May, 20
Gorbachev, Mikhail S., 60
Gore, Tipper, 33
government
  press freedom damages, 63-64, 65,
    66, 69
  con, 55-56, 58, 60-61, 86
  press leaks damage, 107, 108
  con, 102-105, 111-114
  should regulate broadcasting, 73, 74
  con, 77, 78
  should restrict pornography, 179,
    209, 210
  con, 173-174, 175-176, 177, 212
Grant, S. McClelland, 127
Great Britain, 55
  justice system, 81, 89-90
  official secrets act, 100, 113
Green, Robert L., 80
Grenada invasion, 60

Hackney, Sheldon, 152, 153
Hague, Frank, 24, 148-149
Halperin, Morton, 108
Hamilton, Alexander, 58
Harper's Magazine, 59-60
Harrington, Ollie, 19
Hart, Gary, 60
Helms, Jesse, 35, 36, 43, 44
Hentoff, Nat, 26, 147
Herblock, 112
Hillocks, George, Jr., 157
Hinckley, John, 20
Hitler, Adolf, 21, 142
Hobbes, Thomas, 215
Hofoss, Dan, 24
Hollings, Ernest, 76
Holmes, Oliver Wendell, 151-152
Holt, Rinehart and Winston, 159

Institute of Contemporary Art, 37, 39
Iran-Contra scandal, 56, 104
Islam, 158

Jane's Defence Weekly, 107
Jasper, William F., 154
Jay, David Gerald, 150
Jefferson, Thomas, 59
Jehovah's Witnesses, 24
Jesus, 25
  in art, 37-38
  textbooks ignore, 156, 157, 158
Jews, 25, 26, 152, 153, 204-205, 216
Joan of Arc, Saint, 156-157

John Paul II, 163
Johnson, Lyndon B., 104
Jones, Ernest, 131
Jordan, Hamilton, 80
Joseph, Burton, 131
Judaism, 157, 158

Kant, Immanuel, 67, 68, 69, 218
Kaplan, Sheila, 148-149
Kelley, Steve, 99
Kennedy, John F., 104
King, Martin Luther, Jr., 18, 24
King, Stephen, 163-164
Kinison, Sam, 150
Kirk, 103
Kirk, Jerry R., 182
Klein, Norma, 130
Klunk, Wally, 123
Kramer, Hilton, 44, 46
Ku Klux Klan, 191
  should be silenced, 18, 20-21,
    204-205, 206
  con, 23, 26, 27, 148

labor unions, 20, 23-24
La Haye, Beverly, 161
Lance, Bert, 80
lawyers, 87, 190
Ledeen, Michael, 79, 106
Lehman, John, 81-82
Leishman, Katie, 129
Lenkowsky, Les, 80
Leo, John, 28
libel
  laws should be strengthened, 79-84
  con, 85-91
  suits, cost of, 86, 87, 89
liberals, 43
  and textbooks, 157
  opposition to censorship, 31, 149
  is misguided, 18, 20, 21
  school texts favor, 154-159
  con, 160-165
libraries
  should be censored, 121-125
  con, 126-132, 163
  should reflect majority views,
    133-135
  con, 136-139
Lindner, Eileen W., 204
Linsley, William A., 217
Lipman, Samuel, 44
Locke, John, 89
Lockhart, William B., 183

McCarthy, Joseph R., 46, 80
McClure, James A., 37
McClure, Robert E., 183

235

MacIntosh, Craig, 188
MacKinnon, Catharine A., 190, 215, 216
McManus, John F., 206
Manley, Will, 121
Mapplethorpe, Robert
should be censored, 37, 39, 40, 41
con, 33, 43
Marmor, Judd, 130
Marshall, Thurgood, 173
Matsuda, Mari J., 145
Meese Commission. *See* Attorney General's Commission on Pornography
men
exploit women, 187, 190
con, 215, 216, 218, 219
Merrill, John C., 62
Michigan, University of, 148
Miller, Wiley, 34
Miller v. California (1973), 173, 206, 207
Minnesota Civil Liberties Union, 214
Monroe, Bill, 78
Moral Majority, 212-213
Morgan, Robin, 214-215, 216
Morison, Samuel Loring
should be punished, 107-108
con, 111, 113-114
Moses, 158
music
obscenity in
should be censored, 28-31
con, 32-35

Nader, Ralph, 77
Nation, The, 162
National Association of Broadcasters, 72
National Association of Christian Educators, 161
National Endowment for the Arts
should restrict funding of, 37, 38-39, 40, 41
con, 43, 44, 45, 46, 47
National Enquirer, 89, 90
National Institute of Education, 155
National Lawyers Guild, 150
National Legal Foundation, 161
National Rifle Association, 77
national security
justifies censorship, 97-100
con, 25, 101-105
press leaks damage, 106-109
con, 110-114
Nazis, 44, 148, 191, 216
demonstration in Skokie, Ill., 23
should be silenced, 21

con, 23, 26
Neusner, Jack, 40
news media
broadcasts
should be regulated, 70-74
con, 75-78
freedom of the press
must be limited, 62-69
con, 54-61
libel laws
should be strengthened, 79-84
con, 85-91
see also press freedom
New York Times, The, 18, 59
opposition to censorship, 29, 43, 103, 107
New York Times v. Sullivan (1964), 57
New York University, 150-151
New York v. Ferber (1982), 135, 208-210
Nixon, Richard M., 25, 102, 104

Oboler, Eli, 129, 131
O'Brien, Dennis, 144
Oliphant, Pat, 72
Orwell, George, 153
Oxford Book Company, 158

Page, Clarence, 32
Panama Canal, 59
Parents Music Resource Center, 33
Paris Adult Theatre v. Slaton (1973), 173, 175
Paul, Saint, 129-130
Pell, Claiborne, 78
Pennsylvania, University of, 152, 153
Pentagon Papers, 25, 56, 102-103
People for the American Way, 161, 164
Pilgrims, 155-156
Plato, 127
Playboy, 134, 190
Pollard, Deana, 202
pornography
censorship of
feminism calls for, 186-193
con, 194-201
First Amendment allows, 178-185
con, 172-177
harm justifies, 202-210
con, 211-220
child, 135, 177, 179, 181-182, 204, 208-209, 210
encourages violence, 188, 189
Posner, Richard A., 43
President's Commission on Obscenity and Pornography, 176
press freedom

must be limited, 62-69
  con, 54-61
security leaks
  justify censorship, 97-100
  con, 101-105
  should be punished, 106-109
  con, 110-114
  see also news media
prior restraint, 25, 179
privacy rights, 180-181
property rights, 89-90
prostitution, 188-189, 215
Protestants, 26
Pryor, Richard, 150
Pulitzer, Joseph, 59

Quadaffi, Muhamar, 98-99

racism
  in pornography, 187
  justifies censorship, 18, 21, 140-146
  con, 147-153
Ramirez, Mike, 30
Ramsey, Doug, 58
Randall, Richard, 212, 217, 219-220
rape
  obscene music causes, 34-35
  pornography causes, 187, 188, 189, 190
  con, 215, 217
Reagan, Ronald, 20, 122
  and Fairness Doctrine, 71
  and government secrecy, 102
  and pornography, 179, 185
  and terrorism, 98, 99
Réage, Pauline, 218
Rehnquist, William H., 57
religion
  is victim of censorship, 155, 158
  con, 162, 163, 165
  promotes censorship, 44, 129, 130
Riley, Gresham, 149
Roberts, Gene, 86
Robertson, Pat, 161, 162
Robeson, Paul, 24
Roman Catholics, 24, 26
Roosevelt, Theodore, 59
Roth v. United States (1957), 182-183, 214
Russell, Donald Stuart, 108

St. Louis Post-Dispatch, 81, 82
Scales, Peter, 126
Schlafly, Phyllis, 77, 133, 161
Schmertz, Herb, 83
school textbooks
  are censored
    to favor conservatives, 160-165

to favor liberals, 154-159
Sears, Alan E., 178
Seavey, David, 138
secular humanism, 158, 161-162
Serra, Richard, 44
Serrano, Andres
  should be censored, 37-38, 40, 41
  con, 43
sex, 212, 215
sex education, 129-130
sexual abuse
  censorship protects against, 29, 135
  con, 129
  pornography constitutes, 181-182, 190, 192, 208, 210
  con, 177, 214, 215, 217
Shakespeare, Edward, 26
Shaw, George Bernard, 131
Silber, John, 66, 68
Simons, Howard, 113
slavery, 153
Smith, Mike, 213
Smith, William French, 179
Smith Act (1940), 20
Sontag, Susan, 218
South Africa, 60
Southeastern Center for
  Contemporary Art, 37
Southern, Hugh, 38-39
Soviet Union, 107
  censorship in, 60
  schools in, 158
Speakes, Larry, 104
Spear, Joseph C., 101
speech, freedom of. *See* free speech
Spock, Benjamin, 27
Spotlight, The, 70
Stanmeyer, William A., 208
Stewart, Potter, 102, 133, 173
Stone, Geoffrey R., 172
Student Press Law Center, 148
Swift, Al, 73

Taft, William Howard, 59
Taylor, Stuart, Jr., 108
Teapot Dome scandal, 56
Tebben, Carol, 149
Telephone Decency Act (1987), 185
television
  Fairness Doctrine and, 76
  pornography in, 185, 213-214
  see also broadcasting
Terminiello v. Chicago (1949), 26-27
terrorism, 98-99
Thomas, Norman, 24
Thompson, Jack, 33, 34-35
Toles, Tom, 87
Trever, John, 77

Trudeau, Garry, 43
Turner, Stansfield, 112
2 Live Crew, 29-30, 31, 33-34, 35

Uluschak, Edd, 64
United States
Central Intelligence Agency (CIA),
  20, 113
Congress
  and Fairness Doctrine, 71-72, 76, 78
  and free speech, 124, 184
  and libel law, 80, 81
  and pornography, 185
  leaks from, 113
  should restrict arts funding, 37, 41
    con, 43, 45, 46, 47
  should restrict press freedom,
    99-100
    con, 114
Constitution
  and women, 180, 192
  First Amendment
    allows censorship, 31
      con, 26, 33, 35
    for national security, 98, 108
      con, 102-103, 113
    in libraries, 123, 124, 134
      con, 137
    of pornography, 178-185, 191,
      203, 206-209, 210
      con, 172-177, 214
    of racist speech, 20, 21
      con, 23, 25, 27, 148, 149, 151
    of the press, 66
      con, 55, 57, 58, 61
    and arts funding, 43, 45, 48
    and Fairness Doctrine, 72, 73
    and libel law, 82, 86, 89
  Fourteenth Amendment, 151
  freedom to read, 137
  interpretation of, 56-57
  "right to know," 66
  Thirteenth Amendment, 152-153
courts, 89-90
Declaration of Independence, 89
defense contracts, 83-84
Defense Department, 83, 112
Federal Bureau of Investigation
  (FBI), 20
Navy, 111
State Department, 20, 112-113
Supreme Court
  and censorship, 109, 113
  and Fairness Doctrine, 76-77
  and free speech, 23, 26-27

"fighting words" test, 25, 149
First Amendment exceptions, 203,
  204, 149
and pornography, 135, 173-174,
  177, 181, 182-183, 206-210, 214
and press freedom, 56-58, 61

Vietnam War
  press freedom and, 102, 103
  protests against, 24, 162
violence
  against women, 34-35, 192, 203-204
  in music, 29
  in pornography, 205-206, 207-208,
    209
  racial, 18, 141
Vitz, Paul C., 155-156, 157
Voltaire, François Marie Arouet de,
  23, 34, 131

Warren, Earl, 212
Washington, George, 59, 131
Washington, Harold, 40
Washington Post, The, 29, 110
  and national security leak, 99
  and opposition to censorship, 103,
    107
Washington Project for the Arts, 39
Wasserman, Dan, 128
Watergate scandal, 56, 104
White, Byron R., 57
Whitman, Bert, 180
Whitney Museum of Modern Art, 39
Wicker, Tom, 29, 60
Williams, Juan, 29-30
Williams, Linda, 213, 219
Wilson, Woodrow, 59
Wobblies (International Workers of
  the World), 23-24
Wolfe, Alan, 211
women
  Constitution and, 180, 192
  obscene music harms, 29-30, 31
    con, 33, 34-35
  pornography harms, 181, 187-193,
    203, 207, 210
    con, 214-218, 219
  sexism and, 148
World War I, 23
Wright, Don, 56

Zillmann, Dolf, 174
Zola, Emile, 26
Zumwalt, Elmo R., 97
Zumwalt, James G., 97

238